501-650·3767

SOCIAL DIVERSITY WITHIN MULTILITERACIES

"Boyd and Brock and the educators they've assembled have created a framework for teachers to, first of all, develop a vivid and lucid understanding of how issues of social diversity transact with the concept of multiliteracies. They then pull out their ace card and show how these transactions can and should play out in classrooms."

Bob Fecho, University of Georgia, USA

Using a multiliteracies theoretical framework highlighting social diversity and multimodality as central in the process of meaning making, this book examines literacy teaching and learning as embedded in cultural, linguistic, racial, sexual, and gendered contexts and explores ways to foster learning and achievement for diverse students in various settings. Attending simultaneously to topics around two overarching and interrelated themes— languages and language variations, and cultures, ethnicities, and identities—the chapter authors examine the roles that multiliteracies play in students' lives in and out of classrooms.

In Part I, readers are asked to examine beliefs and dispositions as related to different languages, language varieties, cultures, ethnicities, and identities. Part II engages readers in examining classroom and community practices related to different languages and language varieties, cultures, ethnicities, and identities. As a whole, this book provides a framework for challenging top-down standardized educational approaches and offers examples of literacy teaching and learning that build on, rather than ignore, students' diverse backgrounds and experiences.

Fenice B. Boyd is Associate Professor, Literacy Education, Graduate School of Education, University at Buffalo, SUNY, USA.

Cynthia H. Brock is Lecturer, Literacy Studies, School of Education, University of South Australia, Australia.

SOCIAL DIVERSITY WITHIN MULTILITERACIES

Complexity in Teaching and Learning

Edited by
Fenice B. Boyd and
Cynthia H. Brock

Routledge
Taylor & Francis Group

NEW YORK AND LONDON

First published 2015
by Routledge
711 Third Avenue, New York, NY 10017

and by Routledge
2 Park Square, Milton Park, Abingdon, Oxon OX14 4RN

Routledge is an imprint of the Taylor & Francis Group, an informa business

Library of Congress Cataloging-in-Publication Data
  Social diversity within multiliteracies : complexity in teaching and learning / edited by
  Fenice B. Boyd, Cynthia H. Brock.
    pages cm
  Includes bibliographical references and index.
  1. Literacy—Social aspects—United States. 2. Language arts—Social
  aspects—United States. 3. Sociolinguistics—United States. 4. Multicultural
  education—United States. I. Boyd, Fenice B. II. Brock, Cynthia H.
  LC151.S63   2014
  370.1170973—dc23   2014016223

ISBN: 978-1-138-02196-9 (hbk)
ISBN: 978-1-138-02198-3 (pbk)
ISBN: 978-1-315-77738-2 (ebk)

Typeset in 10/12 Bembo
by codeMantra

Printed and bound in the United States of America by Publishers Graphics,
LLC on sustainably sourced paper.

CONTENTS

Foreword   *vii*
Beryl Exley
Preface: An Overview of the Book   *xi*

1   Reflections on the Past, Working within the "Future":   1
    Advancing a Multiliteracies Theory and Pedagogy
    Fenice B. Boyd and Cynthia H. Brock

PART I
**Exploring Languages, Language Varieties, Culture,   11
Ethnicity, and Identities**

2   Language Study in Teacher Education: Cultivating Teachers'   13
    Understandings of Language Variation
    Debra Goodman

3   "Deadly Ways to Learn": Language Variation, Ideology, and   30
    Learning Literacies
    Cynthia H. Brock, Jenni Carter, and Fenice B. Boyd

4   My Life in Stories, My World in Pictures: A View of   42
    Multiliteracies from the Outside In
    Rachel G. Salas and Julie L. Pennington

5   White Male Teachers Exploring Language, Literacy, and   58
    Diversity: A Self-Study of Male Perceptions of Diversity(ies)
    Mary B. McVee, David Fronczak, Jay Stainsby, and Chad White

6 Embracing Sexual Diversity in Classroom Teaching 74
Lynda R. Wiest

7 Designing Safe Places to Talk about Contentious Topics 89
Fenice B. Boyd and Andrea L. Tochelli

PART II
Exploring Languages, Language Varieties, Culture, **107**
Ethnicity, and Identities in Classrooms and Communities

8 Code-switching and Contrastive Analysis: Tools of Language 109
and Culture Transform the Dialectally Diverse Classroom
Rebecca Wheeler and Rachel Swords

9 Tangled in *Charlotte's Web*: Lessons Learned from 127
English Learners
Claudia Christensen Haag and Margaret Compton

10 Culture and Identity: Promoting the Literacies of a 144
Sudanese Father and Son
Doris Walker-Dalhouse and A. Derick Dalhouse

11 Social Equity Teaching in Action: My Community Is 154
My Classroom
Gwendolyn Thompson McMillon and David Benjamin McMillon

12 Transforming Locked Doors: Using Multiliteracies to 168
Recontextualize Identities and Learning for Youth
Living on the Margins
Sean Turner

13 "That Teacher Just Uses Her Mouth": Inviting Linguistically 186
Diverse Students to Learn
Zaline M. Roy-Campbell

PART III
Lessons Learned about Social Diversities within **199**
Multiliteracies

14 Transforming Practice in Action 201
Cynthia H. Brock and Fenice B. Boyd

Index *213*

FOREWORD

The 1996 edition of *Harvard Educational Review* hosted the now seminal article from the New London Group, "A Pedagogy of Multiliteracies." Coining the term 'multiliteracies' to describe the advent of new technologies as well as the rapidly-changing social and cultural literacies of the emerging new world order, the New London Group proffered an ambitiously new educational agenda constituted by four non-hierarchical and non-linear components of pedagogy: situated practice, overt instruction, critical framing, and transformed practice.

Since this time, interpretations of the New London work have been trialed in a range of projects by hundreds of teachers working in diverse communities of practice across a range of year levels and in different disciplinary fields. For many of these projects, the central focus on multiple designs of meaning—linguistic, audio, spatial, gestural, and visual design and their intermodal coupling—has had broad and productive uptake. The strength of this project work has been instituting a practice of (1) experiential immersion across a range of text designs; (2) carefully crafting a technical metalanguage for the requisite content knowledge and text designs; (3) analyzing the cultural and social consequences for a range of stakeholders; and (5) critically remaking real-world texts for real-world audiences for real-world social, cultural, and intellectual purposes (Exley & Luke, 2010).

After nigh on two decades of cogent analyses, I am encouraged by the number of teachers who have applied the multiliteracies model to their contexts and, moreover, returned significant contributions to the profession by publishing accounts and analyses of their efforts alongside discussion about problematics and challenges. In the chapters that follow, Boyd and Brock and authors who contributed to this edited collection have advanced this evolving discussion, promoting what I see as two of the most fundamental outcomes of a transformative orientation: the production of new knowledge discourses and new pedagogic identities for teachers and students. To do so, each chapter of this collection carefully contextualizes the wide-ranging work of teachers and students in particular periods of social and cultural time and place and efficiently delineates the 'what' and 'how' of pedagogical practice to show the affordances of an agentive educational agenda. To this end, the chapters that follow recount powerful locally contextualized projects focused around literacy digs (Goodman), bi-dialectical teaching (Brock, Carter, and Boyd), visual communication (Salas), the architecture of language (McVee, Fronczak, Stainsby, and White), diverse sexual orientations (Wiest, and Boyd and Tochelli), treating linguistic diversity as difference not deficit (Wheeler, Swords), writing about frustrations (Haag and Compton), autobiographies (Walker-Dalhouse and Dalhouse), community farming (McMillon and McMillon), playwriting with incarcerated youth (Turner), and building shared background knowledge (Roy-Campbell). In sociological terms, each of these projects marks out different relations of knowledge and power, and control over social relations for groups of students, their teachers, and, in many cases, extended communities. As Bernstein (1996) recognizes, classification of knowledge and framing of social relations is not the artefact of curricula, schools, and classroom pedagogy alone.

In keeping with the theme of the importance of pedagogic identity, I too introduce my narrative to you, the reader. I identify as a white Australian, born in the 1960s on *Wiradjuri*[1] land in rural New South Wales in Australia to monolingual English-speaking, working-class parents of Norwegian and Irish heritage. As a child, I was raised as a monolingual English speaker on the red clay of *Yuggera* land, what Europeans call the Redland Shire (South-East Queensland), along the edges of *Quandamoopah* (Moreton Bay). It is here that I watched the dolphins in their habitat and the Stradbroke Island ferry travel between *Minjerribah* (Stradbroke Island) and the mainland. Like many shire students, I regularly traveled to *Minjerribah* to compete in interschool sports, undertake geography excursions, and learn about contemporary Indigenous culture, in particular, the Elder, poet, writer, artist, and educator *Oodgeroo Noonucal* (Kath Walker). This is not to suggest that in any way I came to 'see' or 'be' Indigenous. To the contrary, our geography assignments on the sand-island formation of *Minjerribah, Bummeria* (perched Brown Lake), and *Myora* (Freshwater Springs) were founded on the Western knowledge system of land-forms. Our learning about contemporary Indigenous culture never included learning from or deep questions about other ways of knowing. After completing secondary schooling, I undertook tertiary studies and became a primary school-teacher in the mid 1980s.

During the next two decades, periods of time spent in Europe and Asia and connecting with my mother's kin in Norway and visiting and teaching and researching in Australian mainland and island Indigenous communities, including those that are a physical, emotional, and/or spiritual connection for my Indigenous relations on my mother's side and my father's side. The social and cultural identity (singular) I carried through childhood and my late twenties was rapidly becoming very unfamiliar to me. It is only now, after two decades of working in teacher education and exploring my concern for the sociology of education

---

1 Indigenous place names are presented in italics.

and literacy teaching and learning as a social justice issue that I have started to explicitly validate social and cultural identities (plural) as a crucial part of a robust and fulfilling educative process.

The chapters in this edited collection tell stories of success from different times and places and of different societies and cultures. No matter how ideal a project might seem, its success is always rooted to local conditions. Having YOUR class take up some of these projects as they are articulated here will, more likely than not, fail to connect to your students' interests. If bi-dialectical language teaching or a community farming project has no connection to your locality, then there is the very real possibility that such a project could slip into a crisis of irrelevance for your students. Theorizations of effective practice, however, have much portability. This should be the message of import from this volume.

The one constant of each and every chapter of this volume is the way highly expert teachers continue to shift the pedagogic repertoire. As each chapter unfolds, we learn how each teacher expertly 'weaves' everyday and technical knowledges (see Cazden, 2006) and weakly and strongly framed modes of interactional discourses (see Exley & Richard-Bossez, 2013) to systematically build new knowledges and ways of knowing and in so doing, act as facilitators of a transformative education for disparate groups of students in different educational spaces. This edited collection gives me hope that future teachers and system administrators can learn from these accounts and muster the courage to challenge themselves to make a difference, not so much by being a technocrat, but by being one who empowers their young charges as new thinkers affirmed by their social and cultural identities (plural) for a changing world order. Facilitating students' "capacity to speak up, to negotiate, and to be able to engage critically with the conditions" (New London Group, 1996, p. 67) of their lives now and into the future should be the primary goal for all teachers.

Beryl Exley, PhD
Associate Professor, Faculty of Education
Queensland University of Technology, Australia

References

Bernstein, B. (1996). *Pedagogy, symbolic control and identity: Theory, research, critique*. Oxford, UK: Rowman & Littlefield Publishers.

Cazden, C. (2006, January 18). Connected learning: Weaving in classroom lessons. Keynote address, *Pedagogy in Practice 2006 Conference*, University of Newcastle, Australia.

Exley, B., & Luke, A. (2010). Uncritical framing: Lesson and knowledge structure in school science. In D. Cole (Ed.), *Handbook of research on multiliteracies and technology enhanced education*. London, UK: Routledge.

Exley, B., & Richard-Bossez, A. (2013). The ABCs of teaching alphabet knowledge: Challenges and affordances of weaving visible and invisible pedagogies. *Contemporary Issues in Early Childhood, 14*(4), 345–356.

New London Group. (1996). A pedagogy of multiliteracies: Designing social futures. *Harvard Educational Review, 66*(1), 60–92.

PREFACE
An Overview of the Book

Chapter 1, the Introduction, opens the book by addressing educators' beliefs and dispositions.

Part I: Exploring Languages, Language Varieties, Culture, Ethnicity, and Identities

In chapter 2, Debra Goodman looks at in-service and preservice teachers' engagement in a descriptive, systematic language study project implemented in the communities where they teach. Class engagements, field projects, and readings challenge and expand teachers' unexamined assumptions and cultivate a linguistic knowledge base that informs teachers' appreciation of learners' language and ability to support them in expanding their linguistic repertoire. Examples of studies address regional and social dialect and discourses within varied language communities. Through these studies, teachers consider pedagogy that expands learners' linguistic and cultural repertoires while respecting and cultivating students' home and community language practices.

Cynthia H. Brock, Jenni Carter, and Fenice B. Boyd (chapter 3) explore relationships between language variation and ideology. The chapter begins with a short thought experiment designed to ask the reader to consider her or his ideological stance toward language varieties. Then the authors explore two different cases of ideological stances toward language varieties—the Oakland Ebonics Case in Oakland, California, and the bi-dialectical language approach enacted in Western Australia. They end the chapter by inviting readers to consider their own ideological stances, and the implications of those stances, toward different language varieties.

The NLG (1996) argues that in a world where differences of identity and affiliation are becoming more prominent, the "challenge is to make space available so that different lifeworlds—spaces for community life where local and specific meanings can be made—can flourish" (p. 70). Rachel G. Salas and Julie L. Pennington (chapter 4) explain how they taught and supervised preservice teachers in a teacher education program to bridge the gap from theory in their university classroom to practice within the local community. They begin by narrating who they are, noting their ethnic and cultural origins, home and school languages, and professional journeys. These family and life experiences led them to rethink teacher preparation programs and to design and implement a community literacy course to include a variety of situated learning experiences for their preservice teachers. Salas and Pennington convey how they provided opportunity for their preservice teachers to probe their uninformed and unexamined assumptions about their students' culture, identity, and community.

As teaching is still an overwhelmingly female profession, especially in elementary grades, voices of male teachers are often muted or absent in studies exploring the relationships between language, literacy, and culture. Mary B. McVee, David Fronzack, Jay Stainsby, and Chad White (chapter 5) examine the learning of three white male teachers as they reflect on their learning in a graduate course titled *Language, Literacy, and Culture.* These male voices brought important perspectives into classroom discussions of racial, ethnic, and linguistic diversity, and several were outspoken advocates of equity while working in challenging, diverse environments. In this chapter, we read David, Jay, and Chad's stories as they analyze their own learning in the course to explore significant and potentially troubling insights and how these insights helped them to think about teaching and learning.

Literacy teaching and learning occurs through interactions across a variety of spaces and includes moments of interaction that are unmarked and/or unintended as literacy acts. Lynda R. Wiest (chapter 6) provides an overview of ways educators can create classrooms that are inclusive of sexual identity of both students and their parents. The author establishes a rationale for attending to sexual identity as a personal characteristic that matters in multiliteracies teaching and learning and presents suggested strategies for instructional approaches. Wiest ends her chapter by providing practical resources that are inclusive of sexual identity that teachers may consult for additional support.

Using the multiliteracies framework as a lens, Fenice B. Boyd and Andrea L. Tochelli (chapter 7) describe what it means to design a safe place for graduate students to talk about contentious topics, specifically LGBT young adult literature (YAL). The authors look at their students' written products and class discussions to understand how they critically approach texts to think about their own beliefs about LGBT YAL, an author's development of characters, and the story arc presented in the novel. The authors look at the importance of reading LGBT novels and end with suggestions for creating safe classroom environments to include literature that is not typically discussed in the secondary classroom.

Part II: Exploring Languages, Language Varieties, Culture, Ethnicity, and Identities in Classrooms and Communities

After exploring the nature and consequences of traditional literacy instruction that presumes and enforces a monolithic Standard English literacy, Rebecca Wheeler and Rachel Swords (chapter 8) chart a path toward classrooms that honor and build upon the multiliteracy skills of contemporary students. The authors focus on new ways of understanding and responding to the bi-dialectalism of linguistic minority students who speak historically stigmatized vernacular dialects and examine how teachers can lay aside the "ineffective red pen" and instead contrast the grammar of the home to the grammar of the school.

When a researcher situates herself in the classroom as the teacher, it can be a valuable learning experience. In chapter 9, Claudia Christensen Haag and Margaret Compton focus on three key lessons learned from English learners (ELs) when Haag left her university teaching position for a year to return to an elementary classroom to teach ELs full-time. Using vignettes and artifacts from her teaching experience, the authors illustrate how Claudia came to understand the need to value student identity and life experiences and the need to incorporate these experiences in instruction. To promote students' sense of agency, the authors incorporated multimodal paths to learning and included students in the problem-solving process when instructional practices did not meet their needs.

Doris Walker-Dalhouse and A. Derick Dalhouse (chapter 10) examine the literacy practices of a Sudanese father and son to understand the extent to which culture and family literacy practices influenced the son's reading identity, acculturation, and use of multiliteracies. The authors convey the necessity for increased teacher use of a multiliteracies approach that builds upon the cultural literacy practices of refugee students in U.S. public schools. This work contributes to the paucity of research that exists about the cultural literacy practices of refugee families and the influence they have on the racial socialization and reading development of their children.

Looking outside of the traditional classroom setting, Gwendolyn Thompson McMillon and David Benjamin McMillon (chapter 11) provide a portrait of a K–8 summer program in an impoverished community that is considered a food desert. A community gardening project became a summer classroom where students were taught gardening and entrepreneurial skills while utilizing research techniques and comprehension strategies learned in school. Students were encouraged to become self-sufficient, promoting the highest form of social equity teaching.

In chapter 12, Sean Turner retells a multifaceted artistic event whose ambition, at its most fundamental level, sought to transform a space where the imagination takes on its most expressive and volatile potentialities: jail. Turner examines ways in which incarcerated youth shaped notions of self and the imaginary within an arts-based exploration into their own lives and then recontextualized and transformed that knowledge through multimodal design and production activities situated around the building of a hypervisual theatrical performance set.

Zaline M. Roy-Campbell (chapter 13) contextualizes the experiences of Afron and Mumina, two sisters, as a case to examine challenges some ELs encounter in teacher-centered classrooms. By drawing on research literature to illustrate the affordances of a multiliteracies pedagogy, the author considers alternative ways teachers can communicate with and teach linguistically diverse students to actively include them in the learning process.

Part III: Lessons Learned about Social Diversities within Multiliteracies

Cynthia H. Brock and Fenice B. Boyd (chapter 14) bring the chapters together by delving into the lessons learned about social diversity within multiliteracies. They consider transformed practices and embodied actions of the work presented, noting how a multiliteracies perspective with respect to social diversity is instantiated and how, as a literacy field, we might transform conceptions of social diversity to strengthen teaching and learning.

1

REFLECTIONS ON THE PAST, WORKING WITHIN THE "FUTURE"

Advancing a Multiliteracies Theory and Pedagogy

Fenice B. Boyd and Cynthia H. Brock

Introduction

It has been almost twenty years since the literacy field was introduced to the now eminent article written by The New London Group (NLG). Published in 1996, *A Pedagogy of Multiliteracies: Designing Social Futures* presented a theoretical overview of the nexus between the changing social environments and communication systems as related to literacy teaching and learning. NLG's analysis was trailblazing, particularly as the scholars predicted that redesigning social environments and communication systems would transform the future of literacy teaching, ways we communicate and collaborate, and how we construct meaning. In just seventeen short years, for instance, we can co-construct a text on our computer by screen sharing, collaborate with our colleagues through FaceTime, Google Hangout, or Skype, and teach our students to use and apply digital tools and technology to develop their literacy teaching and learning skills (e.g., iPads, clickers, Smart Boards, and online classes). We submit our manuscripts and grant proposals for scholarly production online. On our smartphones, whether we are riding in a car or flying on a plane, we can read *The Help* or the *New York Times*, text family and friends, or play Angry Birds. Predicted by the NLG in 1996, in all aspects of our lifeworlds, these communication systems give us the capability to work in time and space in future-oriented ways.

Cope and Kalantzis (2000) note that one goal for the group's collaboration was to focus on the big picture relative to literacy teaching and learning; the ten academics had different national and cultural experiences and different areas of expertise. Their intent was to stimulate important discussions about the *what* and *how* of literacy pedagogy given the evolving and diverse meanings of the word "literacy" and the "new demands being placed upon people as makers of meaning in changing workplaces, as citizens in changing public spaces, and in the changing dimensions of our community lives—our lifeworlds" (p. 4). The NLG's work redefined literacy as multiliteracies with the potential to build learning conditions "that lead to full and equitable social participation" (Cope & Kalantzis, 2000, p. 9). These scholars argued that a pedagogy of multiliteracies centers on modes of representation that reach beyond language alone, differ according to culture and context, and have specific cognitive, cultural, and social effects.

A multiliteracies pedagogy views language and other modes of meaning-making as dynamic representational resources. Users constantly remake these representational resources as they work to achieve their various social and cultural purposes, including their goals for literacy achievement and lifelong learning. Jacobs (2012) argues that a multiliteracies pedagogy is more than integrating digital tools and technology, multiple modalities, or popular culture into an existing curriculum. Rather, as a field, we are asked to reconceptualize the very notion of what constitutes the curriculum; it should no longer consist solely of traditional literacy (e.g., reading, writing, speaking, and listening) and technology cast in ways that privilege white middle- and upper-class students. Rather, the curriculum must include multimodal "literacies" and social practices that honor the vast array of linguistic, racial, cultural, sexual, and gendered identities of children in our classrooms. In short, a multiliteracies curriculum must include careful attention to social diversity as well as digital and non-digital multimodal tools. But promoting a multiliteracies pedagogy and curriculum does not forgo reading and writing basics such as decoding and encoding, literal level comprehension, and the use of canonical texts; it requires all stakeholders (e. g., teachers, school leaders, teacher educators, researchers, and policymakers) to rethink *why* we teach what we teach, *what* we teach, and *how* we teach content to ensure the success of *all* students.

What might this rethinking of pedagogy from a multiliteracies perspective look like? Boyd and Tochelli (2014) illustrate how one teacher used a multiliteracies approach to teach her students how different text types can represent the same historical event in vastly different ways. For analytical purposes, the teacher used three texts—a memoir, a documentary, and a docudrama—to help students think about the depiction of an event and how different modes influence representation, point of view, and meaning. Each text gave a different portrayal of the integration of Little Rock Central High School by nine students, a key historical event. The authors narrate the pedagogical moves where Deborah, the teacher, placed side by side multiple text types to convey how different modes of communication have the potential to shift meaning in significant ways. By providing these multiple readings of the memoir and visual images, Deborah's instruction was consistent with the multiliteracies approach because she focused "on modes of representation much broader than language alone" (Boyd & Tochelli, 2014, p. 64) to include visual images as dynamic representational resources to assist students in redirecting points of view about the historical events to desegregate Little Rock Central High School. In the next section, we examine the impact of multiliteracies.

Exploring the Reach of a Multiliteracies Framework

The NLG spawned a blitz of professional conversations about theoretical perspectives, critiques about literacy teaching and learning, and discussions about students' meaning-making experiences, as well as the role that social diversity plays in literacy pedagogy. The extent to which multiliteracies has been taken up within the literacy field is extraordinary, and as a concept, the idea has traveled far beyond the small town of New London to become a worldwide reality (Guo, Cope, & Kalantzis, 2009). Leander and Boldt (2013) note, "More than any other text, *A Pedagogy of Multiliteracies* streams powerfully through doctoral programs, edited volumes, books, journal reviews, and calls for conference papers, as the central manifesto of the new literacies movement" (p. 22). The concentrated efforts behind this one article have been monumentally significant.

We conducted a general search on Google Scholar as one approach to test the extent to which the publication is being utilized. We found an approximate yield of 244 citations. We also entered the term "multiliteracies" into three databases including *Education Full Text*, *Education Research Complete*, and *Psych Info*. This yielded over 300 references. We sorted through these references to identify empirical work pertaining to multiliteracies, which narrowed our list of articles to 121 studies published in peer-reviewed journals. Several features of the studies stand out as particularly compelling. First, scholars from around the world are using multiliteracies to frame their work conceptually. For example, we found studies from Greece, Singapore, South Africa, the United States, Canada, Australia, and the United Kingdom. Second, scholars are using a multiliteracies conceptual framework to explore literacy learning-related topics across a broad age span including pre-K, lower and upper elementary, middle grades, high school, and undergraduate and graduate education. We found a range of topics being studied using a multiliteracies conceptual framework including, but not limited to, the following:

- A bridge between school and community literacies
- An exploration of bilingual French and Chinese development in French language schools
- The learning of Aboriginal adolescent students in an alternative school
- An exploration of fan fiction
- Pre- and in-service teachers' learning about new literacies
- Pedagogical innovations in dual-language early childhood classrooms

As one final example of the prevalence of multiliteracies, we entered the term "multiliteracies" in Google Books Ngram Viewer. When key terms are listed in Ngram, it displays a graph showing how frequently the terms have been displayed in Google Books during the years selected. One-word terms are called unigrams; two-word terms are bigrams. So, for example, if the unigram "diversity" is entered into Ngram Viewer, it compares how frequently "diversity" appears in Google Books for the specified time period compared with all other one-word unigrams used in the same time period in Google Books. The same principle is applicable to digrams. If we entered the digram "social diversity" into Ngram, it would compare the digram "social diversity" with all other two-word digrams in all Google Books during the specified time frame. Ngram models are typically used in disciplines such as computational linguistics, communication theory, and probability. For instance, statisticians create ngram language models to explore letter combinations at the phoneme, syllable, letter, or word levels. Figure 1.1 displays the results of a multiliteracies unigram when we entered it into Ngram Viewer.

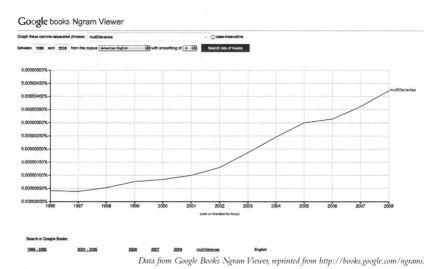

Data from Google Books Ngram Viewer, reprinted from http://books.google.com/ngrams.

FIGURE 1.1 Ngram Results for the Unigram "Multiliteracies."

As illustrated in the graph displayed in Figure 1.1, between 1996 and 2008 (which is the latest year available for Ngram Viewer), the use of the unigram "multiliteracies" has risen steadily from 1996, when its use was virtually zero, to 2008 when compared with all other unigrams in Google Books.

Clearly, there has been a consistent and steady rise in the development of a multiliteracies framework for teaching and learning. With the heightened use, application, and integration of digital tools and technologies, a great deal of this rise can be attributed to multimodality (cf. Miller & McVee, 2012). Multimodality is one facet of multiliteracies; social diversity is another. Kress and Van Leeuwen (2001) define multimodality as "the use of several semiotic modes in the design of a semiotic product or event" (p. 20). Today we are not only consumers of multimodal texts, but also producers of digital tools and technologies that enable us to make meaning in new and innovative ways. The distinction warrants consideration because "meaning is made in ways that are increasingly multimodal in which written-linguistic modes … interface with oral, visual, audio, gestural, tactile, and spatial patterns of meaning" (Kalantzis & Cope, 2012, p. 2). While for centuries written and oral language has been the privileged standard form of communication, in recent times, multimodality has received prominent attention and ups the ante on representation, communication, and interaction to move beyond the comfort zone of oral and written language, as well as print-based text only, as the principal forms of meaning-making.

Advancing a Multiliteracies Theoretical Framework

Our theoretical framework centers on multiliteracies and the ways in which social, linguistic, cultural, and economic identities complicate as well as intersect with literacy teaching and learning. Figure 1.2 presents an overview of the key theoretical elements we explore within and across all chapters: multimodality, social diversity, teaching, and learning. The word "multiliteracies" is listed in bold at the bottom of the figure to indicate that it is the primary theoretical foundation on which the chapters rest. The three major concepts pertaining to multiliteracies on which we focus, represented by the three circles in the cone, all converge on multiliteracies. We chose a cone as the frame for the three major concepts to illustrate that they transact with one another in a dynamic and cyclical manner. Moreover, all of the chapters center on literacy teaching and learning; hence, all of the topics are funneled through the lens of teaching and learning. We opted to place social diversity at the top of the cone to highlight the fact that it is a concept within multiliteracies that we highlight throughout the book.

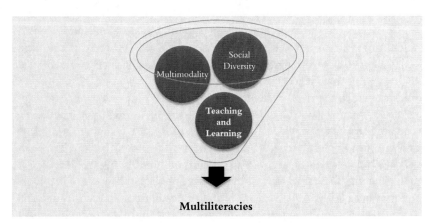

FIGURE 1.2 Social Diversity within a Multiliteracies Framework.

According to Kalantzis and Cope (2012), "A *multiliteracies* approach attempts to explain what matters in traditional reading and writing, and what is new and distinctive about the ways in which people construct meanings in contemporary communication environments" (pp. 1–2). A multiliteracies approach accomplishes these tasks by focusing on two interrelated and significant aspects of meaning-making: multimodality and social diversity. Social diversity centers on "the variability of conventions of meaning in different, cultural, social, or domain-specific situations" (Kalantzis & Cope, 2012, p. 1). It is especially significant because meaning-making fluctuates based upon the social context in which one deliberates; participates in life experiences; understands subject matter knowledge; constructs specialist knowledge; functions in a disciplinary domain area of employment; and understands one's own linguistic, cultural, gendered, and ethnic origins in relation to self and others.

In what ways does a multiliteracies perspective ask us, as a field, to think differently and in new ways about social diversity? Much of the diversity-related literature in the past focused on and was situated within what Kalantzis and Cope (2012) call the "old basic" approach to literacy, which centers on traditional and back-to-basics reading and writing using paper and pencil as tools. More current and important research in literacy and diversity acknowledges the importance of traditional conceptions of literacy, but also focuses on different digital, multimodal, and textual tools as well as unique ways to engage in the use of these tools for meaningful literacy teaching and learning (Albers, Holbrook, & Harste, 2010; Pahl & Rowsell, 2012). Here we focus on these latter new literacy tools and their unique uses in what Kalantzis and Cope (2012) refer to as the "new basics" whereby different people with different skills and backgrounds become privileged and those in positions of power (including teachers, principals, professors, district-level administrators, and so forth) actively and openly question and challenge their own perceptions about race, ethnicity, language, sexual, and gendered identities (p. 5).

Two themes run throughout the chapters in this book, making unique contributions to work on social diversity within multiliteracies. First, the authors demonstrate how literacy teaching and learning is an "emergent practice" (Cole & Pullen, 2010). By emergent practice, we mean that literacy learning is co-constructed with key participants in the moment. This contrasts with literacy practices that are scripted and do not attend to unique aspects of context and culture. For example, Haag (chapter 9) did not use a set program containing scripted lessons with her English learners in her elementary classroom; rather, she worked with her children in agentive ways to co-construct the lessons and activities the group undertook. Second, the authors in this book problematize what counts as literate behavior with respect to social diversity. For example, correcting children's speech is a common practice when working with children who speak non-dominant varieties of English such as Aboriginal English or African American Vernacular English. Rebecca Wheeler and Rachel Swords (chapter 8) educate readers about effective ways to work with children who speak non-dominant varieties of English. Likewise, Goodman (chapter 2) and Brock, Carter, and Boyd (chapter 3) ask educators to examine their own perceptions about non-dominant varieties of English. Taken together, these three chapters help readers to explore what counts as literate behavior with respect to language variation. Both of these aforementioned themes serve as a foundation for transforming literate identities of students and educators. Consequently, the authors of this book illustrate how social identities might be valued in different ways when the definition of literacy is expanded from the "old basic" approach to a "new basic" approach. It is to this end that we now turn.

Multiliteracies and Identities

In this book, we emphasize social diversity aspects of multiliteracies that have been historically marginalized with respect to identity and literacy practices. We focus on dialect differences and the acquisition of marginalized languages, sexual identity, race, ethnicity, and culture. While the authors highlight particular aspects of identity, all are cognizant that identity construction and development are far more complex than any single dimension. Over forty years ago, Cazden, John, and Hymes (1972) argued that students make connections and find continuity in their own literacy learning when teachers understand and draw on their students' unique backgrounds. When that continuity is present, there is a flow and progression between students and the topics and concepts introduced during instruction. In a similar fashion:

> One of the fundamental goals of a pedagogy of multiliteracies is to create the conditions for learning that support the growth of … a person comfortable with [self] as well as being flexible enough to collaborate and negotiate with others who are different from [self] in order to forge a common interest.
> *(Guo, Cope & Kalantzis, 2009, p. 174)*

To illustrate these points, we draw on our own identity development.

I (Fenice) am an African American female. My maternal grandparents and single mother raised my two brothers and me in the rural Jim Crow South. My grandparents were sharecroppers, and my mother was a factory worker. When I am in informal settings among family and friends, I speak African American Vernacular English (AAVE). Cindy's background is European American and Catholic. Both her parents raised her and her eight siblings in the rural Pacific Northwest. Cindy's father was a farmer and blue-collar worker. We have both been divorced. Cindy remarried and is now a stepmother. I am still single. As a single mother, I raised my two sons on my own. So far, we have shared with you only one aspect of our identity development.

Our respective backgrounds are based on engagement in different semiotic domains and social languages. We draw on Gee (2003) in our conceptualization of semiotic domains; they are any "set of practices that recruit one or more modalities (e.g., oral or written language, images, equations, symbols, sounds, gestures, graphs, artifacts, and so forth) to communicate distinctive types of meanings" (p. 31). So with respect to the examples we just shared, Cindy's background as a Catholic means that she was socialized in that particular semiotic domain. As a concrete example, there are over a billion Catholics in the world. Cindy has attended Mass in Thailand, Chile, Spain, Costa Rica, England, and Australia. While there may be slight variations in the enactment of Mass from country to country, many of the practices pertaining to the semiotic domain of Catholicism (e.g., making the sign of the cross when entering the church, norms around receiving Holy Communion, the meaning and use of holy water) have similar meanings in Catholic churches around the world. Social languages refer to the specific styles of languages that different social groups use. With respect to the examples we just shared, Fenice's facility with AAVE represents a social language that she knows and can use effectively. Clearly, based on these examples, we have facility with different semiotic domains and social languages.

However, this brief description of aspects of our past histories is not all there is to each of us and, therefore, does not fully explain our respective identities. We are academicians; we became friends and colleagues when we were doctoral students at Michigan State University (MSU) in the early 1990s. We have been privileged to work and study with many outstanding and prominent researchers. Our shared history as graduate students and later professors at different universities represents another characteristic that is different from our past personal histories. Our histories have played a role in the ways we have become university professors, collaborators, mentors, leaders, and lifelong learners. Our respective histories have also played a role in expanding our repertoires of semiotic domains and social languages and in shaping our perspectives on language, literacy, and learning (Gee, 2003). Growing up in the rural South and rural Northwest played a role in shaping our identities in ways that are no less meaningful than the identities we have constructed as a result of our experiences as doctoral students at MSU and subsequently as university professors.

We are not just African American and white females, nor simply American academics, and although we are all of these things, we are what we do and what we have made and will continue to make of ourselves. We are "simultaneously members of multiple lifeworlds" (NLG, 1996, 71), and our identities have numerous layers that are intricately related to each other. As stated by the NLG, "No person is a member of a singular community. Rather, they are members of multiple and overlapping communities" (p. 71). Our identities are dynamic and multifaceted; they are constructed and developed. What is more, they evolve as a result of our history and biology, our past experiences, and our past and future encounters with individuals and social groups (Moje & Luke, 2009). The different facets of our identity development and construction shape and impact the ways we live and make meaning in the world (Moje & Luke, 2009).

What is valued as literate identities in a "new basic" approach? It is the repositioning of people from being in static, past-oriented categories (e.g., worker, struggling student) into more dynamic, current, and future-oriented active positions. Social diversity promotes the notion that we are looking at the present and future in our lifeworlds; identity is dynamic, fluid, and active. Our audience will see how this idea plays out in Haag and Compton's work (chapter 9). While the young children struggle to learn English, they learn to advocate for themselves to learn English differently and in a completely different context. Likewise, Haag's students' advocacy repositioned her as a different English as second language (ESL) teacher. Her identity was dynamic, fluid, and active. Similarly, readers will see another shift in identity in Turner's chapter (12) as he examines the multimodal performance of incarcerated youth where they (re)story themselves and act as active agents in their world, constructing their own ways of being. The young ELs and adolescents presented in these chapters did not simply use the tools they were provided to make meaning. Rather, they asserted their right to become full meaning-makers and remakers of the symbols and tools given to them to transform meaning cognitively and of self. As stated by Moje and Luke (2009), "Learning from a social and cultural perspective involves people in participation, interaction, relationships, and contexts, all of which have implications for how people make sense of themselves and others, identify, and are identified" (p. 416).

People's unique characteristics combine in different ways that shape and define the ways they make meaning. A social diversity within a multiliteracies lens affords us the opportunity to shift our focus from one way of *seeing* and *being* to an examination of the many complex and nuanced similarities and differences within, across, and between us as individuals and members of different groups. Exploring and understanding the varied ways that people make meaning can help us, as a field, to assist students to understand, moderate, and actively create their spaces and places in the world. Given that identity and literacy teaching and learning are closely connected, it stands to reason that identity should be examined through the avenue of social diversity and multiliteracies. We argue that what is missing in our own work as teachers and researchers, however, is also absent in the field: a more thorough examination of the nature of and the intersections between students' multifaceted social, cultural, racial, linguistic, ethnic, and gendered identities. The chapters in this book focus on these important matters.

References

Albers, P., Holbrook, T., & Harste, J. C. (2010). Commentary: Talking trade: Literacy researchers as practicing artist. *Journal of Adolescent & Adult Literacy, 54*(3), 164–171.

Boyd, F. B., & Tochelli, A. L. (2014). Multimodality and literacy learning: Integrating the common core state standards for English language arts. In K. A. Hinchman & H. K. Sheridan-Thomas (Eds.), *Best Practices in Adolescent Literacy Instruction* (2nd Edition) (pp. 291–307). New York: The Guilford Press.

Cazden, C. B., John, V., & Hymes, D. (1972). *Functions of language in the classroom.* New York: Teachers College Press.

Cole, D. R., & Pullen, D. L. (2010). *Multiliteracies in motion: Current theory and practice.* New York: Routledge.

Cope, B., & Kalantzis, M. (Eds.) (2000). *Multiliteracies: Literacy learning and the design of social futures*. London: Routledge.

Gee, J. P. (2003). Opportunity to learn: A language-based perspective on assessment. *Assessment in Education, 10*, 27–46.

Guo, L., Cope, B., & Kalantzis, M. (2009). Multiliteracies: Introduction to the special issue. *Pedagogies: An International Journal, 4*, 159–163. doi: 10.1080/15544800903075939

Jacobs, G. (2012). The proverbial rock and hard place: The realities and risks of teaching in a world of multiliteracies, participatory culture and mandates. *Journal of Adolescent & Adult Literacy, 56*, 98–102. doi: 10.1002/JAAL 00109

Kalantzis, M., & Cope, B. (2012). *Literacies*. New York: Cambridge University Press.

Kress, G., & Van Leeuwen, L. (2001). *Multimodal discourse: The modes and media of contemporary communication*. Oxford: Oxford University Press.

Leander, K., & Boldt, G. (2013). Rereading "a pedagogy of multiliteracies": Bodies, texts, and emergence. *Journal of Literacy Research, 45*, 22–46.

Miller, S. M., & McVee, M. B. (Eds.) (2012). Multimodal composing in classrooms: Learning and teaching for the digital worlds. New York: Routledge.

Moje, E., & Luke, A. (2009). Literacy and identity: Examining the metaphors in history and contemporary research. *Reading Research Quarterly, 44*, 415–437.

New London Group (1996). A pedagogy of multiliteracies: Designing social futures. *Harvard Educational Review, 66*, 60–92.

Pahl, K., & Rowsell, J. (2012). *Literacy and Education* (2nd edition). Los Angeles: Sage.

PART I

Exploring Languages, Language Varieties, Culture, Ethnicity, and Identities

2

LANGUAGE STUDY IN TEACHER EDUCATION

Cultivating Teachers' Understandings of Language Variation

Debra Goodman

I have to admit, I was always embarrassed by my father's Bronx accent growing up. When he would say that he drove "trew da tunnel," I would cringe. To me, it represented a lower-class way of speaking when in fact it was just his accent.

When a child speaks incorrectly in the classroom, they should not be "corrected" right there and then in front of everyone, but I do believe that they should be made aware of the mistake. Students learn so much of the "wrong" or unconventional way of speaking outside of the classroom (hallways, peers, and even their families) that they need a place to learn or at least hear English spoken correctly. (Teachers' reflections posted on electronic "discussion board.")

These quotes were posted on an electronic discussion board in my course Language, Culture, and Identity: Issues for Teachers and Children. The graduate students in this course are in-service and preservice teachers in Literacy Studies and Teaching of English to Speakers of Other Languages (TESOL) programs. As described in the introduction to this book, a multiliteracies framework focuses on social diversity and multimodality. In this chapter, I describe my efforts to engage teachers in exploring relationships between *linguistic diversity*, language learning, and teaching. When teachers describe with shame the language variations spoken in their own home communities or insist that children's home language needs to be corrected, it reaffirms the importance of engaging teachers in a study of the complex relationships between language, culture, and identity.

While most teachers have the best intentions toward children and their literacy learning, teachers' responses to students' language differences are often based on unexamined hunches or "commonsense" beliefs about what's "proper" or "improper." For this reason, teachers I've worked with tend to show more tolerance of language development than they do of language variation. A survey on the first night of class provides insights into teachers' beliefs and attitudes. In one graduate class, for example, not one teacher agreed with the statement that "invented spellings and miscues should be corrected so that students will not form bad habits." However, almost half of the teachers agreed that "second language speakers should be corrected if they make mistakes in grammar and pronunciation" and that "children's use of improper English should be corrected." One teacher wrote on the back of the survey, "I have never thought in depth about some of these statements. I had a difficult time choosing a side. I think most of these statements are opinion based on knowledge." Teachers who are knowledgeable about the role of approximation or invention in literacy development still believe that variations from standard English should be corrected.

In my experience, many *language teachers* haven't really given much thought to *language*. Few have taken a linguistics course. Teachers' beliefs are supported by casual observations, and we tend to notice examples that confirm our current theories. The linguist Peter Fries (personal communication, 2005) points out that "Even professional linguists who have studied the language for many years … have commented that often something they 'knew' about English was shown to be wrong when they looked at the data." In the course, we cultivate a linguistic knowledge base so that teachers working with children and young adults will be more likely to make informed decisions about day-to-day language learning and teaching. We study language like linguists and anthropologists: through class experiences and field projects engaging teachers in close, systematic study of language in use. Our interpretations are informed by readings, discussion, and multimodal engagements.

Given the discrepancy in teachers' attitudes toward literacy development and linguistic diversity, language variation is a major course focus. We also study language learning and consider the limited role of correction in learning our home language(s). Having explored the role of parents and other experienced speakers within first language learning (i.e., immersing children in demonstrations of how language is used, rather than correcting their speech), we can consider the role of the teacher as children with diverse language backgrounds come to school. As educators, we all want children to leave their school years with the linguistic facility to move between various language communities, including those of their home, work, and neighborhoods. Whether educators favor inquiry and experiential language study (i.e., Y. Goodman, 2003; Wells, 2001), culturally pluralist or culturally responsive perspectives (Gilyard, 1991; Ladson-Billings, 1994; Nieto, 1996), or a more culturally explicit approach to teaching language (Delpit, 1995; Reyes, 1992), most language educators agree that language teaching starts with respecting and understanding the language children bring to school.

A multiliteracies perspective suggests learning occurs as students use a range of modalities to engage with family, peers, and community in varied contextual experiences. Meaning-making is situated within social practice, and "patterns of meaning" shift as we move across social contexts and language communities. According to Kalantzis and Cope (2012), "Negotiating these language differences and their patterns or designs becomes a crucial aspect of literacy learning," and they argue that literacy teaching cannot focus on "the rules of a single, standard form of the national language" (p.1). Yet, teachers continue to be asked to teach aspects of language such as grammar or phonics outside of meaningful linguistic and cultural contexts.

Halliday (1973) writes, "We take language all too solemnly—and yet not seriously enough" (p. viii). I discuss this favorite quote with teachers to share my wonder of language differences, to help them feel confident that we all have intuitive expertise as language users, and to encourage them to document (not denigrate) language and cultural repertoire of learners and their families and to look for competence rather than deficits. Studying language provides teachers with expertise for evaluating and critiquing the linguistic and socio-cultural premises underlying instructional materials and pedagogical approaches. Both experienced and novice teachers find that systematic, descriptive language inquiry—focusing on actual language in use—leads them to reconsider old assumptions and gain new insights about their own and their students' language usage. Throughout the course, teachers use first-hand language data to explore language, moving from language stories and language journals to more in-depth field studies. In this chapter, I share our experiences in the hope that other educators find it informative for their own teaching.

Cultivating a Linguistic Knowledge Base through Observation and Documentation

We begin with our own *language stories*, the funny (or not so funny) incidents that we laugh (or cry) about with family and close friends. The wide range of experiences and expertise that graduate students have with home communities and the multilingual settings where they teach are valuable and largely untapped resources for language study. For example, when speaking to Alabama teachers about the value of multiple sign systems (art, music, etc.) for learning, I suggested encouraging children to explore different media such as colored pencils, crayons, and paint. After the talk, a teacher asked me what I had said besides paints and pencils. I said, "crayons," which in my midwestern U.S. dialect is pretty much one syllable, "crans." After several puzzled exchanges, she finally understood. "Oh you mean CRAY-ons."

We use these anecdotes to get to know each other and to begin to tease out the linguistic patterns in our collection of stories. The distinction between "CRAY-ons" (Alabama) and "crans" (Michigan) is an example of a regional dialect variation involving phonology (or accent). The story illustrates that dialect differences sometimes result in confusion or miscommunication. On the other hand, the teacher clearly understood the rest of my talk, suggesting that our southern and midwestern dialects have many more commonalities than differences.

These language stories point out that phonics relationships vary depending on your spoken dialect, a concept very familiar to linguists (i.e., K. Goodman, 1993; Wilde, 1997; Strauss 2005) but ignored by instructional programs. The Alabama teacher and I have different phonics rules for "crayon," allowing us to interpret the letters in our own dialect. The Alabama pronunciation may appear more phonetic, but I don't experience difficulties understanding "crayon" when I read. A focus on systematic direct instruction of phonemic awareness and phonics simplifies language and may cause confusion for readers. New York City/Long Island (NYC/LI) teachers are frustrated when they try to get children to identify "log" and "dog" as rhyming pairs. Do these rhyme in your dialect? In Long Island, children (and adults) say these words differently: lahg with the vowel sound in "hot" and dawg with the vowel sound in "bought." In Phonics Phacts (K. Goodman, 1993), "phonics" is described as the complex set of relationships between written and oral language within a speaker's dialect. My own observations and research indicate that linguistic diversity may influence reading comprehension, but variations in pronunciation do not cause difficulties for readers unless specific pronunciations are prescribed (Goodman & Goodman, 2000).

Teachers' heritage language stories remind us of relationships between language and everyday cultural practices: "Throughout my whole life I called a strainer or colander a 'sculapasta,' which is Italian for strainer. I never knew the English word for it, and whenever I needed one, I would say, 'You know the thing for the macaroni—to get the water out.'" Language stories help us examine our linguistic pet peeves. One student wrote, "When we moved to New Jersey in seventh grade, my sister, who is a year younger than me, started saying all her sentences as a question. It drove me crazy." A common pet peeve involves the childhood pronunciation of "mine:" "The one thing that drives me nuts is when my kids say mines instead of mine." In this example, the unconventional form (or "mistake") may indicate the overgeneralization that occurs in language development. We say yours and hers, so why not mines? The masculine form ("His jacket is his.") is also inconsistent. As we analyze these examples, we notice the complexities of language learning across our lifetimes.

Unlike the students I worked with in Michigan, who believe they speak "standard English," teachers from the NYC/LI area realize they speak a distinct dialect as soon as they leave home. Another teacher writes:

> When I started going to school in Central NY, I came to find out I had a very strong Long Island accent. I would say things like "walk" or "call" and they literally had no idea what I was talking about. And then they would say things like "sucker" and "pop" and it would be like they were speaking German to me. I found that the longer I spent there, the less "thick" my Long Island accent would become, but when I got back to the island

it would come right back. I came to realize how thick my accent was and how much of a difference it makes what part of New York State we live in.

This story illustrates our perception that people who speak a different dialect have an accent; the more differences, the "thicker" the accent. In fact, all English speakers grow up speaking a dialect of English, including a specific accent. Teachers' stories often involve being teased because of their home language. One student writes, "When I went away to college, my friends who are not from New York made fun of me for not pronouncing my 'r's in words. This made me much more conscious of how I speak." Another story describes the prosodic variation (pitch and rhythm) of an immigrant-influenced language community: "Because Italian was my first language, and because I still speak it at home, I was always made fun of [in terms of] the way I spoke. They said I have this 'sing song' way of speaking."

Other stories explore semantic variations in wording between NYC/LI and other regional dialects:

> I went to Penn State University where the majority of students are from Philadelphia or Pittsburgh. My first year, I was in culture shock. People spoke differently from what I was used to in Long Island. Heros are hogies or subs. Sprinkles are jimmies. Diet Coke is not called soda, but pop! My all-time favorite is "Yinz." Yinz is like saying "You guys." (Or in Brooklynese "yous guys.") I can thankfully say I didn't pick up any of this Pennsylvania Jargon!

In discussing these stories, we refine understandings of language systems and processes, aspects of language variation (regional, cultural, generational, gendered, etc.), and language learning. Language stories also raise issues of relationships among language, community memberships, and linguistic identities. It is striking when highly educated professionals tell stories of feeling insecure about their own language, of being chastised by administrators for saying "you know" too much, or of being discriminated against because of an "immigrant accent." Some speakers cling to their New York speech patterns, while others work to be rid of them. In maintaining her social identity as a New York speaker, the student above derides "Pennsylvania Jargon." This may represent playful banter among college students; however, language attitudes can reflect stereotyping and discrimination, especially when power relationships are in play. In discussing our own language stories, we see that language change and variations do not only occur in isolated (other people's) language, but are patterns across languages and speech communities.

Once teachers begin to observe language, they find it is very hard to stop. We jot down stories and speech samples in language journals and share them in class discussions. Student postings about "heroes" (NYC/LI) and "hoagies" (Philadelphia) began a class inquiry throughout one semester. Students uncovered additional terms for what one student defined as "anything on a long roll," such as "sub" (Midwest) or "Italian" (Maine). One student wondered whether the term "hero" was related to the Greek "gyro," which is pronounced "yero." A curious colleague found that "The submarine originated in Groton, Connecticut, among employees of the Electric Boat Corporation, a manufacturer of actual submarines." Informal language stories and examples piqued our linguistic curiosity and helped us to appreciate, enjoy, and celebrate the language variations that we notice.

Informing Our Inquiry with Readings and Resources

Our inquiries into language in use are informed by a variety of resources, including linguistic texts, published research, newspaper articles, poetry, documentaries, literature, and film clips. On the first night of class, we read McWhorter's (1998) introduction to *The Word on the Street*, addressing discrepancies between "commonsense" views of language and beliefs generally accepted among linguists. (While McWhorter's vehement criticisms of progressive education and critiques of African American culture make me somewhat reluctant to recommend his works, his linguistic writings are written with a direct, humorous, and informative style that interrupts linguistic stereotypes and gets teachers thinking about language differently almost immediately.) He argues that all languages and dialects are equally logical, rule-governed, and complex, explaining that any language is a "bundle of dialects" that all "arise from the same process of gradual, unstoppable change" within our multilingual, global society and that "language mixture is a natural and inevitable part of how languages have changed, now change, and will change" (McWhorter, 1998, pp. 3, 4).

A *New York Times* article, "Disco Rice and Other Trash Talk," is fun to read and sparks interest in language study. It describes how New York City sanitation workers create insider communities through specialized language, such as "disco rice" (maggots) (Urbina, 2004, p. B1). The article illustrates how language develops in a specific discourse community (Gee, 1991) and explores language as a badge of social membership within a marginalized group.

In Inada's (1994) poem *Rayford's Song*, the author narrates a school experience where Rayford, a black student, interrupts the third-grade music class and asks if he can sing his own song. While Rayford's rendition of "Swing Low, Sweet Chariot" stuns and inspires his classmates, the teacher responds by correcting his pronunciation. The teacher's action lets the children know that there is a canon of literature, even in music class, and the songs (and language) of their home communities are not included. One teacher, Kathryn, reflects, "*Rayford's Song* is an example of how a teacher can silence his or her students. This story allows teachers to understand how children and even adults feel while being corrected."

Over the next weeks, we view the video *American Tongues* which, while a bit dated, provides extensive firsthand examples of regional dialect and language attitudes. The PBS series *Do You Speak American?* (and related website) provides a wealth of information and resources on a wide range of issues. We also read

Spreading the Word: Language and Dialect in America, McWhorter's (2000) highly readable book for opening discussions with teachers about language diversity. (For reasons mentioned above, I use additional texts to expand on the discussion of *Spreading the Word*, which is somewhat simplistic.) Through these initial explorations, teachers reconsider long-held attitudes about language.

Amanda writes, "I thought people that spoke a slang version of English were either being lazy or were uneducated. McWhorter made us see that slang is in fact the natural change of language." One teacher questions the language attitudes prevalent among her colleagues:

> As a teacher, I always hear my colleagues comment on their students' manner of speaking in a derogatory way, and while in the past I have agreed, I am at this point more inclined to question why the children speak this way. … I think all teachers should read this book and explore language so that they will be better informed about the variations that exist in the English language. I think this study would help teachers to be more understanding and less condemning when their students use slang instead of the standard in English language.

Lauren perceives a shift of awareness in the class: "I think from what we've learned in only two weeks of this course, we are all going to reevaluate how we respond to students who speak differently from the rest of the bunch." In discussion and reflections, students tease out relationships between language variation and communication. Darlene writes, "No matter how language is used through different dialects, slang, sounds, structure, and whether it's logical or not, the bottom line is that this is how we are able to communicate and make meaning of our world." Gina describes home language as part of a person's identity as well as a resource for learning: "I agree with McWhorter that a person's dialect may be different from yours, but it is not necessarily bad grammar or bad English. It is their own and it is hard to change it, not that you should. It is their own way of understanding something."

Teachers pose questions based on their everyday encounters with language variation and concerns about whether or not they should teach a "right way" to speak:

> I teach four- and five-year–olds. … Now when one of my kids asks me "Bathroom please," do I correct them or do I let them just go without correcting them? I must say for the most part I do correct them. I don't want them to feel hurt or shut down by my corrections. I also don't want them to move on to kindergarten speaking incorrectly.

In response, I point them to McWhorter (2000), who writes, "The idea that there is one 'best' English shining in the sky is so intuitively plausible and so relentlessly hammered into us throughout our lives that it is natural for teachers [and parents] to consider part of their jobs to be upholding standard English" (p. ix).

We all struggle with this issue, recognizing that our students live in a world where negative attitudes toward some dialects and languages are prevalent. Chanda writes:

> As a third-grade teacher, I find myself wavering back and forth on the topic. I guess it would be great if we could have the best of both worlds. However, the reality of the situation is that there is a standard that we have to live up to and children today are being called upon not only to reach the standards set by others but to surpass them. While I agree with McWhorter's theory that we are experiencing an evolution of language, and that all the languages are equal, the reality is that there is a standard and probably in our lifetime that standard won't change. Therefore, it is our responsibility as educators to respect these variations in our students' speech and to build upon it. We can do this by teaching them the "correct" way to speak in a way that lets them be themselves and be able to reach their goals in the world of standard English.

Chanda, an African American teacher, reflects Delpit's (1995) concerns that African American children need to learn the codes or rules of the "culture of power" in order to succeed in mainstream America (p. 24). Children who enter school speaking stigmatized dialects (such as AAE or Appalachian English) are generally expected to adopt "school language" (or Academic English) for learning, even in the earliest grades. Such practices may further privilege students who come to school speaking a variation of English considered appropriate in school. On the other hand, Chanda points out that children's home language is part of "being themselves." Our language stories suggest that we, as teachers, maintain home and community language to honor our cultural histories and identities and to sustain our memberships in social communities. How do we provide children opportunities to expand linguistic and cultural repertoires without losing home language and culture?

While teaching questions come up throughout the semester, we place them on hold and then often find that inquiry studies challenge and contradict some of our basic assumptions. Through language study, questions are revised and made more explicit: When are students using specific variations? What is the role of correction in language learning? If we find, as I describe later, that young children are already code-switching adeptly between home and "school" English, a host of new questions can be raised about the goals and foci of language arts pedagogy.

Informing Our Understandings through Systematic, Data-Based Study

Teachers often find linguistic inquiry daunting, feeling they lack the expertise and understandings to collect and interpret data. Informal observations, class explorations, and small group studies help them feel more comfortable as "novice linguists." Language study in the course begins informally through language stories, language journals, and shared expertise. Students start a more formal data collection process by recording and transcribing a five- to ten-minute oral sample of an adult family member, friend, or colleague. This provides the class with a range of language samples from our New York City/Long Island speech communities. When transcribing these short recordings, students realize, for example, that all speakers use informal language features (e.g., "gonna," "you know").

After listening to recorded language samples in small groups, we use sticky notes to record specific examples of language features that distinguish one dialect or variation from another. For example, the spoken sentence, "I spent *tree dollas*," provides examples of two different phonological features of a Brooklyn speaker that we can explain linguistically. We can group the language samples into categories such as phonology, syntax, semantics, pragmatics, or discourse—furthering our understandings of these linguistic systems or aspects of language. Next, students work in groups with a set of Post-it samples representing the same linguistic feature to construct a linguistic rule or pattern.

This process makes it clear that the features of regional dialects or informal speech, even those considered "poor grammar," are systematic and rule-governed. For example, "r-lessness" occurs at the end of a syllable and following a vowel. (In fath*er* or fo*r*get about it, but not in *r*ice or un*r*eliable.) Among some NYC/Long Island speakers, the /r/ shifts to "uh" so that door sounds like "doah." This pronunciation is different from the r-less feature in African American English (AAE) made famous through the rap term "ho" (whore).

Following these exploratory discussions, small group studies focus on a specific feature of language variation or aspect of language study. Some groups looked closely at a specific dialect feature among some NYC/Long Island speakers. For example, the "interdental fricatives" group looked at pronunciation of "th" phonemes among various New York communities. The group found that shifting from the voiced interdental fricative (*th*e, *th*en) to the voiced alveolar stop /d/ is common in many working-class New York communities as well as African American and immigrant communities. Students found that /t/ can be substituted for the voiceless interdental in words like "three" by speakers from Brooklyn. However, while African American English (AAE) speakers may say "den" for "then," they do not typically say "tree" for "three" (unless they also come from Brooklyn).

Adger, Wolfram, and Christian (2007) provide guidelines for teachers to engage in systematic study of language features within their school community. A group focusing on Long Island's famous "open o" in words like "coffee" asked varied speakers to read a passage where words such as "dog" or "coffee" each occurred twice. The "r-less" group hypothesized that r-lessness is a low-status feature that occurs only in working-class New York City communities and among African Americans. Through observation and reading, the teachers found r-lessness is present in many American and British dialects, including some high-status speech communities. They discovered that r-lessness was considered high status in the first part of the twentieth century and that early movie actors were coached to remove the /r/ from their speech. In addition, r-lessness occurred in the speech of four U.S. presidents, each representing different speech communities.

Other group studies have focused on semantic variations (pop/soda, lollipop/sucker, etc.), youth slang, and discourse markers (such as *you know* or *like*). One impressive group study focused on code-switching, or shifts between languages, dialects, or registers. A Korean American student observed language in her own family to see when Korean and English were spoken during a family gathering. A bilingual teacher studied code-switching between Spanish and English among students in her fifth-grade classroom. A European American teacher studied the dialect code-switching of African American students in her classroom. Another teacher focused on shifts in formal and informal speech styles within a university office. The group presentation and handout provided many examples and extensive information about code-switching for their colleagues.

Independent Field Projects

Following group projects, teachers engage in focused language studies with new confidence. Selecting an inquiry study from a menu of options, each graduate student develops in-depth understandings and expertise in a specific field or area of linguistics. When projects are shared, the class benefits from many areas of language study. Data analysis workshops also provide time for teachers to share resources, processes, and interpretations.

Providing choices for language studies supports differences in teaching levels (pre-K to high school), research experiences, backgrounds, and interests. Students select a topic that interests them, puzzles them, or perhaps worries them. One young mother was concerned because her son was labeled "language delayed." At 18 months, he spoke infrequently and had about twenty words in his speech repertoire. Through close study of video recordings of her son interacting with family members in varied contexts, she found that his small number of "words" were resources for expressing a wide range of meanings depending on social function and context.

Students have examined commercial discourse in exchanges between staff and customers in a supermarket, bar, drug store, and jewelry store. Studies have documented language teenagers are developing in instant messaging. One student compared greetings at her synagogue to greetings at the college library. Students have studied language within many New York City/Long Island immigrant speech communities, including Irish, Spanish Queens, Haitian, Greek, Italian, and in regional communities such as Bonacker (a language community of East Hampton locals). Students also study language in literature, films, and TV shows, such as *My Cousin Vinny, Sweet Home Alabama, Fargo, Moesha*, and *The Sopranos*. Classroom studies, such as the one described below, have focused on discourse, second language learners, or speakers from stigmatized speech communities.

A Study of AAE Features of One Fifth-Grade Girl

Doreen Noone Wheeler's study provides a specific example of how teachers may challenge and refine their beliefs and knowledge base through language study. Doreen, a European American teacher, decided to study African American English in her classroom:

> because I work in a multicultural neighborhood and many of my students each year use this form of speaking … Throughout my four years of teaching in a predominately African American and Hispanic community, I would continuously correct my students' Black English during class time and even in the schoolyard. This whole way of speaking really bothered me, and I wanted my students to sound more educated. I felt like it was a reflection on me if I could not "improve" their way of speaking. What I was sadly failing to realize was that this is who they are, this is a piece of their heritage.

[Although I've elected to use African American English (AAE), borrowing from recent titles, Doreen uses Black English (BE) based on earlier readings. Other descriptors include Black English Vernacular (BEV), African American Language, or Ebonics.]

Doreen selected one fifth grader, Jasmine, "Not only because she's outgoing and personable, but mainly because she is constantly using Black English both inside and outside of the classroom." Doreen writes:

> My original hypothesis was that this girl used Black English in all situations and never deviated or code-switched, whether she was involved in either a formal or informal conversation. The other part of my hypothesis was that this form of speaking was holding her back and making her education suffer.

It is common for teachers to report that all of their urban students speak Black English, which is equated with the language of rap music. African American English may influence the language of Hispanic students in integrated communities, but these are distinct communities. Systematic observation and conversations with children and with adults from a particular community help teachers gain an understanding of students' linguistic and cultural backgrounds.

Doreen recorded a writing conference focusing on a poem Jasmine had written. Since writing conferences are common in Doreen's classroom, this should provide an authentic data sample. Doreen believed one recorded conversation would provide sufficient examples of AAE features. However, she was "kind of disappointed" with the recording because she did not hear nonstandard features. Doreen also found very few examples of AAE features in Jasmine's writing. At this point, Doreen "started to think I was going crazy." In her mind, she hears

"Jasmine's loud voice," using AAE features throughout the day. She wondered, "Did she secretly figure out what I was studying for my class project?"

Doreen's study replicated a characteristic finding of sociolinguistic studies (i.e., Labov, 1972; Wolfram, 1993), documenting that speaker's usage of distinct dialect features may vary depending on linguistic and social context. This is particularly true for stigmatized features (e.g., "ain't") that are characterized as "nonstandard" forms. A teacher's characterization of a student's language based on casual rather than systematic observations colors the teacher's perceptions of the child's actual language use. Having heard AAE features in Jasmine's language, Doreen perceives them as occurring all the time. When documenting identifiable phonological or grammatical variations systematically, Doreen finds they occur much less frequently than predicted. More subtle distinctions, such as intonational rhythms and rhetorical patterns, may signal AAE usage and influence teachers' perceptions.

Faced with contradictory evidence, Doreen began to revise her hypotheses:

> Two things occurred to me: 1) She was not using her normal form of Black English because we were talking about her writing piece and maybe she does not use Black English in her writing, or 2) The conference was very stiff and structured, and she changes or code-switches her dialect when she is put one-on-one with her teacher.

Doreen gathered more data, starting with a "casual interview, where I asked her friendly yet personal things you might discuss with a new friend." Aside from calling her mother "moms," Jasmine still did not use any identifiable features of AAE or even informal English. Doreen then recorded a conversation between Jasmine and an African American boy in her class, telling the students "to just go ahead and talk among themselves about the class trip we had just gone on." Doreen had to leave the room before the two students began to speak more casually, providing the following examples of AAE:

*   He be acting all gangsta.
*   She live in, like, a house.
*   We wasn't yelling, we was talking.
*   Why you all don't still go to Rye Playland no more?
*   We respected where we come from.

Doreen also noticed examples of informal spoken English common across American dialects, such as "I'm gonna have fun" and "This movie is kinda nasty." This informal language further highlights Jasmine's awareness, whether conscious or intuitive, that interactions with her teacher call for more formal English. Doreen concluded that "Jasmine uses a colloquial dialect when she is speaking to her friends, working in a group, or when she is angry. However, when speaking to me or another educator, she code switches to what is considered standard dialect or 'Proper English.'"

Doreen's study influenced her views of Jasmine and her home language. She writes that:

> My original hypothesis was wrong and that Jasmine does not use the Black English features in all settings. I also reject my initial ideas that all people that use Black English features are ignorant. Just from the conversations I had with Jasmine alone, both formal and informal, it is extremely apparent that Jasmine is anything but ignorant. In fact, she is a very bright child, especially in the reading and writing areas. She has a very creative mind that is always working.

Doreen's study also had an unexpected (and remarkable!) side effect: "I have to say that I really learned a lot about Jasmine that I would never have known without doing this study." She reflects, "I was not aware of code-switching or the fact that someone as young as fifth grade not only can do this but now also knows when to do this. I now look at my students in a different light with a newfound hope for their extended education." In the future, Doreen will work to be a teacher "who doesn't try to change my students' language or dialect, but instead just helps them to understand when they should use it or not."

Reconsidering Language Learning and Teaching

In school, language study often focuses on phonics and grammar from a prescriptive stance. The goal is for students to adopt a standardized version of English determined (or prescribed) by the teacher, textbook, or program. Observing language in use challenges misconceptions about idealized "standard English," as well as views of nonconventional English variations. When teachers believe strongly in the importance of "Standard English," I encourage them to identify a group of "standard" speakers, listen to them speaking, and carefully analyze what they hear. Invariably, they find that all speakers use forms considered nonstandard, even within professional settings. One recent group study on informal standard English looked at features such as "gonna" for "going to" and "wanna" for "want to" provides an example of how systematic study continues to challenge our preconceptions. While "gonna" tends to vary depending on formality of setting, documenting the use of "wanna" in Obama's formal speeches made us consider that "wanna" is actually the standard pronunciation.

Doreen's study illustrates that initial perceptions and hunches about children's language use are often inaccurate. Through inquiry study, teachers (and their students) don't have to take linguists at their word, but can investigate areas where they have puzzles and let the data speak for itself. Looking systematically at language in use with a descriptive stance, we come to appreciate the complexity and flexibility of children's linguistic understandings and language development. The research studies we read are more significant when we use them to inform our observations and understandings.

One goal for teachers is to support learning and language development, recognizing that development and sophistication in the use of a variety of genres occurs over time and that mistakes in conventional usage are a part of the process. Experiences in analyzing speaking, listening, reading, and writing in various genres and social contexts prompts teachers and children to consider the language styles and forms appropriate in particular settings. Social conventions vary if a writer is composing a rap song, a science report, a letter to the editor, a poem, a diary, an email, and so on. Similarly, process is a consideration; for example, rough draft writing focuses on meaning rather than conventions.

Language study helps teachers to observe and document language development, appreciate and support children's outside-of-school language communities, evaluate the validity of assumptions about language that underlie pedagogical programs and practices, and develop pedagogy that supports language learning. Halliday (1973) writes:

> If we (and this includes teachers) can learn to be more serious about language, and at the same time a great deal less solemn about it … then we might be more ready to recognize linguistic success for what it is when we see it, and so do more to bring it about where it would otherwise fail to appear. (p. viii)

Language Study in the Classroom

Taking a multiliteracies perspective, looking at multimodal practices in diverse language communities, both teachers and their students can explore the complex ways we make meaning within varied social contexts available to learners today. Kalantzis and Cope (2012) contrast the "old basics" of phonics and grammar instruction with a "new basics" involving "multiple literacies for a world of multimodal communication" and "many social languages with and variation in communication appropriate to settings" (p. 5). As a veteran whole language teacher, my work on language study in the classroom is also informed by research in reading and writing as language processes and constructivist studies of early child development. The book *Valuing Language Study* (Goodman, Y., 2003) provides a wealth of ideas for studying language with students.

Language pedagogy informed by linguistic study is additive rather than subtractive (Valenzuela, 1999). Children's home language is a resource they bring to each new language experience, and young children as well as English Language Learners need opportunities to think and learn in their own language or dialect (Ruiz, 1988). For example, employing the ethnographic approaches of literacy researchers such as Taylor (1993) and Moll et al. (1992), teachers engage students in "literacy digs" exploring the texts in their homes and communities. Students might gather texts posted on their refrigerators or take community literacy walks.

Young children can use these texts to appreciate what "we can read" while older students explore the uses of texts in a variety of contexts. Teachers and students can study language together, investigating language functions and forms, exploring linguistic and cultural diversity, and addressing linguistic stereotypes. Exploring language variation in literature, such as in McKissack's (1986) *Flossie and the Fox*, raises sociocultural and sociopolitical issues that teachers and students can address together. Learners, like their teachers, can come to see that while all variations are rich means of expression, some variations are privileged in our society. And, yes, children and youth can explore a variety of language forms in their own writing (even before they become published authors). The book *Valuing Language Study* (Y. Goodman, 2003) is a resource for exploring these learning experiences with students.

When exploring language study with their students, I encourage teachers to study language like linguists, shifting from a prescriptive to a descriptive stance in the classroom. Rather than teaching kids that "log" and "dog" rhyme, young children might explore the "og" family (dog, log, frog, etc.), investigating which pairs rhyme or don't rhyme in their home communities and how these words are pronounced in other language communities. This kind of linguistic inquiry places phonemic awareness in a context that addresses children's extensive home language knowledge within studies that provide more accurate metalinguistic understandings than a "standard" phonics workbook is capable of describing. Children's intuitive understandings become explicit when teachers and children study language together.

Studying language through inquiry changes the relationship between teachers and learners, whether in the college classroom or the elementary school classroom. When teachers and children engage in language inquiry together, learners and their families often become the "expert speakers" with knowledge to be shared rather than inadequate speakers with language forms to be subtracted (Valenzuela, 1999) or eradicated (Gilyard, 1991). When my colleague Terry McGinnis (McGinnis et al., 2007) and a group of teachers examined the explored multimodal and transnational practices of youth engaged in online literacies, they found that the digital natives in our classrooms have much to teach us. They conclude that schools "should consider a range of ways to bridge youth's digital worlds with their academic worlds; to find space for all youth to express and share their concerns and challenges related to local, national and global issues and politics; and to encourage and build upon such transnational literacy practices" (p. 302). In her courses, McGinnis encourages teachers to use inquiry study and digital stories with students to explore critical issues and topics through multimodal compositions.

Engaging in language inquiry helps teachers to tease out linguistic complexities, revise and refine their beliefs, and inform their own teaching with a greater awareness of how language matters in everyday life and learning.

Author's Note

1 "Language Study in Teacher Education: Cultivating Teachers' Understandings of Language Variation" is a revised version of "Language study in teacher education: Exploring the *language* in language arts," originally published in *Language Arts*, 84(2), 145–156, copyright 2006 by the National Council of Teachers of English.

References

Adger, C., Wolfram, W., & Christian, D. (2007). Exploring dialects. In *Dialects in schools and communities* (2nd Ed.). Mahwah, NJ: Erlbaum.

Delpit, L. (1995). *Other people's children: Cultural conflict in the classroom*. New York, NY: The New Press.

Gee, J. P. (1991). *Social linguistics and literacies: Ideology in discourses*. New York, NY: Falmer.

Gilyard, K. (1991). *Voices of the self: A study of language competence*. Detroit, MI: Wayne State University Press.

Goodman, D., & Goodman, Y., (2000). I hate 'postrophes: Issues of dialect and reading proficiency. In J. K. Peyton, P. Griffin, W. Wolfram, & R. Fasold (Eds.), *Language in action: New studies of language in society* (pp. 408–435). Cresskill, NJ: Hampton.

Goodman, K. (1993). *Phonics phacts*. Portsmouth, NH: Heinemann.

Goodman, Y. (2003). *Valuing language study: Inquiry into language for elementary and middle schools*. Urbana, IL: NCTE.

Halliday. M.A.K. (1973). Foreword. In *Breakthrough to literacy* by D. Mackay, B. Thompson, & P. Schaub. Glendale, CA: Bowmar.

Inada, L. (1994). Rayford's song. In B. Bigelow, L. Christensen, S. Karp, B. Miner, & B. Peterson (Eds.), *Rethinking our classrooms: Teaching for equity and justice* (p. 108). Milwaukee, WI: Rethinking Schools.

Kalantzis, M., & Cope, B. (2012). *Literacies*. Cambridge, UK: Cambridge University Press.

Labov, W. (1972). *Language in the inner city: Studies of Black English vernacular*. Philadephia, PA: University of Pennsylvania Press.

Ladson-Billings, G. (1994). *The dreamkeepers: Successful teachers of African American children*. San Francisco, CA: Jossey-Bass.

McGinnis, T., Goodstein-Stolzenberg, A., & Saliani, E. (2007) "indnpride": Online spaces of transnational youth as sites of creative and sophisticated literacy and identity work. *Linguistics in Education*, 18, 283–304.

McKissack, P., & Isadora, R. (illustrator). (1986). *Flossie and the fox*. New York, NY: Dial Books for Young Readers.

McWhorter, J. (1998). *The word on the street*. New York, NY: Plenum.

McWhorter, J. (2000). *Spreading the word: Language and dialect in America*. Portsmouth, NH: Heinemann.

Moll, L.C., Amanti, C. Neff, D., and Gonzalez, N. (1992). Funds of knowledge for teaching: Using a qualitative approach to connect homes and classrooms. Theory into Practice, 31(2). *Qualitative Issues in Educational Research*. (Spring 1992.) pp. 132–141. Taylor and Francis.

Nieto, S. (1996). *Affirming diversity: The sociopolitical context of multicultural education* (2nd Ed.). White Plains, NY: Longman.

Reyes, M. (1992). Changing venerable assumption: Literacy instruction for linguistically different students. *Harvard Educational Review*, 62: 427–446.

Ruiz, R. (1988). Orientations in language planning. In S. L. McKay & C. W. Sau-ling (Eds.), *Language diversity—problem or resource?: A social and educational perspective on language minorities in the United States* (pp. 3–25). Cambridge, UK: Newbury House.

Strauss, S. (2005). *Silent "e" speaks out: The linguistics, neurology, and politics of phonics.* Mahwah, NJ: Erlbaum.

Taylor, D. (1993). *From the child's point of view.* Portsmouth, NH: Heinemann.

Urbina, I. (2004, July 31). Disco rice and other trash talk: Picking up the garbage means picking up the lingo. *New York Times*, p. B1.

Valenzuela, A. (1999). *Subtractive schooling: U.S.–Mexican youth and the politics of caring.* Albany, NY: State University of New York Press.

Wells, G. (Ed.). (2001). *Action, talk, and text: Learning and teaching through inquiry.* New York, NY: Teacher's College Press.

Wilde, S. (1997). *What's a schwa sound anyway? A holistic guide to phonetics, phonics, and spelling.* Portsmouth, NH: Heinemann.

Wolfram, W. (1993). Dialects, language variation, and schooling. In L. M. Cleary & M. D. Linn (Eds.), *Linguistics for teachers* (pp. 4–22). New York, NY: McGraw-Hill.

3

"DEADLY WAYS TO LEARN"

Language Variation, Ideology, and Learning Literacies

Cynthia H. Brock, Jenni Carter, and Fenice B. Boyd

A few years ago when searching for studies about language variation, Cindy came upon an article with the following title (emphasis in original): "*Deadly Ways to Learn* … a yarn about some learning we did together" (Cahill & Collard, 2003). As we begin this chapter, we invite you to take a moment and answer the following questions:

1. Why do you think Cahill and Collard entitled their article "*Deadly Ways to learn* … a yarn about some learning we did together"? Why is the title significant?
2. Why do you think we are asking you to think about this title at the onset of our chapter? What does this experience have to do with the focus of our chapter?

Now having posed the above questions and having asked you to take a moment to consider how you might answer them, we address each question in turn. First, Cindy found the aforementioned title compelling, and prior to reading the article, she assumed that the article would be a research report about some ineffective ways that teachers in the study taught their students about language variation. It turns out that her prediction was not correct. The Cahill and Collard (2003) study was conducted in Western Australia. Cahill is a *Wadjella* (Wadjella means "white fella" in Aboriginal English); Collard is an Aboriginal person. The term "deadly" means "really good" in Aboriginal English. In their 2003 work, Cahill and Collard reported the positive and powerful results of a teacher action research study pertaining to language variation conducted in Western Australia that occurred as a result of Aboriginal people and *Wadjellas* teaming up to study the impact of two-way bi-dialectical teaching (i.e., Aboriginal English and Standard Australian English) on the literacy learning of children in their schools.

Why might we introduce this article title at the beginning of our chapter? Unless you know Aboriginal English, you were likely as stumped as Cindy about the title of the article. For us, discussion about the title is a powerful reminder that the cultural, linguistic, and ideological lenses we use to view the world shape what we see, hear, and understand. Sometimes, for example, we forget that as academics from the United States and Australia, Standard *Academic English* is one lens through which we (i.e., Cindy, Jenni, and Fenice) view the world culturally, linguistically, and ideologically. We also emphasize that the three of us speak other language varieties. For example, Cindy grew up in the rural western United States with family members who speak and write a version of rural American English. Jenni grew up in the state of South Australia, and she speaks South Australian English (which is more British than the English spoken in other Australian states). Fenice grew up in the rural southeastern United States; she speaks and writes a version of Standard English, but she also grew up speaking African American Vernacular English. The *Deadly Ways to Learn* example reminds us that we may be missing important understandings by not questioning the affordances and constraints underpinning our own cultural, linguistic, and ideological lenses (Osborne, 2014). Additionally, this example sheds light on the fact that we interpret new language varieties through our existing cultural, linguistic, and ideological lenses. In short, interpreting across language varieties is more than merely understanding the definitions of different vocabulary words used in different language varieties. Language varieties, like all language practices, are situated within specific cultural and ideological practices that have nuanced local meanings (Malcolm, 2013; Osborne, 2014; Pennycook, 2007). As you read the ideas we share in this chapter, we invite you to consider how your own cultural, linguistic, and ideological lenses shape the interpretations you render of the ideas we share.

Overall, this chapter focuses on the literacy education of children who speak varieties of English that are traditionally marginalized in public schools and in societies in general. Specifically, we discuss how a multiliteracies conceptual framework paves the way for more just and equitable perceptions of language varieties. Although we discuss a number of language varieties in this chapter, we focus primarily on African American Vernacular English (i.e., AAVE) and Aboriginal English. We are mindful that there are many versions of AAVE and Aboriginal English (Delpit, 2012; Malcolm, 2013). Additionally, we are aware that AAVE is considered to be a dialect by some scholars and a separate language by others (Perry & Delpit, 1998). As well, we explore what we, as a field, know about language varieties, and we examine how our understanding of language varieties informs our beliefs and practices with respect to children's literacy education. Finally, throughout this chapter, we weave a discussion of the role that politics, power, and ideology play in discussions of language-related issues (Gee, 2012; Postman, 1970).

We include a brief discussion of ideology here since we refer to ideology as we discuss language variation throughout this chapter. We draw on Mannheim (1964), who argues that ideology relates to the "picture of society" that "individuals carry around in their heads" about the nature of that society (p. xxiii). Kavanagh (1995) suggests that another central piece of the ideology picture is individuals' recognition of "their place in that society" that they "carry around in their heads." The "society that individuals carry around with them in their heads" includes beliefs about race, class, gender, sexual identity, languages, language varieties, ethnicity, religion, and so forth (p. 309). Moreover, various combinations of these different social/cultural/biological markers can distinguish between who is and is not considered elite in different societies (Janks, 2010). Drawing on Marx (1967), Gee (2012) argues that ideology relates in particular to power differentials between the elite in societies and all others. Additionally, Gee (2009) argues that elites paint a picture of reality that (1) is in their best interest, (2) helps them to sustain their power, and (3) convinces others (i.e., the non-elite) that the way things are is normal. The problem here is that when sets of beliefs are considered "normal," they may be taken for granted and not questioned or challenged. And unfortunately, according to Gee (2009), "The elite and powerful in a society fail to realize that their views of reality follow from, and support their positions of power" (p. 28). One of our central goals is to elucidate ideologies about language varieties, interrogate them, and consider the ethical implications of those ideologies in our work as teachers (Faber, 2004). Additionally, we emphasize that language-in-use can serve as a powerful vehicle for maintaining ideological positions.

In the next section, we discuss the two aspects of multiliteracies that we draw on to frame this chapter. Then we ask you to take a short quiz comprised of two questions. Finally, there are two sections structured around each question.

Multiliteracies Conceptual Framework

In chapter one, Fenice and Cindy provided an overview of multiliteracies. Here we look more closely at specific ways that a multiliteracies perspective can inform our thinking about language variation. Working in conjunction with a group of like-minded colleagues that comprised the New London Group (1996), Kalantzis and Cope (2012) coined the term "multiliteracies" in an attempt "to explain what still matters in traditional approaches to reading and writing, and to supplement this with knowledge of what is new and distinctive about the ways in which people make meanings in the contemporary communications environment" (p. 1). Scholars have argued that efforts to understand meaning-making in the present time must include attention to two central issues. First, as teachers, we must consider the social diversity present within and across cultural and linguistic contexts (New London Group, 1996). Second, in the new communications environment, "meaning is made in ways that are increasingly multimodal—in which written-linguistic modes of meaning interface with oral, visual, audio, gestural, tactile, and spatial patterns of meaning" (Kalantzis & Cope, 2012, p. 2).

Kalantzis and Cope (2012) argue that serious attention to these two central issues will bring about a shift in the ways we think about our work as teachers as well as the ways that we think about our students as learners. They discuss this shift in terms of moving from "old" basics to "new" basics. Two central language-related ideas that mark the shift from old basics to new basics are of particular concern to us. First, whereas one aspect of the old basics focused exclusively on correct spelling and grammar, new basics acknowledge the "many social languages and variation in communication appropriate to [different] settings" (Kalantzis & Cope, 2012, p. 5). Second, whereas old basics focused solely on standard forms of English, new basics shift the focus to learning to "communicate with different kinds of people who can innovate, take risks, negotiate diversity, and navigate uncertainty" (Kalantzis & Cope, 2012, p. 5). We discuss each of these language-related shifts from old to new basics in the sections that follow as we talk through answers to the quiz.

Quiz: Language Variation and Literacy Learning

You may want to jot down your answers to the questions below and keep your answers handy as you read through the remainder of this chapter.

Question #	Question:	Type of Answer:
1.	What is language variation, and what does it have to do with ideology?	Short Answer
2.	Our central goal as teachers should be to teach all students Standard English.	True/False
Please answer the two questions above before continuing.		

FIGURE 3.1 Language Variation Quiz.

We address each of the questions in Figure 3.1 in the following manner. First, with respect to question number one, we begin by defining language variation. Then we use a case study of the Oakland, California Ebonics Debate to illustrate the central role that ideology plays in people's perceptions of language varieties. As you read through the Oakland Ebonics case study, pay particular attention to (1) the way that Ebonics is characterized by different groups of people and (2) the role that Ebonics should play in the learning of standard varieties of English according to advocates of the Oakland Ebonics Resolution.

Second, with respect to question number two, we use a case study of language variation educational practices in Western Australia to explore the role that Standard English might play in our work as teachers. As you read through our answer to the second question, pay attention to your own thoughts about the role of Standard English plays in your instruction. Also ask yourself what is different about the role that Standard English varieties play in the Western Australia case study as compared with the Oakland Ebonics case study.

Language Variation: What Does Ideology Have to Do with It?

We briefly discuss language variation in this section; however, for a more comprehensive overview of language variation, we refer you to chapter 2 by Debra Goodman and chapter 8 by Rebecca Wheeler and Rachael Swords. Typically, differences *across* languages (such as French, Spanish, German, and English) seem starkly obvious; however, significant differences also exist *within* languages (Adger, Wolfram, & Christian, 2007). Scholars (e.g., Wardhaugh, 1998) suggest that language variation refers to the non-uniform nature of language. Language varies with respect to "sociocultural characteristics of groups of people such as their cultural background, geographical location, social class, gender, or age" (Wolfram, Adger, & Christian, 1999, p. 1). Language varies in other ways, too. For example, language variation may also refer to the different ways that a speaker uses language in different contexts. For example, when we (the three of us as authors) present a research paper at a conference, we present ourselves more formally than when we are talking with family members at the dinner table. Referring back to the beginning of this chapter, we presented an example that illustrated differences between a variety of Aboriginal English and a variety of Standard Australian English. Linguists typically use the term "dialect" to refer to a type of language used by a particular group of people associated with a geographical region or social group (Adger, Wolfram, & Christian, 2007).

Wolfram and Schilling-Estes (1998) distinguish between popular, general-public-type viewpoints about dialects and linguists' conceptions of dialects. In Figure 3.2, we present a comparison between the general public's conceptions of dialects and Wolfram and Schilling-Estes' (1998) conceptions of dialects.

MYTH: General Public's Conceptions of Dialects:	REALITY: Linguists' Conceptions of Dialects
"A dialect is something that SOMEONE ELSE speaks."	"Everyone who speaks a language speaks a dialect of the language; it is not possible to speak a language without speaking a dialect of the language."
"Dialects have no linguistic patterning in their own right; they are deviations from standard speech."	"Dialects, like all language systems, are systematic and regular; furthermore, socially disfavored dialects can be described with the same kind of precision as standard language varieties."
"Dialects result from unsuccessful attempts to speak the 'correct' form of a language."	"All speakers of languages speak dialects; moreover, dialect speakers acquire their language by adopting the speech features of those around them, not by failing in their attempts to adopt standard language features."

(Wolfram and Schilling-Estes, 1998, pp. 7 and 8.)

FIGURE 3.2 Differences between the General Public's Conceptions of Dialects and Linguists' Conceptions of Dialects.

To this point, our comments about language variation likely seem benign. Discussions about language varieties are often far from benign, however (Delpit, 1995). Consider, for example, the Oakland Ebonics Debate. African American

Vernacular English (AAVE) is sometimes called Ebonics. An intense national debate occurred in the United States in the 1990s when the School Board of Oakland, California sanctioned the use of Ebonics as a tool to teach African American children in Oakland to learn to speak standard varieties of English. What is Ebonics, and why did the Oakland School Board want to sanction its use in Oakland schools? Although there are debates as to whether Ebonics is a dialect or a language (see Baldwin, 1998), according to renowned linguist Geneva Smitherman (1998), Ebonics is

> neither "broken" English, nor "sloppy" speech, nor merely "slang," nor some bizarre lingo spoken only by baggy-pants-wearing Black kids. Rather, the variety of Ebonics spoken in the United States … is rooted in the Black American Oral Tradition and represents a synthesis of African (primarily West African) and European (primarily English) linguistic-cultural traditions. (p. 30)

The Linguistics Society of America weighed in during the Oakland Ebonics Debate crafting a resolution identifying Ebonics as viable, rule-governed, and valuable, supporting the Oakland School Board decision. (See the Linguistics Society of America Resolution on Ebonics at http://www-personal.umich.edu/~jlawler/ebonics.lsa.html. See the original Oakland Ebonics Resolution at http://linguistlist.org/topics/ebonics/ebonics-res1.html. See the revised Oakland Ebonics Resolution at https://linguistlist.org/topics/ebonics/ebonics-res2.html.)

Why did the Oakland School Board propose using Ebonics to teach standard varieties of English in the first place? The Oakland School Board sought to improve the school success of children in the Oakland School District. While African American children made up over half of the student population, they received the lowest grade point average of any other group of children in the district (1.8 compared with white children, 2.7, and Asian American, 2.4), received four-fifths of the overall school suspensions, and were grossly overrepresented in special education (Perry & Delpit, 1998). Prescott Elementary School stood out because the African American children there were consistently more successful than African American children at any other school in the district. Prescott Elementary teachers had voluntarily adopted an approach to teaching, the Standard English Proficiency Program, that acknowledged "the systematic, rule-governed nature of Black English and takes the position that this language should be used to help children learn to read and write in Standard English" (Perry & Delpit, 1998, p. xi). The members of the Oakland School Board sought to expand this successful instructional approach to other schools.

Let us return to one of the questions we asked you to ponder as you read the Oakland Ebonics case study: How was Ebonics characterized by different groups of people involved in the Oakland Ebonics debate? Clearly, since Ebonics is considered a viable and valuable language by linguists and since educational scholars (e.g., Delpit, 1995, 2012; Gonzalez, Moll, & Amanti, 2005) have long argued that education is most effective when teachers value, draw on, and build instruction from children's linguistic and cultural backgrounds, the Oakland Ebonics Debate was much more about persistent, deficient views of African American language and culture than anything else. What might we as teachers do about deficient views of language varieties such as Ebonics? We propose adopting a shift from the notion that there is one standard form of English to the notion that there are many viable languages and language forms as discussed by Kalantzis and Cope (2012). Moreover, this shift requires, at minimum, a two-pronged approach: First, the more we learn about language, the more we value different languages and language varieties. Second, language practices, like all human endeavors, are infused with ideology. Consequently, it would serve us well to interrogate our own ideological perspectives, and those of others, with respect to language and language varieties.

The second question we asked you to ponder was the following: According to advocates of the Oakland Ebonics Resolution, what role should Ebonics play in the learning of standard varieties of English? Although advocates of the Oakland Ebonics Resolution saw Ebonics as a valuable tool to draw on as children were taught standard varieties of English, the end goal was the learning of standard varieties of English. In essence, even though Ebonics was valued, it was seen as a stepping-stone to learning standard varieties of English. We argue that a shift from old to new basics would precipitate a shift in our thinking about Ebonics. Advocates of new basics would see Ebonics as a valuable dialect to learn in its own right.

Now that you have finished reading this section and before we move on to the second question in the next section, we invite you to compare the original answer you wrote to the first question: What is language variation, and what does it have to do with ideology? How does your original answer compare with what you just read? Would you change any or all of your original answer? Why or why not?

Should Our Central Goal Be to Teach All Students Standard English?

Referring back to Figure 3.2, it is likely clear that from a linguistic perspective, dialects are systematic, rule-governed versions of a language. When considering dialects from a clinical linguistic academic perspective, if all dialects are equally viable, should one of our central goals be to teach all students Standard English? In a more equitable world where all language varieties are valued and respected, we suspect that a logical answer to this question would be no. Why? If linguists consider all language varieties to be equal from a scientific perspective, then no one language variety is more important than any other; consequently, we might ask ourselves why one language variety (i.e., Standard English) should be *the* language variety of choice for everyone to learn. However, as the Oakland

Ebonics example illustrates, the general public does not see language varieties and practices from a clinical academic linguistic perspective. In fact, language practices are ideological, and many Americans see language varieties such as AAE through ideological lenses clouded by racism. We wish to point out here that all of us, including linguists, operate from ideological perspectives (e.g., Redd & Schuster Webb, 2005).

Scholars such as Lisa Delpit (1995) and Maria de la luz Reyes (1992) have long argued that teachers have a responsibility to teach Standard English to all children, especially children from non-dominant backgrounds. Two terms in the previous sentence, "Standard English" and "non-dominant," point us to the reason that scholars argue for teaching all children a version of Standard English. We address the latter term and then the former. Gutierrez (2008) uses the term "non-dominant" to highlight the politics of dominance, especially in U.S. society. People from dominant backgrounds are white, middle to upper class, heterosexual, native English speakers. People from this dominant group speak standard varieties of English and hold positions of power in society. A problem with the term "standard," of course, is that it implies that anything that sounds different must not be "standard" and therefore must be deficient (Macedo, 1994). Having raised these issues, however, those in positions of power in society hold standard varieties of English in higher regard. Consequently, it is imperative that educators help children learn standard varieties of English. Not doing so precludes them from having access to positions of power and authority in society (Delpit, 2012, de la Luz Reyes, 1992).

A question worth asking, however, is whether it can be otherwise? Can other language varieties besides standard varieties of English be considered as useful/valuable as varieties of Standard English in school and societal settings? We return to the example from the beginning of this chapter to answer with a resounding *yes*, it can be different! In fact, it *is* different in the state of Western Australia. Well over a decade ago, fourteen schools in Western Australia began taking part in the "Deadly Ways to Learn" project (Cahill & Collard, 2003). In a nutshell, the goal of this project is two-way bi-dialectical teaching and learning. Two-way bi-dialectical teaching means that two target dialects are equally valued in teaching and learning. In the case of Western Australia, the two target dialects include varieties of Aboriginal English and standard Australian English. This dual focus of the "Deadly Ways to Learn" project sets it apart from other related projects. Namely, a central feature of the project is "to promote Aboriginal English and Standard Australian English as being of equal value" (Williams, 2011, p. 25). Aboriginal English varieties are not seen solely as a gateway to teaching Standard Australian English; rather, both dialects are considered indispensable. Contrast this approach with the Oakland Ebonics Resolution in California. In that context, although the proponents of the Ebonics Resolution saw African American English (AAE) as valuable, the focus of the Oakland Resolution was using AAE as a vehicle for teaching Standard English.

A second unique feature of the "Deadly Ways to Learn" project is the teacher action research component of the project, whereby Aboriginal educators are teamed up with non-Aboriginal educators. In this context, educators work with and learn from one another about their respective languages and cultures. While the process of crafting this bi-dialectical approach to language varieties in Western Australia has not been a trouble-free venture, it is widely seen as an important and successful endeavor (Cahill & Collard, 2003; Malcolm & Truscott 2012; What Works Program, 2010; Williams, 2011). In fact, Malcolm (2013) asserts:

> [T]wo-way bidialectical education has become a reality within the Western Australian education system, supported by the recently-launched 14-volume training resource *Tracks to Two-Way Learning*. … This forms a basis for Aboriginal and non-Aboriginal educators to work in two-way teams, showing mutual respect and receptivity, to the end that Aboriginal and non-Aboriginal learners will learn in linguistic and cultural partnership. (p. 51)

For a detailed look at some of the important bi-dialectical work being done in Western Australian schools, please see the following link: http://www.whatworks.edu.au/4_2_1.htm.

Let's return to the original question used to frame this section: Should our central goal be to teach all students standard English? We propose that *a* central goal in both the United States and Australia should be to teach all students a variety of Standard English. After all, standard varieties of English are the language of power in both contexts (Delpit, 2012; Malcolm, 2013). However, we argue that *the* central goal should be bi-dialectical teaching and learning in both the United States and Australia. The work in Western Australia serves as a model to follow for other regions and states in Australia and the United States. This shift in focus from Standard English to bi-dialecticalism as the instructional aim represents a shift in focus from "old" basics that focused on one "correct" version of English to "new" basics that place value on facility with a variety of different linguistic and cultural practices (Kalantzis & Cope, 2009). It is likely apparent that a shift from "old" to "new" basics requires a shift in ideology as well as practice. We discuss ways to foster shifts in ideology and practice in the final section of our chapter.

Concluding Comments: Language Variation, Ideology, and Learning Literacies

David Foster Wallace begins his book, *This is Water* (2009), as follows:

> There are these two young fish swimming along and they happen to meet an older fish swimming the other way, who nods at them and says, "Morning boys. How's the water?"

And the two young fish swim on for a bit, and then eventually one of them looks over at the other and goes, "What the hell is water?" (pp. 3–4)

In many ways, ideology is like the two young fish swimming in water. It (the water) is *there*, and we (the fish) are *there*, but we may not really be consciously aware of *it* or being *there*. A central task of this chapter has been to ask us to ponder, question, and critique the water and our place in it. Recall that for the purposes of this chapter, we drew on Mannheim's (1964) and Kavanagh's (1995) notions that ideology is the picture of society that we carry around in our heads plus our recognition of our place in that society. We end this chapter with concrete ideas for interrogating our own ideological perspectives as well as the ideological perspectives of others. As well, we share examples of ideas and approaches for learning about ideology as it relates to language and language use.

It is not just reflection/recognition we propose, but conscious, critical self- and other-interrogation. Examples of critical questions we might ask ourselves and others include the following:

- How do I view different language dialects, and whose interests are best served by my particular views?
- How do my views of different language dialects "square" with the academic views of trained linguists, and whose interests are best served by my particular views of this relationship?
- How do I view speakers of different dialects, and whose interests are best served by my particular views?
- How do others with whom I associate view different language dialects and the speakers of those dialects, and whose interests are best served by their views?

Critical reflection is one important step in helping to alleviate the dialect prejudice that Adger, Wolfram, and Christian (2007) argue is still a pervasive form of prejudice in society. We also recommend reading the chapters in this edited volume by Debra Goodman (chapter 2) and Rebecca Wheeler and Rachael Swords (chapter 8). Both chapters are replete with myriad ideas for providing quality dialect-related instruction in classrooms.

Additional ideas for studying dialect and ideology and implementing bi-dialectical approaches to teaching and learning include the following:

- See the materials entitled *Tracks to Two-Way Learning* for an example of a quality resource about the bi-dialectical teaching and learning being carried out in Western Australia (Department of Education and Department of Training and Workplace Development 2012).
- See the publication by Hilary Janks entitled *Language, Identity, and Power* (1993). This teacher resource provides valuable activities that you can do in your own classroom with your students to help them explore relationships

between language practices and ideology. In this work, Hilary Janks, an educator from South Africa, identifies how language played an important role in maintaining a set of race relations that were embedded in the practices of apartheid.

• Work with small groups of colleagues to explore the curriculum materials you use in your own classroom. What ideologies undergird these documents? Consider the language policies in your own districts and states. What ideologies undergird these policies? You may find the "Rethinking School Website" (http://www.rethinkingschools.org/index.shtml) helpful as you interrogate these curricula and policies.

• Work together with a small group of colleagues interested in exploring language practices and ideologies. Consider reading and discussing books such as Shirley Brice Heath's *Ways with Words* (1983) as well as *Words at Work and Play: Three Decades in Family and Community Life* (Heath, 2011). Other important books include Lisa Delpit's *Other People's Children* (1995) and *Multiplication Is for White People* (2012).

References

Adger, C.T., Wolfram, W., & Christian, D. (2007). *Dialects in schools and communities*. Mahwah, NJ: Erlbaum.

Australian Department of Education, Employment and Work Relations (2010). What Works Program (program description). Retrieved from http://www.whatworks.edu.au/dbAction.do?cmd=homePage

Baldwin, J. M. (1998). If black english isn't a language, then tell me what is? In Perry, I. & Delpit. L. Eds. *The real Ebonics debate: Power, language, and the education of African American children*. Boston, MA: Beacon Press. 67–71.

Cahill, R., & Collard, G. (2003). *Deadly ways to learn* ... a yarn about some learning we did together. *Comparative Education*, 39(2).

de la Luz Reyes, M. (1992). Challenging venerable assumptions: Literacy instruction for linguistically different students. *Harvard Educational Review*, 62, 427–447.

Delpit, L. (1995). *Other people's children: Cultural conflict in the classroom*. New York, NY: The New Press.

Delpit, L. (2012). *Multiplication is for white people: Raising expectations for other people's children*. New York, NY: The New Press.

Faber, L. (2004). The trope as trap: Ideology revisited. *Culture, Theory and Critique* 45(2), 133–159.

Gee, J. P. (2009). *Social linguistics and literacies: Ideology in discourses* (3rd Ed.). Bristol, PA: Taylor and Francis.

Gee, J. P. (2012). *Social linguistics and literacies: Ideology in discourses* (4th Ed.). Bristol, PA: Taylor and Francis.

Gonzalez, N., Moll, L. & Amanti, C. (2005). *Funds of knowledge: Theorizing practices in households, communities and classrooms*. New York, NY: Routledge.

Gutierrez, K.D. (2008). Developing a sociocritical literacy in the third space. *Reading Research Quarterly*, 43(2), 148–164.

Heath, S. B. (1983). *Ways with words: Language, life and work in communities and classrooms.* New York, NY: Cambridge University Press.

Heath, S. B. (2011). *Words at work and play: Three decades in family and community life.* New York, NY: Cambridge University Press.

Janks, H. (1993). *Language, identity, and power.* Johannesburg: Hodder & Stoughton in association with Witwatersrand University Press.

Janks, H. (2010) *Literacy and power.* New York and London: Routledge.

Kalantzis, M., & Cope, B. (2009). Multiliteracies: New literacies, new learning. *Pedagogies,* 4(3), 164–195.

Kalantzis, M., & Cope, B. (2012). *Literacies.* Cambridge, MA: Cambridge University Press.

Kavanagh, J. H. (1995). Ideology. In F. Lentricchia & T. McLaughlin (Eds.), *Critical terms for literary study* (pp. 306–320). Chicago, IL: University of Chicago Press.

Macedo, D. (1994). *Literacies of power: What Americans are not allowed to know.* Boulder, CO: Westview Press.

Malcom, I. G. (2013). The ownership of aboriginal English in Australia. *World Englishes,* 32(1), 42–53.

Malcolm, I. G., & Truscott, A. (2012). English without shame: Two-way Aboriginal classrooms in Australia. In Androula Yiakoumetti (Ed.). *Harnessing Linguistic Variation to Improve Education* (pp. 227–258). Bern: Peter Lang.

Mannheim, K. (1964). *Ideology and utopia.* New York, NY: Harvest.

Marx, K. (1967). *Capital: A critique of political economy, Three Volumes.* New York, NY: International Publishers.

New London Group (1996). A pedagogy of multiliteracies: Designing social futures. *Harvard Educational Review,* 66, 60–92.

Osborne, S. (2014). At the heart of learning: Imagining the future. *AlterNative: An International Journal of Indigenous Peoples,* 10.

Pennycook, A. (2007). *Language as local practice.* New York, NY: Routledge.

Perry, T., & Delpit, L. (Eds.). (1998). *The real Ebonics debate: Power, language, and the education of African American children.* Boston, MA: Beacon Press.

Postman, N. (1970). The politics of reading. *Harvard Educational Review,* 40, 244–252.

Redd, T. & Schuster Redd, K. (2005). *African American English: What a writing teacher should know.* Urbana, IL: National Council of Teachers of English.

Smitherman, G. (1998). Black english/ebonics: What it be like? In Perry, I. & Delpit. L. Eds. *The real Ebonics debate: Power, language, and the education of African American children.* Boston, MA: Beacon Press. 29–38.

Wallace, D. F. (2009). *This is water: Some thoughts, delivered on a significant occasion, about living a compassionate life.* New York, NY: Little Brown & Company.

Wardhaugh, R. (1998). *An introduction to sociolinguistics.* Malden, MA: Blackwell Publishers.

Western Australia Department of Education (2012). Tracks to Two-Way Learning: A Bidialectical Approach (program description). Retrieved from http://det.wa.edu.au/curriculumsupport/eald/detcms/navigation/english-as-an-additional-language-or-dialect-for-aboriginal-students/teaching-and-learning-resources/tracks-to-two-way-learning

Williams, L. J. (2011). Australian dialects and indigenous creoles: Is there a place for nonstandard Australian English in the lower secondary English classroom in Australia? *English in Australia,* 46(1), 21–30.

Wolfram, W., Adger, C., & Christian, D. (1999). *Dialectics in school and communities.* Mahwah, NJ: Lawrence Erlbaum.

Wolfram, W., & Schilling-Estes, N. (1998). *American English.* Malden, MA: Blackwell.

4

MY LIFE IN STORIES, MY WORLD IN PICTURES

A View of Multiliteracies from the Outside in

Rachel G. Salas and Julie L. Pennington

A class of second graders sit as their preservice teacher, Alice, reads to them from the book *In My Family* by Carmen Lomas Garza (2000). Emilo says:

> I love the picture about the empanadas (turnovers). It reminds me of La Esperanza, the bakery by my house. I can smell the empanadas as I walk home from school. They smell so good! My nose tells me they are baking apple and *calabasa* (pumpkin), my favorite empanadas! I can sit outside and smell that all day long! I love the story about the *cascarones* (Easter Eggs).

Isabel says excitedly:

> I do exactly what they do in the story! After church on Easter we take out the *cascarones* painted bright colors and break them on my brother and his friend's heads! The *confeti* (confetti) pours out all over their faces; it's so funny! The boys act like they are upset, but they like it too! It's a little sad too because the eggs are so pretty I really don't want to break them. I want to keep them and look at the beautiful colors! I like the story about the *Virgen de Guadalupe*.

Lupe seriously interjects:

> It's my name too, and you can see her picture painted on the wall by where my mama and I do laundry. I go outside and look at it all the time. It has mirror pieces on it, and she looks like she is shining and glowing while she protects us! It makes me proud to be named Guadalupe too!

The class silently mulls this over for a few minutes before Daniel chimes in:

> Well, I like the story about the *milagro* (miracle). I like it because the tortilla store by my *abuela's* house is named Milagro! Watching those tortillas come out so fast, and knowing my mom is going to turn them into the best enchiladas ever, well that's just a *milagro!*

The class laughs and all agree with Daniel's comments.
Tita asks:

> You know what the best part is, teacher? This book is my life in stories and my world in pictures! It's where I live and someone thought it was important enough to make a book about it. *Imaginaté* (imagine that)!

The students all murmured their agreement to Tita's profound comment; they were amazed to see their stories and their community told in a picturebook.

The outstanding and articulate connections that you just read in our opening vignette were made by second-grade English Learners (ELs). Alice, who read the book *In My Family* by Carmen Lomas Garza (2000) to this group of second graders, is amazed. She had no idea that the children would eagerly make so many connections to a simple story. Alice recounts:

> I can't believe they know so much, where did they learn all this? Last week, I read *Chrysanthemum* (by Kevin Henkes) and Temo (Cuauhtémoc), whose real name is long and I can't pronounce, and Marguerita were the only two who made any connections to the story! I just can't believe what happened today!

This chapter is about how we, Rachel and Julie, taught and supervised preservice teachers in a teacher education program at a large public institution in the southwest to bridge the gap between their classroom practicum experience, where they worked with students in a classroom setting and then hurried back to the university, and the dynamic local community setting, where most of their students lived. It also includes a compilation of experiences we have had throughout the years working in different university settings where we have attempted to craft quality, diverse, and experiential preservice literacy programs. We begin this chapter by providing a brief narrative of who we are as teacher educators, followed by a short description of the teacher preparation program that served as a context where we began rethinking preservice teacher education. It was this program that led us to discuss the possibility of a situated learning experience for preservice teachers and finally to the creation of a community literacy course.

While I, Rachel, use my voice to write and share the majority of this story, it is important to note that it was the constant open dialogue I held (and still hold) with Julie that enabled me to articulate and actualize the vision we had for providing a situated learning experience for the preservice teachers in our cohort. Julie and I came from different socioeconomic strata and linguistically diverse homes, yet our lives paralleled in some interesting ways, and it was the desire and common goal to help our students achieve that brought us together and made us a perfect team.

In the following section, we chose to juxtapose a brief snapshot of our parallel narratives to provide a glimpse into our lives and to share the path that led us to work with EL students, preservice teachers, and ultimately with each other. Working collaboratively allows us to cross cultural and linguistic borders. We navigate issues of power and negotiation in this collaborative process. This dual narrative in Figure 4.1 highlights our contrasting meaning-making processes within our sociocultural, contextual, and linguistic domains (Kalantzis & Cope, 2012).

Rachel	Julie
I am of Mexican descent, born and raised in Los Angeles, California. My father, who was born in Mexico, was bilingual in Spanish and English, having spent most of his childhood in the United States, but my mother only spoke Spanish for most of my formative years. My first language was Spanish, and I learned English, like many of the ELs I talk about in this chapter, through older siblings, by watching TV, and in U.S. schools.	I am a seventh generation Texan, born and raised in Texas. My parents only spoke English, yet for the first thirteen years of my life I lived in Kingsville, Texas where many people spoke English and Spanish. Garza's book is set in Kingsville and I remember eating at El Jardin. My first language was English, but I was surrounded by Spanish. My caregivers spoke Spanish, our morning cartoons were in Spanish, and we had Spanish in school starting in kindergarten.
It was in kindergarten that I had my first reality check with being "foreign" when my teacher changed the Spanish spelling of my name to English without consulting me or anyone in my family and began calling me by this new name. Funny, in my five year-old mind my first reaction was to blame my family for having gotten it all wrong and calling me by the wrong name! But the new name stuck and fifty years later I still use it.	I did not have to learn Spanish. Yet it was in college that I had my first reality check with being a monolingual English speaker when my university placed me in a predominately Spanish speaking community and school for my student teaching semester. Funny, in my twenty-two year-old mind my first reaction to coming to the school was to blame my university for having gotten it all wrong by sending me to a school in a neighborhood where I was unable to speak to many of the students in my class! But the school stuck and fourteen years later I was still teaching there.
In first grade I realized I "talked" funny thanks to my wonderfully attentive yet misguided teacher. With only the best intentions for my academic progress my first grade teacher kept me after school several days a week for the entire school year practicing the pronunciation of the digraphs "ch" and "sh." While I truly admire her patience and tenacity, had she had a class in language acquisition she would have realized that she had set upon a difficult task, and even today I have to concentrate and slow down my speech to attempt	In the first year at the school, I realized I was limited by my lack of Spanish thanks to my past experiences which allowed me to exist in a world where English was dominant. With only the best intentions for my academic progress my family, my teachers, and my

Continued

to pronounce the "sh" digraph correctly. I believe these early educational experiences set me on the path to teaching my first bilingual multiage 4th – 5th grade classroom in East Los Angeles.

I shared a culture and language with my students but it was through their stories I realized how different and difficult their academic journey was from my own. And the research data bore it out: many of them would score poorly in reading and just as many would dropout by high school. I remember asking my older sister, "How did we do 'it'?" Just like my students, we had come from a low socioeconomic (SES) background, we spoke Spanish, and our parents had some education but no college experience?

By "it" I had meant, how did we successfully navigate the labyrinthian corridors of academia. "Hard work, parents who cared and pushed us, and ultimately fear of failure," she told me. But that wasn't it and I knew it.

My students had all of the values and qualities that my parents instilled in my sisters and me. Nelson, at age 10, worked harder than any kid I had ever met. I had spent time with Carlos' family during my home visits and they were supportive and inquisitive about finding ways to ensure his success. And Luz, if she missed one problem on a math test would skip recess to go over the problem to figure out where she misunderstood or miscalculated and then come to me to explain exactly why she had missed the problem. I remember looking at her thinking "what a mind, what an incredible and beautiful mind!" She amazed me with her inner strength and her mental acuity. (So much so that years later I would use her name for my daughter's middle name. I never wanted to forget her).

As an educator, I had to figure out how to help my students and other ELs compete successfully in the academic arena. This desire to continue my work with EL students led me to graduate school and ultimately to negotiate change within a preservice teacher education program with Julie's help and assistance.

community kept me safely speaking English with some Spanish in high school. While I truly admire their goals of ensuring that I went on to college, had I had more classes in Spanish I would have realized how my own language and culture influence my knowledge. So today I have to concentrate and slow down my speech to attempt to unearth the Spanish I do remember correctly.

I believe these early educational experiences set me on the path to teaching at my school in a bilingual multiage 1st – 2nd grade classroom in Texas. I did not share a culture or language with my students, but it was through their stories I realized how different and difficult their academic journey was from my own.

I carried a deficient view of their possibilities and saw their inability to speak English and their differing knowledge base as a hinderance to their learning.

And the research data bore it out; many of them would score poorly in reading and just as many would dropout by high school. I remember asking myself, "How do I do this?" Unlike my students, I had come from a cultural and linguistic background that matched my school, we all spoke English and our parents had educational and college experience. By "this" I had meant, how do I successfully help my students navigate the labyrinthian corridors of academia when I do not understand their experiences and their experiences do not match with the school's?

Yet over time I came to realize that my students had all of the values and qualities that my own parents had instilled in my sister and me. One of my students, Benjamin, at age 7, was reading in English and Spanish by the end of first grade; skills I had not mastered at twenty-two. I had spent time with Leticias' family during home visits and I witnessed their dedication to her education and plans for her to attend college. As an educator, my English learners (ELs) taught me that they were capable of more than I thought possible and it was my job to figure out how to help them compete successfully in the academic arena. This desire to continue my work with ELs led me to graduate school and ultimately to negotiate change within a preservice teacher education program with Rachel's help and assistance.

FIGURE 4.1 Rachel and Julie's Narrative Histories.

As the glimpse into our lives above shows, Julie and I ultimately had similar reasons to enter graduate school. It was in graduate school while working with and observing preservice teachers like Alice that we spent hours talking about better methods to prepare preservice teachers to work with and teach literacy to ELs and culturally and linguistically diverse CLD children. After supervising preservice teachers in the field and sitting through our own graduate coursework, we would find ourselves late in the evening in the literacy office getting ready for the next day. We talked about what we had observed and the comments that Alice or other preservice teachers (PTs) had made after working with EL and CLD students at Julie's school. We spent hours planning how we could scaffold instruction and experiences to help them better understand themselves and their students. For the most part, the preservice teachers were able to keep a significant distance between themselves and the EL students. They came to the school, took courses, and taught lessons. At the end of the day, they went home with only an understanding of how the students responded to school-determined tasks. They never saw them in their own community, and they held onto their deficient perceptions of the EL students.

It was during one of our late night talks that we realized there were many things we wanted to accomplish within a preservice teacher education program, but we had three concrete ideas we felt could be brought forth and implemented immediately for our literacy cohort of preservice teachers. We envisioned a transformative process that provided preservice teachers with three specific learning opportunities:

1.   Situated learning experiences that were in authentic community literacy learning environments
2.   Multimodal experiences in situated learning environments within the community, such as community walks to see forms of literacy (e.g., murals, storefronts, Spanish newspapers at local convenience store, etc.)
3.   Guidance targeted specifically to assist them in understanding the intersection of community literacy and classroom literacy instruction

We will use these three learning opportunities to tell the story of developing and implementing a situated learning experience for preservice teachers in a community literacy course. The stories are framed within a multiliteracies perspective to show how preservice teachers gained experience in working with EL and CLD students within a community environment (Kalantzis & Cope, 2012).

First Key Idea: Developing a Literacy Course about Drawing outside the Lines and Looking within the Community

In traditional teacher preparation, students enrolled in elementary certification programs will take three to four literacy courses to become certified teachers. The courses usually focus on Early Literacy (grades K–3), Adolescent Literacy (grades 4–8), and Reading Diagnosis. If students are fortunate, they may have a children's literature course—hopefully with a heavy dose of multicultural children's literature included—and a writing across the curriculum course. Many of the literacy courses require a practicum where preservice teachers visit classrooms to work with students during the reading and language arts block. This allows them to go into a school, focus on literacy methods, and return to the confines of the university walls or their middle-class neighborhoods without deeply reflecting on their dispositions on teaching CLD and EL students or understanding the students' home, language, and community environments.

In contrast, a program that seeks to provide preservice teachers (PTs) with authentic situated learning experiences teaches the traditional literacy courses in a CLD community school where PTs interact with teachers, students, and their families in the everyday school setting. Furthermore, courses outside the traditional literacy band are developed to provide a broader lens on literacy throughout the students' home and community. A community literacy course should be situated within the community and look at the literacies needed for everyday sustenance, survival, and economic and academic advancement (Boyle-Baise & McIntyre, 2008; Cooper, 2007; Garcia, Arias, Harris Murri, & Serna, 2010).

A Course in Community Literacy

Reflecting on beginning her community literacy volunteering at a local ESL program, Alice honestly describes her thoughts and feelings:

> At first I thought the volunteering was going to be another burden because of my course load this semester. I was not looking forward to it at all. When I first started in the class, I was a little bored. I mainly helped one person, a native Farsi speaker, and the class he attended was very structured. I thought all the worksheets were very boring, but the students seemed to like it. So I hung in there.

The community literacy course we created offered practical readings, materials, and successful models of adult literacy found in research to help guide and prepare PTs to work and teach in a variety of adult education settings throughout the CLD community. The situated learning experiences included adult ESL, GED, and literacy programs housed in community centers, local libraries, churches, the community college, and alternative high school programs. We met the students in our community literacy course once a week for two hours at the same elementary school in the local CLD community where the PTs tutored second through sixth graders during the week. Prior to each class session, the students read literature and materials that discussed community literacy programs and research. We offered the PTs a list of adult literacy placements within the community that had been arranged prior to the class meeting. Once they selected a program from the list, they were responsible for making the initial contact to set up their volunteer service. We wanted them to be able to talk to the volunteer coordinator, see if the program was a good fit for them and their schedule, introduce themselves, and set up their service hours on their own. They were required to volunteer a minimum of two hours a week for twelve weeks. Once they began volunteering, we visited them at their community site to offer support and guidance. As the PTs volunteered, we continued to meet weekly as a class to discuss further readings and research and the students' situated learning experiences. At one class meeting, Alice offered:

> I did not think I would be so impressed with them (adult ELs), but I can't help but be impressed. They are accomplishing so much and most of them do not realize it. I also thought that because I do not speak any other language it would be impossible to help them. I now know that is not true.

While we visited all the PTs in their community literacy placements multiple times, I found myself drawn to Alice's class of ESL learners. I watched Alice, a shy young woman from the dominant culture, work with adults from Mexico, Iran, Hungary, Russia, Japan, and China. I saw her understanding of literacy within the context of communication develop and grow. Alice was beginning to understand the importance of adapting communication patterns across contexts (Kalantzis & Cope, 2012). One day, after she had been volunteering in the adult ESL class for several weeks and had her own small group of students to teach, she told me:

> I really admire the people in the class; it made me think about all the studies we read about Mexican Americans and the resiliency that exists within them. I could not imagine living in another country and not knowing the language. It has to be very difficult for them. How brave they are to come and learn something new. I also admired the way they helped each other. This mainly happens between Spanish speakers because they have that common language bond. To watch them switch into their native language to help another student who was behind was amazing. It really made me rethink bilingual education. I think that we have to keep that support structure in place for the students, as it allows them to reach the other side. I think that we are foolish if we think otherwise. I think I am learning the most from this experience!

Alice seemed to internalize what we were reading in class and what she was witnessing and experiencing firsthand in the ESL program. She was making connections, reevaluating her assumptions, and beginning to change her views on education and CLD populations. But in any course and venture, there are always challenges and unknown variables that can skew perceptions and experiences.

The Many Forms of Literacies

Stephie, a young, white preservice teacher, was not happy that she was not teaching traditional "literacy" defined as reading and writing. Stephie was battling the negativity demon and labeling her community literacy placement as "useless."

> I did not do much work involving literacy. I was working with math the majority of time. I helped students with math problems. I did learn a lot about the students in the class. Many times I would talk to the students to learn about why they were in class. I could relate some of their stories to our class readings, which was interesting. I felt like I met some amazing people in that class. They were willing to learn and appreciated any help that I had to give. I learned about a part of society that I did not know much about.

For her, the community literacy placement was a disappointment.

I think one of the biggest "aha" moments for me as a teacher educator was understanding that many PTs saw and accepted literacy as it is narrowly defined. Stephie did not recognize the language of math as a form of literacy with very specific linguistic terms, structure, and academic English. She also didn't value the informal discussions she had with the students she helped with math in the GED class, nor did she accept these discourse patterns as a form of literacy. I realized it was my job to show Stephie and the other PTs how other forms of literacy exist. The PTs needed to understand that literacy today goes beyond phonics generalizations and the five-paragraph structure. Literacy outside the confines of the traditional "three r's" was rich, complex, digital, auditory, visual, and most definitely multimodal. They especially needed to experience how "literacy and numeracy" are essential and necessary skills for all learners (Kalantzis & Cope, 2012, p. 5). I realized that in order to better prepare my PTs, I needed to explicitly help them make connections to multiple forms of literacy, expand their understanding of literacies, and guide them on the path as they engaged in multiliteracy praxis. I believed that in order to help the PTs gain a deeper understanding of the multiple forms of literacy, I had to go outside the walls of the classroom and take it to the street (Boyle-Baise & McIntyre, 2008). I had to provide my preservice teachers with multimodal experiences.

Kalantzis and Cope (2012) argue that meaning is constructed through all aspects of text whether written, oral, audio, gestural, or visual. It is the visual and audio sensory communications of the community I wanted the preservice teachers to acknowledge and experience as authentically as possible.

Second Key Idea: The Writing on the Walls—Multimodal Experiences in Situated Learning Environments

When Alice first read *In My Family* by Carmen Lomas Garza (2000) to her second-grade students, she was amazed at all the connections they made to the story. Through her situated learning experience in an adult ESL classroom, she learned to acknowledge the power of knowing and using multiple languages. While these literacy experiences helped her develop a better understanding of the literacies her students brought with them and used to make meaning within different situations, it was obvious that Alice, Stephie, and the other PTs needed to gain a deeper understanding of "literacy" ways of knowing. When the students came to class to tutor their elementary students or to attend their community literacy class, they always drove into town. Listening to them talk as they prepared for class, I caught bits and pieces of their chatter. "Did you see all the writing on the walls on the corner store? There is no respect for property!" "I know, did you see the big, bright, gaudy painting of the Indian on the tire shop? They think that's art?" "Well, if that's art, no wonder there is so much tagging on the walls!" The chatter was rarely positive when describing the surrounding community. They talked about the run-down houses, the unkept yards, and the neighborhood drug dealings. They seemed to avoid mentioning all the nicely kept homes, the trimmed yards with religious statues with floral offerings to *La Virgen de Guadalupe*, and how parents and neighbors were taking on the drug dealers.

It was time to tour the streets; it was time to read the walls and to highlight the cultural, historical, and religious artifacts of a vibrant and robust community. Stephie had clearly shown us how her narrow definition of literacy prevented her from understanding the rich literacy experience she was having with her GED students she tutored in math. What had we, as literacy educators, done to disrupt this singular notion of literacy? Not enough and perhaps not much. It was time to see literacy in a new light and through a multimodal lens. While I knew I would not be able to take the PTs throughout the entire community, I could begin the process by walking with them, highlighting the imagery, and teaching them how to "read" the literacy on the local walls (Freire, 1993).

Walking the Road to Multimodal Understanding

I led the PTs to the main street, just a few blocks from the school, so we could all view the "painting of the gaudy Indian." (See Figure 4.2.)

I informed the PTs:

> Most Mexicans have indigenous blood. The Mexicans are very proud of their Indian lineage and many associate strength with the Aztec warriors. The Aztec warriors were called "eagle warriors" and were feared infantry soldiers. These soldiers were a select group of men and they could come from either nobility or commoner populations. The Aztec warriors were considered the bravest soldiers. So this depiction of an Indian with an Eagle headdress represents strength, courage, and pride in their heritage.

My students silently studied the image of the proud, strong, fierce Indian depicted on the wall. I know what I had heard them say about the "gaudy Indian" artwork, so I was

Photograph by Barbara Falconer Newhall, BarbaraFalconerNewhall.com. Used with permission.

FIGURE 4.2 Mural of Aztec Warrior.

hoping by explaining the warrior Indian, they could begin to see the cultural heritage of the community come to life. My goal was to avoid being preachy and moralizing. I did not want them to shut me out, but to hear and think about what I said.

As we continued on the walk, I pointed to the writing on the walls and tried to explain or describe what they saw. I wanted the PTs to read the walls, to listen to the sounds and music coming from the local bodegas or stores, and to appreciate the multiliteracy event. I also wanted them to see the different newspapers and periodicals written in Spanish so that the community could stay informed and politically active and engaged and to realize this community had access to print media. While many of the adults they had met and worked with could not speak English, I wanted my PTs to realize that many were literate in their native language and read to stay informed and entertained. I also wanted to walk to the laundromat so that Alice could see the mural of *La Virgen de Guadalupe* painted on its side wall. I wanted her to see why Lupe was so excited about the story *In My Family* by Carmen Lomas Garza (2000). While I knew Alice would neither experience nor understand the significance of the mural in the same way as Lupe, I wanted her to see Lupe's and the other second graders' world in pictures, sounds, and text. I wanted all the PTs to realize that the students they taught in the local community school could all go beyond the text and make text-to-world connections given the opportunity. (See Figure 4.3.)

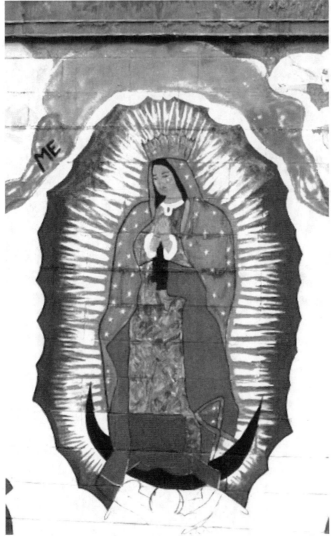

FIGURE 4.3 Mural of *La Virgen de Guadalupe*.

As we all stood and observed the mural of *La Virgen de Guadalupe*, I explained to my students the deep and respectful connection and commitment the Latino population has with *La Virgen*:

> We have named her Gudalupe but she is the same Virgin Mary, mother of Jesus, honored and celebrated by Catholics and Christians throughout the world. You do not have to be religious to have faith and belief in La Virgen's

power and presence. You will find her image in many places throughout this community. Her image is ubiquitous, she is depicted on walls, on calendars, tattooed on bodies of young men and women, and small statues of her likeness can be found in yards and homes throughout the neighborhood. She represents inner strength, serenity, and peace and some pray to her daily and others reach out to her in their hour of need. We see her as a channel to the Lord.

After the initial community walk, I charged my students to locate and view several other powerful murals in the community. I told my students:

> These murals offer an important historical perspective, tell stories, and depict images that go to the soul and fiber of this community. We will study these images so we can begin to better understand the students and their community. I will meet you at the murals or you can go on your own on a different day. If you need me to take you, I will, let me know. We cannot have an honest and in-depth discussion if we do not all go and experience the artwork. We will talk about the murals in class, but perhaps you should ask the local people and your students about their significance.

I had selected a few murals I thought would be powerful portrayals of the community's beliefs in social justice, integrity, and historical perspective. We went to see the image of Cesar Chavez painted against the backdrop of fields of lettuce on a local car dealership's building. Not all my students knew who he was, his commitment to Mexican and itinerant farm workers and their families, or his involvement in the peace and social justice movement brought to the forefront by the Reverend Martin Luther King Jr. They had heard his name and saw it on the street sign that led them into the heart of the community where they tutored. But they were not curious, nor did they ask about the man and what he meant to this community. (See Figure 4.4.)

Photograph by Everdayzac, reprinted from Wikipedia, Wikimedia Commons.

FIGURE 4.4 Mural of Cesar Chavez.

The last place we visited had several murals, and I wanted the PTs to study them all, but there was one I wanted them to focus on. I wanted them to study the bright, vibrant mural of the indigenous person with open arms stretching over Earth and engulfed in powerful fists breaking chains in the background. (See Figure 4.5.) What did this "story" say to them? What did they "read" on the wall? Did the imagery make sense to them at all?

Photograph of mural by Raul Valdez, reprinted from La Nueva Raza, http://nuevaraza.wordpress.com/2010/02/22/austin-sacrifice-for-justice-immigrant-rights-activist-rama-carty-resistencia/.

FIGURE 4.5 Mural of Earth and Chains.

We returned to class and discussed the images, stories, and powerful representations communicated by the "walls." I was asked what some of the images meant and represented. I gave my students historical and technical explanations, but I wanted them to be able to make the connection of the literacy on the wall to their classroom and students. I wanted to know what the walls had said to the PTs. At first, I felt the PTs were giving me answers I wanted to hear. Finally, after much discussion and interpretation Alice offered:

> The single most important thing I have learned that I feel will help me as a teacher is the importance of culture on an individual, and how important it is to recognize, honor, and value that culture. I learned this in the classroom, in theory, and saw it in practice in the community. And finally, I have learned as a teacher, I will be able to open a mind or close it, depending on how I view diversity. Whether it's diversity of culture, gender, political views or any other—honor and value and acceptance of that diversity is the key.

Stephie added:

> I have learned how important it is to seek out the schemas that accompany the students. It is these schemas on which I can build and extend the student's knowledge. I have learned that I can come to know a student's schema through knowing his or her world. One of the ways to know a student's world is by making myself familiar with his or her cultural, home, and community environment.

Walking the road to multimodal understanding is not always an easy venture. It requires planning, patience, trust, and translation. But it is a task worth attempting and undertaking even if it is just for a brief glimpse into the heart of a community. I learned as a teacher educator that I had to be willing to share my stories with my students and be willing to commit time and energy to guide them figuratively and literally through the process of understanding the community. I did not always lead them successfully, but each attempt taught me something new and added to my repertoire for the next opportunity. I found that sometimes we come to understand something much better if we have a guiding hand to help us cross into the unknown.

Third Key Idea: Sometimes All It Takes Is a Guiding Hand—Understanding the Intersection of Community Literacy and Classroom Literacy Instruction

We knew creating the community literacy course was a a good place to start, a venue to help students begin to see the importance of multiliteracies and a forum where they could begin to ask questions and attempt to use new literacy strategies. Although it wasn't perfect, it was a learning experience for all of us. What we did learn was that helping the PTs make connections both intellectually and physically was important. Going into the field with them as a support, guide, and translator was vital. I don't think the PTs would have learned as much if we had just assigned them the community walk activity and asked them to go out on their own to see, listen, and communicate with the community. Walking with them, taking them metaphorically by the hand, and guiding them down the road and translating unknown words and images was necessary. I learned not to get angry with their comments no matter how hurtful and pointed they could be. I wanted them to be free to articulate their thoughts and feelings so I could help guide them to a deeper understanding of the multiliteracies within the dynamic community environment.

I know I learned from the experience too. I had driven through the community admiring the murals and artwork on the walls but had not walked the streets and really listened to the sounds and the vibrations coming from the shops, houses, and people on the street. To be true to myself and acknowledge the power of the multimodal experience, I needed to be on the street with my PTs.

It is so easy for us as academics to sit in our offices and pontificate about the power of experiencing other cultures and the richness of literacies throughout the community. It is equally easy and noble for us to get on an airplane and work in other countries to help develop world literacy. It is also very easy to send our preservice teachers out into the community to teach and work with CLD populations on their own without proper support and supervision. What we must do is walk the road with our PTs, travel on the journey along with them as best we can, and provide guidance so that we learn along with them. Let us cultivate a bountiful literacy garden in our own backyard as well as in other communities and countries. Stephie made it clear that having support along the way was crucial for her:

> I feel that exposure is key. Exposure to the students, the community, and the culture is so important. Stereotypes and false notions often stem from ignorance, I know this. Getting to know people from a different culture and working with them can be very powerful in changing negative views and attitudes. Having said that, I have to be honest and say I was glad to have you [Rachel] come with us into the community to help translate signs, newspapers, the language we heard coming from the music and people talking on the street. Mostly, I felt safe with you there, because I thought, well, we wouldn't look like outsiders.

We believe the scaffolding of situated learning experiences is instrumental in assisting preservice teachers to begin to understand how EL and CLD students learn and develop within social, economic, and linguistic context (Garcia, Arias, Harris Murri, & Serna, 2010).

Conclusion

Our work continues to focus on how best to prepare preservice teachers to work with and teach English learners and culturally and linguisitically diverse student populations in our local community schools. We do not profess to have all the answers, but we are committed to continuously ask questions and seek answers to what works best for our PTs and the EL and CLD students they are working with right now, right here in the community.

Transforming traditional literacy coursework structures can be difficult. Institutional frameworks such as course schedules, licensure requirements, and faculty commitment can inhibit change. Yet, there are ways to incorporate these ideas into literacy courses that are compatible with existing programs. We propose three levels of transformation to accommodate various levels of constraints and resources.

- Level 1: Altering assignments to include at least one community walk and analysis.

- Level 2: Revising all of the literacy courses to include a strong CLD component and teaching within a CLD community.
- Level 3: Co-teaching courses with multicultural education faculty and integrating CLD notions throughout both focus areas to demonstrate the community literacies in the CLD populations.

What we have discovered is the importance of developing literacy coursework for our PTs that includes experiential and scaffolded situated learning experiences that reflect a multiliteracies approach to literacy. We learned there is a need to disrupt commonly held misperceptions and cultural stereotypes brought into the class by white preservice teachers. In order to begin changing and transforming the process, we must provide a new constructive, approachable, and positive vision of the community for preservice teachers to access. Giving our PTs a window into the community helped them better understand their students and ultimately provided them with a view of multiliteracies from the outside in. As we began our chapter with Alice's children's discussion about *In My Family*, we end with her reflection:

> I, also, have learned many things that are important to me as a person. I have learned that I can make a difference in this world. I have learned about my own ability to persevere; this semester has not been easy.

References

Boyle-Baise, M., & McIntyre, D. J. (2008). What kind of experience? Preparing teachers in PDS or community settings. In M. Cochran-Smith, S. Feiman-Nemser, & D. J. McIntyre (Eds.), *Handbook of research on teacher education: Enduring questions in changing contexts* (3rd ed., pp. 307–330). New York, NY: Routledge.

Cooper, J. (2012). Strengthening the case for community-based learning in teacher education. *Journal of Teacher Education*, 58(3), 245–255.

Friere, P. (1993). *Pedagogy of the oppressed*. New York, NY: Continuum Books.

Garcia, E., Arias, M. B., Harris Murri, N. J., & Serna, C. (2010). Developing responsive teachers: A challenge for a demographic reality. *Journal of Teacher Education*, 61(1–2), 132–142.

Garza, C.L. (2000). *In my family*. San Francisco, CA: Children's Book Press.

Kalantzis, M., & Cope, B. (2012). *Literacies*. New York, NY: Cambridge University Press.

5

WHITE MALE TEACHERS EXPLORING LANGUAGE, LITERACY, AND DIVERSITY

A Self-Study of Male Perceptions of Diversity(ies)

Mary B. McVee, David Fronczak, Jay Stainsby, and Chad White

re•flec•tion /ri'flekSHən/
1. the throwing back by a body or surface of light, heat, or sound without absorbing it:
   'the reflection of light'
2. serious thought or consideration
   'he doesn't get much time for reflection' (Oxford Dictionary, 2014)

Reflection is a commonly used word in teacher education, and significant work has shown that reflecting upon one's own position in terms of race, social class, gender, and the like is a challenging undertaking (Florio-Ruane, 2001). As we began our journey into reflection, we focused primarily on reflection as pondering, mulling over, and ruminating. But in taking stock of our journey as learners, we were struck by the multiple dimensions of reflection and particularly how our identities are reflections of our own experiences and broader sociocultural-historical contexts. These reflections of ourselves can project who we aspire to be or alternatively can protect us by reflecting or not absorbing painful truths about ourselves. In this chapter, we attempt to explore our learning to represent reflection as the absorption of truths about ourselves and our society. Ultimately, in sharing our stories, we hope to prompt questions and explorations directed toward new understandings.

In this chapter, we (Chad, David, and Jay) explored our learning as we used qualitative research techniques to analyze our learning after completing a graduate course in Language, Literacy, and Culture (LLC). Mary served as guide and as instructor for the LLC course. This chapter presents the valuable but sometimes potentially troubling insights we encountered. We consider how these insights helped us rethink teaching and learning for all students. Through these accounts, we also attempt to counter unidimensional reports in teacher education literature that often present white, male teachers as stereotypically "deficient" or "deficit" (Lowenstein, 2009).

Perspectives from Theory and Research

Despite efforts to recruit more males into teaching, the teaching force in the United States has become increasingly female. In 1969, 69% of teachers were female, but in 2011, 84% of all public school teachers were female (Feistritzer, 2011). Many studies within literacy teacher education have focused on the dilemma faced by white teachers who are instructing students from diverse linguistic, racial, ethnic, cultural, and economic backgrounds (e.g., Florio-Ruane, 2001; McVee, Brock, & Glazier, 2011). Often these studies focus exclusively on white women (Lowenstein, 2009). This is not surprising given teacher demographics and the long-standing positioning of teaching as "women's work" (Apple, 1984; Sparks, 2012). To explore the ways in which male teachers are positioned, this study relied upon positioning theory, which is useful in explorations of identity, narrative, and social interaction (Moghaddam & Harré, 2010). We also drew from related perspectives on multiliteracies (New London Group, 1996).

While there are many facets of multiliteracies, several were integral to this study. First, multiliteracies focused our attention on cultural and social practices and patterns in a globally connected world. A second facet of multiliteracies was that which drew attention to the various modalities of meaning-making and the affordances of meaning design across modes. Finally, while multiliteracies perspectives do not require the use of technologies, multiliteracies advocates have recognized the powerful opportunities currently available to learners who can readily compose complex multimodal texts and rapidly share them with others (Cope & Kalantzis, 2000).

As noted, meaning-making and meaning representation are key elements of multiliteracies. Cope and Kalantzis (2009) identify five questions to guide investigations of meaning-making systems:

- Representational: To what do the meanings refer?
- Social: How do the meanings connect the persons they involve?
- Structural: How are the meanings organized?
- Intertextual: How do the meanings fit into the larger world of meaning?
- Ideological: Whose interests are the meanings skewed to serve? (p. 176)

Each of these questions also implies a set of positions or expected rights, duties, and obligations linked to particular norms (McVee, 2011). As the New London Group (1996) wrote, discourses draw "attention to the diversity of constructions (representations) of various domains of life and experience associated with different voices, positions, and interests (subjectivities)" (p. 78). Positioning theory is particularly helpful in identifying these types of norms and then analyzing the various ways in which teachers (or designers) position themselves and others. The authors of this chapter engaged in this type of analysis as they considered not only their own social positions or lifeworlds, but also the lifeworlds and positions of their students, and ultimately, the relationship between themselves and their students (New London Group, 1996). The collaborative spirit of this endeavor also embodied the notion of situated learning and reflection in and through communities of practice advocated by scholars of multiliteracies (e.g., Gee, 2000; Michaels & Sohmer, 2000).

Background and Course Context

Our work stemmed from a seminar in Language, Literacy, and Culture (LLC) taught by Mary. Typically, this seminar has a male to female ratio 1:24, including Mary as instructor. However, one semester the gender ratio was 5:20. These male voices brought important perspectives into classroom discussions of racial, ethnic, and linguistic diversity, and several were outspoken advocates of equity and were working in challenging, diverse environments. After the course, Mary invited all five males to participate in a self-study research group to analyze their learning across the semester. Four young men agreed to participate; however, one relocated due to a job offer, leaving the coauthors of this chapter: Chad, David, and Jay.

Chad had already had varied teaching experiences, but shortly after the LLC class concluded, during the self-study analysis, he began working for the Freedom Friendship Program, a nonprofit organization that provided academic support for at-risk youth (names of schools and organizations are pseudonyms). Chad assisted at Pine Street High School, supporting teachers and providing one-to-one tutoring. The school population was 94% African American. Approximately 95% of students in this urban school received free or reduced lunch, and 80%–90% of families received public assistance. Approximately 50% of students in the district graduate. While Chad would have continued teaching at this urban school or other schools in the district, few positions were available. Ultimately, in search of work, Chad moved to South Carolina where he obtained a job as middle school social studies teacher.

Jay had been a teacher for five years. After working as a substitute in several rural districts, he accepted a full-time position teaching GED (General Education Diploma) students. Jay taught English, math, and science to help students succeed on their GED. At the time of the self-study, Jay was working with students of diverse cultural backgrounds from traditionally low social and economic status neighborhoods. Interestingly, many of the students who attended Jay's GED classes had come from the same district and even the same school where Chad worked as a tutor. Although attempting to achieve their GED, Jay noted the many challenges they faced on a daily basis just to come to GED classes, such as transportation, childcare, and self-doubt. While teaching GED classes was fulfilling, it was economically challenging, and Jay continued to search for full-time teaching positions. Jay is currently in his first full-time teaching position as a middle school English Language Arts teacher in a suburban district.

At the time of the reflection study, David was in his first year as a full-time teacher at a private Catholic elementary school where, previously, he had been an independently contracted Title I Consultant teacher. David was one of five male teachers; there were thirty-two female teachers. Currently, he works full-time as a literacy specialist at the same school and was recently named head of the reading department. The school, which is in a middle-class suburban neighborhood, serves mostly white, middle-class students from PreK–8, but cultural, ethnic, and linguistic diversity within the school community is increasing as the school adds scholarship opportunities. All faculty are white. David is the only openly gay staff member in his building. David also teaches part-time as a reading instructor at a tutoring center serving a diverse clientele.

Mary is a university professor whose research and teaching focus on helping literacy teachers explore their own beliefs about culture, language, and diversity and develop culturally relevant pedagogies (Ladson-Billings, 1995) to address the needs of all learners. In the LLC class, three primary influences have informed the approach to learning: personal narrative (McVee, Brock, & Glazier, 2011); multimodal design (McVee, Bailey, & Shanahan, 2008; New London Group, 1996); and embodiment (McVee, Dunsmore, & Gavelek, 2005; McVee & Boyd, in process). During the class and the self-reflection study, Mary drew upon her experiences as a teacher of English to English language learners in the United States, China, and Hong Kong and more than 20 years' experience in teaching teachers and assisting them with research using qualitative methods. As a member of a bicultural, biracial family, Mary brings an understanding of the practical issues of teaching and learning and the personal issues of narrative related to identity, language, culture, and literacy.

To carry out the self-study, we examined written book club logs, multimodal responses, written academic reflections, a "What is literacy?" assignment, personal narratives and reflections, and final projects (digital and written). We used techniques from Brock et al. (2006) to help frame our work. Participants first coded their written work for "significant insights." They labeled or described the insight and indicated whether this was "troubling" and if so, how. Finally, participants considered: "How might this significant insight affect your work with children/youth/young adults in future?" All coauthors met to compare their Significant Insights Tables and to identify crosscutting themes and categories.

What Shows in the Mirror? Stories from Chad, David, and Jay

As a group, we have 15 weeks' worth of writing, including multimodal artifacts from the LLC course, and we met an additional eight times where we analyzed and audio-recorded our conversations. Given this large data set, Chad, David, and Jay kept three guiding questions in mind while drafting the chapter: What two or three ideas were most important in my learning? What texts were most powerful? What story do I want to tell about my learning that I think is important for other teachers or students to hear?

Below, Chad, Jay, and David discuss their experiences and learning in relation to these three questions. Following this section, we discuss several themes that pertain to multiliteracies.

Chad

Currently, I am working as a middle school social studies teacher in South Carolina. Shortly after starting there, I was talking with a veteran teacher and a student teacher before observing their class. The veteran teacher turned to me and asked, "So, if you had one piece of advice to give our friend here," he nodded to indicate the student teacher, "one piece of advice before he enters the classroom, what would it be?" Immediately a thousand thoughts rushed through my head, but I wanted to try and pick that one great piece of advice. I don't remember exactly what I said, but I wish I had said: "Always remember who you set out to be as a teacher, and never give up on that goal." Most novice teachers, myself included, believe that we will be able to save every child that walks into our classroom, despite the numerous warnings from veteran teachers that we won't reach every child. Reality eventually sets in after the first week of teaching, maybe even the first day, when we realize that every student in our classroom is unique. Unfortunately, this is when many teachers lose who they set out to be. It is almost what happened to me. As I entered my master's program, I thought I had some things figured out; I "knew" who certain students were when they walked into my classroom, and I made a lot of assumptions.

Language, Literacy, and Culture (LLC) was the first course in my master's program. (Teachers in New York are required to obtain a master's degree after their initial certification. Chad chose a Literacy Specialist master's degree program.) By the time I entered class, I had already experienced my first dose of reality. I had just completed the student teaching assignment for my social studies certification during the previous semester. One of my student teaching placements was a first-ring suburban school that had a diverse student population in terms of race, family background, reading levels, socioeconomic status, and learning abilities. Walking into the classroom for the first time, my anxiety was through the roof, but I was thrilled to finally begin teaching. By the time I left, I was horribly frustrated by the lack of motivation that many of my students exhibited.

Despite our best efforts, my fellow student teachers and I just could not seem to understand "those" kids. Who did they think they were? Did they think they were going to be able to skate by for the rest of their lives? How could they be so disrespectful, especially when we were trying our hardest to give them an education? The list of complaints and implicit judgments would arise whenever we teachers got together. What troubled me the most was that this was the type of school where I wanted to teach permanently. I wanted the challenge of the diverse classroom with students who struggled because I felt that as a teacher, I was caring and dedicated enough to save them all.

When the LLC class began, I was not thinking that it would be helpful in considering some of the problems I faced during student teaching. However, I had switched from social studies to literacy because of the many struggling readers I encountered during teaching. Before I entered the classroom as a full-time teacher, I wanted to expand my knowledge of literacy to better meet the needs of my students. On that first fall day, I had no idea what to expect from LLC, but I immediately became intrigued by the discussions, readings, assignments, and people that made up the class.

It wasn't until the Initial Sketch assignment that I began to connect what I had experienced during student teaching to what I was learning in class. The assignment required us to write a reflection about a time we crossed a cultural border in our lives, and I immediately struggled with the task of coming up with an experience that met the requirements of the assignment. This revelation that I had not crossed many cultural borders became personally unsettling. I had always considered myself to be an open and accepting person. But if I never left the immediate world around me and stepped out of my comfort zone, was I really that open and accepting? Furthermore, if I never had any experiences crossing cultural borders, how could I expect to connect with the diverse population of students that I intended to work with? The assignment became an eye-opening moment for me during the course; throughout the remainder of the assignments, discussions, and readings, I began to reflect on who I was, who I thought I was, and how both of these positions translated into my interactions with those around me, especially students.

In addition to the assignments, we read many influential books; each presented concepts that changed how I viewed my interactions with students. I began to understand how even minor actions by teachers could impact individual students' perceptions of school. For example, in *Holler If You Hear Me*, Greg Michie (2009) described a humbling and humiliating experience where a student had an accident for fear of asking permission to use the bathroom because of Mr. Michie's earlier reprimands. After reading Carger's (1996) *Of Borders and Dreams*, I saw how easily we can mistake our own personal experiences as universal truths and how educators must instead seek to understand the whole student to make informed instructional decisions. When I read Finn's (2009) *Literacy with an Attitude*, I realized that rather than empowering my students with a voice, I was on the verge of fulfilling the status quo of silencing underprivileged students in my classroom. Without realizing it, I had failed to look at each of the unique individuals who entered my classroom and instead had treated them all as one.

As a privileged white male who grew up in a middle-class household, this realization became a major problem. When I treated all of the students the same,

I realized I was treating students the way I would expect to have been treated when I was in school. Obviously, this was not a conscious decision I was making, but it was a mistake I could not afford to make if I was to work with a diverse population of underprivileged students. While my students deserved to have the same high expectations held up for them, I realized that my students may not have had all of the same opportunities and privileges that I had had in my schooling. I became aware that I could not blame students when they were not successful.

The lessons I learned in the LLC also helped me in my tutoring position with the Freedom Friendship Program. Working in a high-poverty urban school was a challenge, but I had learned through the LLC that it was okay to feel uncomfortable and that it was okay to talk about issues of race. For example, when I first started working in the school, my students, who were African American, made fun of my name, Mr. White, a name they found very humorous. I know that to some observers, their actions may be seen as disrespectful, and during my time in the school, I witnessed situations where white teachers misread student conduct or comments as disrespect. These situations often escalated out of control. If I had not had some exposure to talking about race and whiteness in the LLC, I think I too may have reacted differently. But because we had talked about race and whiteness, I was able to find the humor in the situation and joke with the students. They delighted in inventing new names for me so that I wouldn't be known as the white guy whose name was "Mr. White."

After the lessons learned from the narratives and the revelations discovered during the self-reflecting assignments, I came away from the class and our self-study with a much better understanding of who I was as a teacher. I know by now that I won't be able to save every student, but that does not mean we should not try. In my student teaching experience, I realized that my colleagues and I had failed as teachers; we had given up on students who may have needed just one more push. We had prejudged students, assuming that we already knew what the outcomes would be: The students would fail. I also know that trying to save every student with just innovative lessons, integration of technology, or differentiated instruction is not going to work. Through self-reflection, we must constantly monitor who we are as teachers and how our teaching stance impacts the interactions we have with students. We must ensure that we recognize students as individuals while approaching educational decisions from their perspectives in order to empower them to achieve their full potential.

Jay

When entering the LLC course, I was unsure of what to expect. I was thoroughly enjoying my English Education Adolescence graduate studies at the university, but I had never really given any thought to what the LLC course was about other than it satisfied a requirement. That said, I truly enjoyed my experience in the class. Because the course was structured around the use of personal narratives (see McVee & Boyd, in preparation; McVee, Brock, & Glazier, 2011) and a peer-led book club model of interacting with core texts (Raphael & McMahon, 1994), we students took control of our learning and really decided what was important to talk about. It was fulfilling to go into class and have the student and group discussions dominate our time together. In addition, this class allowed students to consider topics that are generally not easy to talk about, specifically, race, class, and socioeconomic status—topics that are essential to teachers, but up to that point seemed taboo in other courses. Given this, I was able to evaluate my own beliefs as an educator but more importantly as a human being. I could see how these ideas influenced my life growing up and my interactions with students in the classroom, while challenging myself to be better overall.

In the fall of 2011 while taking the LLC class, I had been working for exactly a year in a GED program in Buffalo and Lackawanna, New York. Both locations and the students were much different from what I was used to as a student and an educator. Growing up in a predominantly white, suburban neighborhood did not prepare me for the trials and tribulations that my students were going through or had already gone through. The LLC class helped me recognize the "border crossing" that I was doing in order to serve this population of students. I had to learn and understand what the GED students needed, which in turn drove me to change my practice and my demeanor with students. What was good for a cohort of students in a white suburb did not necessarily translate well to the GED students.

We were constantly exchanging our funds of knowledge and adapting what we expected of each other. For example, I had to be realistic that many of my students were young mothers responsible for maintaining the care and well-being of their children. A sick child or needy family member meant that the GED student needed to stay home and care for others. The day-to-day demands could interfere with students' ability to get to class, but it wasn't that they did not care or did not want to learn. At one point, as a scaffold for writing, my students produced a description using words and images in iMovie to represent their lives and communities; this helped me see that the funds of knowledge they needed for survival were often at odds with the funds of knowledge needed to "do school" and be successful in the academic world.

At points, I had to lower my expectations of myself and change what I expected of students. I realized that students sometimes did not have the background knowledge to be successful in the environment that I created for them as a teacher. It was up to me to change my teaching to meet their needs; I couldn't just blame them for not succeeding. What was great about being in the LLC at that time is that I realized that I was not alone in my naiveté. In the communal setting that we established, I was allowed to see what other people were going through and how they dealt with their insecurities and fears working with populations that we may not have necessarily been used to dealing with.

This also showed me that education is a recursive process. We must always be thinking as teachers and improving our pedagogical practices in order to best serve whatever population we are dealing with. Whether it is the GED students from the urban city center or my seventh- and eighth-grade ELA suburban students, it is always important for me to reflect on how a particular day or lesson went and how I can improve. As a teacher, I understand it is important for students to show growth, so it seems logical that as the person teaching the students, I should always be showing growth as well. I know that I am a much better teacher now than when I was student teaching, but also know that I am nowhere near where my highly effective colleagues are. I did realized this before, but the LLC class and my self-study truly helped me deepen my understanding of the importance of teacher reflection and how to effectively put my reflection into practice so that I can transform my instruction.

In addition to growing as a graduate student and a teacher through the class and self-study, I would be remiss to leave out the books that we read, responded to, and discussed. While they all had wonderful insights into class, race, and socioeconomic status, there was one that truly left an impact on me and made me look at how I was treating my student population as a whole. *Warriors Don't Cry* by Melba Pattillo Beals (1995) was a chilling example of the horrors and dangers that racism can lead to, especially systematic, institutionalized racism. Hearing these accounts always made me uneasy, but reading a full-length book about African American students integrating an all-white school in the southern United States made me cringe. With this visceral response, I nearly missed the lesson of reading this story.

The number one takeaway for me was that as teachers, we must treat all students with respect and tolerance no matter their race, origin, or status within the community. It is up to us as teachers to give students what students deserve in the small window of opportunity where we encounter them. If we are not making an environment that is warm and inviting where students can learn and grow, then we are failing as teachers and should perhaps think of another profession. I know that every day I walk into my classes, I am the one who has to set the tone of acceptance as the leader and be the one that students look up to. Without my work in the LLC course, I am not sure whether this would have ever been spelled out so clearly to me or if I would have made such a great effort to look past the rough exterior of some students and get to know them as learners and people. If we do not get to know our students as learners and as people, then what are we really doing?

David

Diversity is my "thing." My family knows it. My friends know it. My colleagues know it. Diversity is the reason why I chose to do graduate work at the university. When I learned that I could fuse my love of literacy with diversity studies through the Advanced Certificate in Teaching and Leading in Diversity (ACTLD), I knew that this was the school where I wanted to continue my education. When I applied and was accepted, I was confident that through taking the eighteen additional credits, I would learn the "right" way to approach diversity. In my admissions essay, I alluded to this by stating that the program would provide me with "advanced diversity awareness and sensitivity training." My use of the word "training" reveals my previous belief that diversity was a technical "thing." I would simply learn the "right" things to do and say while avoiding the "wrong" things to do and say when interacting with others with a cultural background different from my own. I planned to become "culturally competent" by the time I completed my course-work. Over time, I learned that my dichotomy of "right" versus "wrong" was too simplistic. After three and a half years of part-time study, I now know that diversity is not black and white.

The class that helped to bridge this realization for me was one that also bridged my ACTLD and Master's Literacy coursework: Language, Literacy, and Culture (LLC). One of our first assignments called for us to self-reflect on a personal border crossing. It was the first time in my graduate study where I was asked to thoughtfully consider my own diversity. I struggled initially to identify a border crossing. Growing up, I had a pretty happy childhood. I came from a family where education was valued, and I was provided with opportunities to easily access it. College was not a question but an expectation. It was a course reading that inspired my final decision for my border crossing examination. In an article we read, Florio-Ruane (1997) referred to the "'in between spaces' where the self is elaborated" (p. 157). I noticed that my initial self-reflection had been more on the surface level. I wanted to dig deeper, and I needed to; the first sketch was due soon! Reflecting on my "in between" space, I realized that my border crossing was my coming out as a gay man.

I had previously addressed this topic briefly in an undergraduate course on memoir and autobiography reading and writing my senior year of college. However, the unique feature of this particular "border crossing" project was its recursive nature. It was not one-and-done as my undergrad college paper had been; on the contrary, this assignment was one that was revisited and developed throughout the course of the entire semester. This was new. In addition, in the past, I had only explored this topic through a linguistic mode, but this project called for students to respond using multiple modes, intentionally layering semi-otic signs to communicate meaning through three multimodal representations of our border crossing. Through each representation, I was pushing myself to more deeply reflect and unpack my border crossing. My life became the text that I was responding to authentically.

But it was not just me who had the opportunity to respond; it was also my peers. It was through my experience in these small groups that I came to appreciate the diverse backgrounds of each individual in the class. Our dialogue was scaffolded through shared references to course readings we had studied; these shared ideas helped uphold the collaborative culture. For example, a particularly memorable article read was the chapter where Thompson (2011) wrote about high school girls Ava, Miroku, and Kouga who engaged in anime fanfiction writing, recasting themselves as characters in another world. Thompson stated, "This hidden and secret life centered on ... Anime-Ava the purebred, Miroku the monk warrior, and Kouga the silent stealth fighter [and] continued to go unnoticed while the girls continued to be labeled as reluctant readers and writers" (p. 200). "Unnoticed" is the word that broke my heart each time I read this passage. While I would argue that fanfiction is a highly complex form of literate response, their teacher communicated a different message and viewed the students as "reluctant" to engage in reading and writing, without ever realizing they were engaging authentically in authentic literacies on their own.

As teachers, we have the privilege of spending an extensive period of time with students. It is our responsibility to notice our students, appreciate them, and celebrate their differences. As with reflection, this noticing takes time, a precious and limited resource in schools. Even if we do not have the time to confer individually with each child each day, teachers can communicate the daily message that we do not view differences as deficits. As teachers, we can take genuine interest in others' expressions of their unique border crossing(s). In class, my small group modeled this for me through their close attention and responsive language to my work.

I learned that much like crossing geographic borders, cultural border crossings involve movement from one place to another. In order to begin the process, however, teachers must be self-reflective and embrace reflective practices in their pedagogy. Through the completion of the semester-long border-crossing assignments, I expanded my notion of what can be read as a text and realized that our lives and the lives of our students serve as the most powerful texts. We can engage with one another to positively impact outcomes. In *Savage Inequalities*, Kozol (1991) wrote about how our schools are designed to disadvantage certain students and predicted that these conditions "will likely so remain" (p. 270). Over twenty years after its publication, Kozol's prediction sadly holds true. As teachers, we cannot alter every single factor that impacts our students' daily lives. There is hope though. As reflective practitioners, teachers can closely read their own and their students' lives not as black and white texts, but as intricate multimodal ones that are multifaceted and meaning-filled.

Discussion: What Positions Surface through Our Learning? How Can We View These Positions with a Multiliteracies Lens?

Earlier in this chapter, we referenced five questions that Cope and Kalantzis (2009) had introduced in their article about multiliteracies. These five questions related to meaning and meaning-making were addressed within the LLC and are represented in the learning and positions that Chad, David, and Jay describe.

In the section below, we keep these questions in mind as we look across the insights gained by Chad, Jay, and David and broaden our discussion to include crucial elements of learning related to multiliteracies.

Self-Awareness and Self-Reflection

Kalantzis and Cope (2012a, 2012b) trace important elements of multiliteracies and discuss how education as a discipline and as a practice will need to change. In particular, Kalantzis and Cope (2012b) note that each teacher is "a learner—a designer of learning environments, an evaluator of their effectiveness, a researcher, a social scientist and an intellectual in their own right" (p. 28). As we looked across the various products representing learning for Chad, David, and Jay, it was clear they recognized their agency as designers of educational environments. Furthermore, self-awareness and self-reflection were recognized as necessary and recursive processes that educators must foster in order to effectively serve diverse student populations. Chad, David, and Jay observed that their journey of cultural awareness pursued in class interactions with others spurred their self-awareness. By framing their reflections in the context of crossing borders and diversity, they discovered that they consistently became more conscious of cultural awareness over the course of the semester's assignments and their own self-study analysis for this chapter. As they became more self-aware, it spurred further reflection. For example, Chad observed that when he revisited a particular assignment, he found many "flaws" in his cultural awareness but even though his initial insights were limited the assignment still fostered self-awareness. This in turn inspired him to "go deeper with reflections" and to continue designing and redesigning his own learning and the learning environment he created for students.

Teacher and Student Discourses

Since the publication of the first New London Group (1996) article, discourses have been central to multiliteracies:

> A discourse is a construction of some aspect of reality from a particular point of view, a particular angle, in terms of particular interests. … discourse draws attention to use of language [and other semiotic systems of meaning making] as a facet of social practice that is shaped by—and shapes—the orders of discourse of the culture. (p. 78)

Differences between teacher and student discourses were identified as areas that created tensions and challenges for teachers. In some cases, participants (e.g., Chad and Jay) recognized they differed from their students by class, race, and social economic background. They realized that drawing from different discourses and values could pose a challenge that teachers must overcome.

In other cases, Chad, David, and Jay realized that even insider perspectives (discourses) could conflict with one's own identity. As a practicing Catholic, David observed: "I am able to fully participate in the Mass through the call and response oral reading required and feel comfortable praying with my students. … However, as a gay man, this discourse makes me simultaneously an outsider in the community." Discourses are representational given that they point to specific meanings, but they also are social because discourses point to how meanings connect to and thus relationally define the people involved within a particular discourse or set of discourses.

Power and Empowerment

These relational functions of D/discourse carry within them domains of power (Gee, 2014) and notions of inclusion or exclusion. Teachers may not see themselves as powerful beings, but in this chapter, Chad, David, and Jay each came to a greater understanding of the ways that they, as teachers, could empower or disempower students. Whereas Chad, David, and Jay all recognized that discourse norms and values could cause tensions or conflict, they were not content to resign themselves to allowing conflict or tensions to become the status quo. They identified that teachers must take an active stance if they wish to help students empower themselves. Jay described it this way:

> It is essential that I create a classroom environment where a student's discourse does not inhibit them to become a self-fulfilling prophecy, but instead [their discourse] can ultimately work for them. It is imperative that they use their knowledge, not mine alone, to make the curriculum that they are a part of to have the best possible outcome.

All three participants recognized that their white, male identities provided them with specific rights or privileges not always provided to their students. They also recognized that discourses of power and empowerment were not just limited to words but included students' lived realities and the rapidly changing textual forms (e.g., social media, online hypertexts) with which students engaged outside of school.

Border Crossing as Authentic, Situated Learning

Jay and Chad acknowledged that they had not had to cross significant cultural borders in their lives growing up in white, suburban America, but they did encounter these border-crossing experiences after leaving home. Although David's experience as a gay man positioned him uniquely to identify with those who are not included within mainstream American society, he recognized that there were other border-crossing experiences that he could learn from. All three participants recognized that if they wanted to help empower students, they needed to create a multifaceted classroom environment to engage students with curriculum in ways that helped students to cross the borders related to class, race, religion, gender, and culture. Chad, David, and Jay realized that to guide students in such border-crossing experiences, teachers must first be comfortable and able to cross cultural borders themselves. Such border-crossings, whether literal or metaphoric, were not easy, and often they were very uncomfortable. But the recognition of discomfort and challenge indicated that border-crossings were authentic and situated within complex lived, cultural, social, and historical contexts. Acquiring knowledge in this way was an example of what Cazden (2000) had in mind when she observed that "we all live in the contact zone and have to take responsibility for negotiating within it" (p. 266).

Troubling Insights

We recognize that it may appear as if Chad, David, and Jay had things all figured out by the end of the LLC course. However, as part of the analysis, Chad, David, and Jay had identified insights that were troubling to them. Most troubling insights arose when participants realized that they were:

1. not as open to issues of diversity as they had previously thought;
2. not as aware of students' backgrounds as they ought to be;
3. failing to provide differentiated education and supporting the status quo instead;
4. shocked by the history of segregation and racism and de facto segregation in contemporary schools;
5. originally unaware of the causal linkages between poverty and the limited options for some students.

These troubling insights point to the profound emotional and embodied nature of learning as tied to issues of identity, socialeconomic class, gender, race, ethnicity, and culture (McVee & Boyd, in preparation).

Conclusion

As educators in a multicultural, multiliterate, and globalized world, we bear the burden, challenge, and joy of bringing all voices into conversations about literacy and culture. It is our hope that this chapter will spur conversation in two areas in particular. Male voices, particularly white, male teacher voices, must be invited and appreciated in the multiliteracies conversation in new ways. Second, if there really are to be designs for new learning, teachers and researchers must focus on insights and stances of self-reflection that help transform teaching to serve the needs of all our children. A multiliteracies agenda must actively embrace multiple voices, genders, races, and positions.

We opened this chapter with two definitions of reflection. Looking back at those, we believe that educators must engage in deeply reflective processes to ponder, to explore, to question, to be metacognitive, but we must also reflect our transformed pedagogy back into the world of learners and learning. A singular inward focus is necessary at times, but it is not sufficient to accomplish change. Our focus must continue also to be outward toward our students and their individual and collective futures.

References

Apple, M.W. (1984). Teaching and "women's work": A comparative historical and ideological analysis. In E. B. Gumbert (Ed.), *Expressions of power in education: Studies of class, gender, and race* (pp. 29–49). Atlanta, GA: University of Georgia.

Beals, M. P. (1995). *Warriors don't cry*. New York, NY: Washington Square Press.

Brock, C., Wallace, J., Herschbach, M., Johnson, C., Raikes, B., Warren, K., Nikoli, M., & Poulsen, H. (2006). Negotiating displacement spaces: Exploring teachers' stories about learning and diversity. *Curriculum Inquiry*, 36(1), 35–62.

Carger, C. (1996). *Of borders and dreams*. New York, NY: Teachers College Press.

Cazden, C. B. (2000). *Taking cultural differences into account*. In B. Cope & M. Kalantzis (Eds.), *Multiliteracies: Literacy learning and the design of social futures* (pp. 249–266). New York, NY: Routledge.

Cope, B., & Kalantzis, M. (Eds.). (2000). *Multiliteracies: Literacy learning and the design of social futures*. New York, NY: Routledge.

Cope, B., & Kalantzis, M. (2009). "Multiliteracies": New literacies, new learning. *Pedagogies: An International Journal*, 4, 164–195. doi: 10.1080/15544800903076044

Feistritzer, C. E. (2011). *Profile of teachers in the U.S. 2011*. Washington, DC: National Center for Education Information (NCEI).

Finn, P. J. (2009). *Literacy with an attitude* (2nd Ed.). Albany, NY: SUNY Press.

Florio-Ruane, S. (1997). To tell a new story: Reinventing narratives of culture, identity, and education. *Anthropology & Education Quarterly*, 28(2), 152–162.

Florio-Ruane, S. (2001). *Teacher education and the cultural imagination*. Mahwah, NJ: Lawrence Erlbaum.

Gee, J. P. (2000). New people in new worlds: Networks, the new capitalism. In B. Cope & M. Kalantzis (Eds.), *Multiliteracies: Literacy learning and the design of social futures* (pp. 43–68). New York, NY: Routledge.

Gee, J. P. (2014). *An introduction to discourse analysis: Theory and method* (4th ed.). New York, NY: Routledge.

Kalantzis, M., & Cope, B. (2012a). *Literacies*. New York, NY: Cambridge University Press.

Kalantzis, M., & Cope, B. (2012b). *New learning: Elements of a science of education* (2nd Ed). New York, NY: Cambridge University Press.

Kozol, J. (1991). *Savage inequalities: Children in America's schools*. New York, NY: Harper Perennial.

Ladson-Billings, G. (1995). Toward a theory of culturally relevant pedagogy. *American Educational Research Journal*, 32(3), 465–491.

Lowenstein, K. L. (2009). The work of multicultural teacher education: Reconceptualizing white teacher candidates as learners. *Review of Educational Research*, 79(1), 163–196.

McVee, M. B. (2011). Positioning theory and sociocultural perspectives: Affordances for educational researchers. In M. B. McVee, C. H. Brock, & J. A. Glazier (Eds.), *Sociocultural positioning in literacy: Exploring culture, discourse, narrative, and power in diverse educational contexts* (pp. 1–22). Cresskill, NJ: Hampton Press.

McVee, M. B., Bailey, N. M., & Shanahan, L. E. (2008). Using digital media to interpret poetry: Spiderman meets Walt Whitman. *Research in the Teaching of English*, 43(2), 112–143.

McVee, M. B., & Boyd, F. B. (in preparation). *Exploring diversities in teacher education through narrative, multimodality, and dialogue.*

McVee, M. B., Brock, C. H., & Glazier, J. A. (Eds.). (2011). *Sociocultural positioning in literacy: Exploring culture, discourse, narrative, and power in diverse educational contexts.* Cresskill, NJ: Hampton Press.

McVee, M. B., Dunsmore, K. L., & Gavelek, J. R. (2005). Schema theory revisited. *Review of Educational Research*, 75(4), 531–566.

Michaels, S., & Sohmer, R. (2000). New people in new worlds: Networks, the new capitalism. In B. Cope & M. Kalantzis (Eds.), *Multiliteracies: Literacy learning and the design of social futures* (pp. 267–288). New York, NY: Routledge.

Michie, G. (2009). *Holler if you hear me* (2nd Ed). New York, NY: Teachers College Press.

Moghaddam, F. M., & Harré, R. (2010). *Words of conflict words of war.* Santa Barbara, CA: Praeger.

New London Group. (1996). A pedagogy of multiliteracies: Designing social features. *Harvard Educational Review*, 66(1), 60–92.

Oxford Dictionary (2014). http://www.oxforddictionaries.com/us/definition/american_english/reflection

Raphael, T. E., & McMahon, S. I. (1994). Book club: An alternative framework for reading instruction. *The Reading Teacher*, 48(2), 102–106.

Sparks, S. D. (2012). Despite downturn, few men attracted to teaching field. *Education Week*, 31(30), 10.

Thompson, M. K. (2011). Adolescent girls authoring their lives through anime: Fanfiction and identity in Inuyasha Central. In M. B. McVee, C. H. Brock, & J. A. Glazier (Eds.), *Sociocultural positioning in literacy: Exploring culture, discourse, narrative, and power in diverse educational contexts* (pp. 181–203). Cresskill, NJ: Hampton Press.

6

EMBRACING SEXUAL DIVERSITY IN CLASSROOM TEACHING

Lynda R. Wiest

> We still live in a culture in which presumed heterosexuality and traditional messages about gender dominate us from birth. Children and adolescents who violate these norms get the message that they need to keep aspects of themselves hidden, or at least alter them, if they want to be accepted.
>
> *(Sadowski, 2013, p. 1)*

Teaching is a challenging profession that is compensated only moderately well for its labor-intensiveness and societal significance. Presumably, most educators enter such a field because they care deeply about young people and their development. It is thus surprising and worrisome that research shows teachers tend to assume passive roles when it comes to a sector of students who suffer some of the greatest social injustices, maltreatment that seeps into school settings. (See, for example, Kosciw, Greytak, Bartkiewicz, Boesen, & Palmer, 2012, and Puchner & Klein, 2011.) These students are sexual-minority youth, here defined as those who do not fit societal expectations for their externally assigned gender, be that in physical characteristics, self-expressed appearance, behavior, self-identified sex, or romantic attractions. Specifically, variant gender expression, gender identity, and sexual orientation include males who dress or act in feminine ways or identify as female, and vice versa for females, as well as individuals who are attracted to the same sex. Sexual minorities also include intersex individuals, who have both male-typical and female-typical sexual anatomy, occurring in 1 in 1,500 to 1 in 2,000 births (Intersex Society of North America, 2008).

Teachers express many reasons for neglecting sexual diversity as a classroom topic or issue (e.g., Bouley, 2011; Puchner & Klein, 2011). Concern about parent complaints seems to top the list. Other prominent reasons include uncertainty about administrative support, lack of knowledge and resources related to the topic, incongruence with personal beliefs, a perception of this topic being irrelevant to young children, and a belief that this topic falls outside a teacher's role.

In this chapter, my goal is to appeal to educators to recognize the importance of this topic in relation to instructional effectiveness and especially human compassion. Educators wield a great deal of influence to let sexual-minority youth languish under their leadership or to support them to maximize their human potential. I contend that parent resistance should bear no more weight here than if, say, parents or other community members opposed school attention to the civil rights or women's movements. We, as educators, may and should teach the realities of our world, which includes attention to all individuals, with special concern for social justice and human dignity. This cannot happen selectively. Personal religious and cultural beliefs should not infringe upon a teacher's workplace duties or the rights of others to fully and equally participate in life.

Teaching about sexual diversity is important, beginning in the early years. Sources such as www.safeschoolscoalition.org say that primary-grades children should learn:

- there are no "girl" and "boy" things, such as colors, toys/games/activities, chores, and so forth;
- families come in many forms, including foster, adoptive, guardian-headed, single-parented, and same-sex-parented families; and
- it is not okay to call people names or say hurtful things, including sexual-minority put-downs such as "fag," "dyke," or "That's so gay".

After reading this chapter, educators will have a foundation from which to assume a more knowledgeable and proactive stance to address sexual diversity in the classroom and to bring administrators on board as need be, in order to better serve all students who pass through their doors. I make two main points: (1) Sexual minorities have unique needs. (2) Teachers can make a difference. I conclude with resources that can be consulted to support efforts to create a welcoming and inclusive school environment for sexual-minority students.

Multiliteracies as a Conceptual Framework

Multiliteracies, a term coined by the New London Group (1996), is the philosophical standpoint on teaching and learning that guides this chapter. The New London Group and others who discuss the concept of multiliteracies, such as Cummins (2009) and Kalantzis and Cope (2012), posit that social diversity and multimodal pedagogy are key considerations in effective classroom learning today. These authors point out that student diversity is not only to be affirmed, but also is to be viewed as a source of strength that can lead to more powerful learning for all students. Further, they note, contemporary youth learn through varied, blended learning modes, such as oral, visual, audio, and tactile. Digital media, often appearing in multimedia formats, figure largely in accessing and creating information. Both human diversity and learning modes are ever evolving, and thus, a multiliteracies approach is flexible and adaptable to changing contexts. To serve these "new basics" of education, as Kalantzis and Cope (2012) call them, students should research and create real-world information using multiple means, and they should understand and incorporate varied perspectives and approaches in doing so. Collaboration and communication are also integral to the multiliteracies approach: among teachers, among students, and between teachers and students.

Teachers and schools are vitally important in this modern way of conceptualizing effective pedagogy. Schools and classrooms are not considered to be fair or neutral spaces without direct efforts to make them such. The New London Group (1996) states, "Schools have always played a critical role in determining students' life opportunities" (p. 71). Cummins (2009) notes that teacher decisions and actions are vitally important to transformative multiliteracies pedagogy. He says student empowerment "results from the affirmation of student identity in teacher-student interactions" (p. 44).

Multiliteracies tenets hold that education efforts should draw on the strengths of every student and ensure that all students are valued; recognized for who they are; and provided full access to societal resources, benefits, and opportunities. Students should be encouraged and supported to express themselves and to contribute to society in their own unique ways, and they should be accorded the power and status to do so. Therefore, all education professionals are responsible for constructing school environments that foster these important goals for all students, including sexual-minority youth.

The Unique Needs of Sexual Minorities

> Brandon, a gay high school student, reluctantly enters school. He stops by his locker and opens the door. Before he can reach in, he is shoved into the locker from behind and called "fag." Embarrassed and ashamed, Brandon musters the strength to go to English class, where he hears stories of famous people and families that do not mirror his life. Walt Whitman is mentioned. "Wasn't he gay?" a student asks. "That's not really relevant to this discussion," the teacher responds. In mentioning the episode at home, Brandon's father says, "Do we have to talk about that topic again?"

> Elsewhere, an elementary school girl steps into her mother's car at the end of the school day. She is in tears. "What happened?" her mother asks. "Ashley said she isn't allowed to come to my house to play because I have two mommies."

These kinds of experiences, although a fictitious composite of research findings, are all too real and happen routinely to sexual-minority youth and families. Some issues are similar to those faced by other minority groups. Others are unique to sexual minorities, such as those related to same-sex-parented families and erroneous associations of sexual-minority individuals with sexual promiscuity or deviancy. Another critical difference is that sexual-minority youth and their parents often do not share the same sexuality. Instead of having parents who identify with their minority status and can relate their own experiences and discuss possible ways to handle matters, parents themselves may not understand their sexual-minority children and may even reject or distance themselves from them. This results in a vitally important loss of support that affects students in every aspect of their world, including school.

Sexual-minority youth face serious problems at home, in school, and in the wider community. These issues and their consequences, summarized in Figures 6.1 and 6.2, are documented in many studies, such as Darwich, Hymel, and Waterhouse (2012), Kosciw et al. (2012), and Sadowski (2013). Sexual-minority youth are targets of physical and verbal harassment and physical assault. Even routinely hearing homophobic comments, such as "homo" or "lesbo," that are not specifically directed at them takes a toll on their self-image. Sexual-minority youth might be excluded from some social groups and functions, and as noted, their own family might ostracize them. At school, they experience silencing and invisibility due to the failure of curricular materials and classroom discussions to give meaningful or substantial attention to sexual-minority individuals and topics.

In describing the types of skills students need within today's multiliteracies approach, Kalantzis and Cope (2012) note that students should be able to read unfamiliar text and engage in meaning-making "without the barrier of feeling alienated by it and excluded from it" (p. 6). This points to a clear academic disadvantage for sexual-minority youth through their absence in curricular text. Further, many teachers have been shown to redirect sexual minority topics when raised, ignore anti-gay language and behavior, and even contribute to an unwelcoming climate by making homophobic or heterosexist comments themselves (e.g., Kosciw et al., 2012; Puchner & Klein, 2011). One eleventh-grade transgender student described the situation this way:

> Teachers and staff are not educated when it comes to a transgender student and therefore do nothing about it, and most of the time they also question my gender and make me embarrassed, and everyone thinks I'm a freak of nature.
> *(Kosciw et al., 2012, p. 30)*

Issues Sexual-Minority Youth Face
Physical and verbal victimization (harassment, assault)
Social exclusion and rejection
Reduced family closeness and support; less adult support in general
Exclusion from school curricular materials and classroom discussions of sexual-minority issues and topics
Teacher/school passivity and even contribution to issues of concern

FIGURE 6.1 Issues Sexual-Minority Youth Face at Home, in School, and in the Community.

Note that four of the five major issues presented in Figure 6.1 are relational, meaning that they occur in interactions with other people. This makes the issues particularly destructive to sexual-minority students' lives.

Living with the issues noted above can lead to serious personal, social, and educational consequences, as listed in Figure 6.2. Due to strained relations with families, sexual-minority youth are more likely to run away from or be kicked out of their home. One study, for example, found that 40% of homeless youth are sexual minorities (Durso & Gates, 2012, p. 4). Sexual minorities are also more likely to suffer poorer psychological well-being, such as higher levels of depression and lower self-esteem, and to have greater health risks in general due to the stress they experience. They are also more likely to engage in self-harm through substance abuse and suicide. All of these factors combine with negative school social experiences (e.g., mistreatment and exclusion) to create academic issues, including higher school absenteeism and dropout rates, lower grades, and lower college aspirations. One sexual-minority student in Kosciw et al.'s (2012) study reported, "I stopped going to school four months before graduation because I couldn't handle the bullying anymore. I will not get to attend my senior prom and … throw my graduation cap in the air" (p. 41).

Personal, Social, and Educational Consequences of Sexual-Minorities' Life and School Experiences
Greater likelihood of homelessness
Poorer mental and physical health
Increased self-harmful activity
Less supportive and rewarding social experiences
Lower educational engagement, performance, and aspirations

FIGURE 6.2 Consequences of Issues Faced by Sexual-Minority Youth.

It should be clear from the information presented thus far why sexual-minority youth have more of an "uphill climb" than other youth when it comes to succeeding in education. Cummins (2009) asserts a causal relationship in his discussion of multiliteracies pedagogy, which is an approach intended to acknowledge and address such issues. He says, "Societal power relations are directly relevant to understanding why some groups of students experience academic difficulties" (p. 39).

Although the information in Figure 6.2 focuses mainly on sexual-minority youth, it is important to recognize that some students have same-sex parents. These young people also experience issues related to invisibility of their family structure in school settings, as well as prejudicial social issues at school and in the community. Further, because sexual-minority adults are more likely than heterosexual people to be poor, their children are particularly vulnerable to the effects of poverty (Gates, 2014, p. 2). Thus, issues surrounding children of sexual-minority parents add another "layer" to this topic that is important for teachers to understand. Current estimates indicate that as many as six million Americans (2%) have at least one gay parent (Gates, 2013, p. 2), a number that is surely on the rise.

Finally, it is important to note that some students find a way to navigate these challenges and succeed in their personal, social, and academic worlds and at times even become stronger and more successful in response to these hardships. However, these individuals often have important sources of support that come from significant adults, such as parents or teachers. The next section outlines ways teachers can play this important part in sexual-minority youths' lives.

The Important Role of Teachers and Schools

Emily, a middle school student who has recently become aware of her same-sex attractions, enters school and meets a straight friend as she walks down the hall. "Are you going to the GSA (Gay-Straight Alliance) meeting today?" the friend asks. "Yes," says Emily. "See you there." Emily reaches her history classroom, which has a rainbow-striped triangle with the words "Safe Zone" posted by the door. After students settle into their seats, the teacher announces that today students will continue to explore the U.S. civil rights movement. This lesson will focus on gay rights and will include learning about the 1969 Stonewall riots and watching excerpts from the film *Milk*, which chronicles the life of Harvey Milk, who became California's first openly gay politician in the 1970s.

In a nearby elementary school, a teacher engages the topic of family and community. "Today we are going to talk about different types of families. Some families have one parent, such as a mom, a dad, a grandparent, or another adult who heads the family. What other types of families are there?" The teacher is prepared to add two-mom and two-dad families if not offered.

Elsewhere in the school, a student tells another, "You're so gay" as part of a conversation they are having before class starts. The teacher opens the class with a discussion of the comments "That's so gay" and "You're so gay." What do these comments mean? Are they compliments or criticism? Is it okay to use language that describes a whole group of people in a negative way? What can that do to people to whom we say it as well as to others who hear it? What guidelines should we set for our classroom and hallways related to this and other language so that all students in our school feel valued and welcome?

The fictitious but research-based scenarios above show what school can be like for students who have teachers who understand sexual-minority issues and topics and address them proactively. Unfortunately, research shows that school administrators, counselors, and teachers receive little or no preparation in this area and thus tend to demonstrate low competency in relation to how to better serve sexual-minority youth (Bidell, 2012; Jennings, 2012; Kitchen & Bellini, 2012). When the topic is addressed, it is more likely to appear in secondary than in elementary classrooms (Schmidt, Change, Carolan-Silva, Lockhart, & Anagnostopoulous, 2012), although as noted earlier, it should be present at all grade levels in a developmentally appropriate way. Further, the climate for sexual-minority youth is worse in middle school than in high school, in part because middle schools tend to have fewer supports and resources (Kosciw et al., 2012).

In the following sections, I recommend strategies for becoming a proactive, effective practitioner on behalf of sexual-minority students. Elaboration on these suggestions may be found in sources such as Kosciw et al. (2012) and PFLAG's (Parents, Families and Friends of Lesbians and Gays) website (http://community.pflag.org). For these efforts to succeed, university faculty must assume responsibility for preparing school administrators, counselors, and teachers to address sexual diversity in PreK–12 schooling.

Create More Comprehensive Curricula

School curriculum consists of the content we want students to know and the approaches we take in presenting it. Teaching students about the surrounding world in an age-appropriate way is not pushing a particular agenda. Instead, this is education in its truest sense. It is not sanitized or selective; it simply reflects real life. As such, sexual-minority people deserve to be included throughout the school curriculum, although formal inclusion of the topic of sexual diversity is more relevant to some subject areas, such as English/language arts, history/social studies, and health education. Schools still tend to honor heterosexual readings and films such as Shakespeare's *Romeo and Juliet* and Margaret Mitchell's *Gone with the Wind*, while omitting options such as Lillian Hellman's *The Children's Hour* and Annie Proulx's *Brokeback Mountain*. In Kosciw et al.'s (2012) survey of middle and high school students, one student wrote, "My English teacher discussed LGBT [lesbian, gay, bisexual, transgender] issues often in class (in a positive light) and it felt really good to know that she was open and accepting" (p. 61). Three suggestions for developing more inclusive curricular approaches follow.

First, include the full range of human experiences where relevant (e.g., in discussions of family and community).

Second, incorporate use of literature, news media, writing, film, and music. For example, have students read fiction and nonfiction literature that presents facts and portrays fictitious but realistic lives. (For ideas, see Rainbow Books and Stonewall Book Awards in the resource list at the end of this chapter.) It is important to choose material that represents a broad range of types of sexual-minority individuals. News media can include articles such as "When Girls Will Be Boys" by Alissa Quart (*New York Times*, March 16, 2008) and press coverage of "My Princess Boy" (see http://myprincessboy.com/). Writing short essays and journal entries is a good way to process feelings and issues. It is best to create some assignments where students are free to write on any topic of their choice. Sharing writing should be a private matter between the student and teacher except where it is important to share writing for academic purposes, but this should be made known in advance (who will see it and how). Dilg (2010) poignantly articulates the value of writing and literature:

> As writing potentially does for any writer and reader, the history of gay, lesbian, bisexual, and transgender literature in the United States reflects broadly and deeply the way in which both writing and reading have supported lives. ... The act of writing has served not only artistic and literary purposes but psychological and social purposes. (p. 72)

Films on sexual diversity tend to be more relevant to older students and might include analysis of such productions as *The Wedding Banquet, Transamerica, a Aimée & Jaguar* (based on a true story in World War II Berlin) and the documentary *Bullied*. Include sexual-diversity topics among these works, as well as sexual-minority authors, scholars, and filmmakers.

Music tends to resonate strongly with young people. Songs with sexual-diversity themes tend to be most appropriate for older students to analyze the lyrics and/or videos (e.g., "Start Again" by gay Irish singer Ryan Dolan and "Same Love" by Macklemore & Ryan Lewis). However, a song such as "Everything Possible" by the Flirtations (and more recently by Fred Small) that simply mentions "Some women love women, some men love men" within the lyrics is an appropriate song to hear at an early age.

Third, provide curricular materials within the classroom and seek to have resources made available in the school library and perhaps local libraries. Sample material includes historical and biographical information about gays and lesbians and high-quality literature and films.

Discuss Sexual Diversity Openly and Honestly in a Developmentally Appropriate Manner

Sexual-minority topics fit some school subjects better than others, but these topics might also arise informally outside of formal inclusion in the curriculum. However these topics come about, it is important to address and not dismiss them, although the context will dictate the degree to which this occurs. Further, teachers in all classes can make informal statements, such as telling students to draw a picture of or discuss something with their "parent or parents" (not their "mom and dad") or casually mentioning same-sex partners, as in "When Sally Ride and her life partner Tam O'Shaughnessy co-founded the company

Sally Ride Science. ..." In my own graduate schooling, a professor once mentioned an accomplished mathematician who committed suicide in his thirties. He followed, "It's too bad he couldn't accept his sexuality." This simple statement in the course of an entire semester made me feel safe in that classroom and form an affinity for that professor. This exemplifies how powerfully sexual minorities can crave affirmation and support in a predominantly heterosexual world.

Note that informal conversations might also take place outside of class, and some issues might need to be referred to a school counselor or other relevant professional to address if a student's welfare might be at stake or the actions or words of another seem potentially dangerous. Also, because being a sexual-minority youth or having sexual-minority parents can be sensitive and personally risky, it is important to preserve students' privacy by creating a supportive and inviting atmosphere but allowing students to determine what and how much to share, if anything. (Note: Sexual orientation, gender identity, and gender expression are *not* about sexual behavior.)

Develop Supportive Relationships and Safe Spaces

Because families might not be a source of support for sexual-minority youth, as noted earlier, teachers, friends, and community groups can be especially important (Pearson & Wilkinson, 2013). Supportive actions by and relationships with educators have been shown to have a positive impact on sexual-minority students' lives and on school climate in general (Kosciw et al., 2012; Sadowski, 2013). The concept of multiliteracies as a teaching-learning philosophy holds that educators should support members of marginalized groups, such as sexual-minority students, in order to make schools pleasant places for all students (Kalantzis & Cope, 2012). Posting a safe-space-type sign outside and/or inside a classroom is one good way to publicly signal support.

If a school doesn't have a GSA (Gay-Straight Alliance; see www.gsanetwork.org), helping students start one is a good way to create a consistent support group within the school. Helping students find community groups or mentoring programs are other ways to help students find constructive connections, but it is important to first screen these groups to be sure they are willing and able to support sexual-minority individuals in positive, affirming ways rather than, for example, trying to silence or change them.

Other example messages of support include planning schoolwide activities (e.g., related to gay civil rights) and posting pictures of diverse families or of famous people that include sexual minorities in the classroom or school hallways. One sexual-minority student in Kosciw et al.'s (2012) survey research stated:

> I was lucky enough to have staff that are understanding and respectful of LGBTQ [lesbian, gay, bisexual, transgender, queer/questioning] teens,

because even though some of the students aren't … I knew I would always have a few teachers to talk and share with. LGBTQ teens need that. They need to know that they're safe. (p. 51)

Address Stereotypical and Offensive Comments and Behaviors

Comments showing heterosexism (e.g., "Only a man and woman can/should get married" or "I wonder if that singer [female] has a boyfriend"), homophobia (e.g., "I don't want to go in the restroom with her because she's a dyke" or "He's a fag so he deserves to be beat up"), or ignorance/thoughtlessness (e.g., "That's so gay" or a joke with heterosexist/homophobic undertones) should all be challenged. Sometimes a simple comment or question is enough, such as (in relation to wondering if a particular female singer has a boyfriend), "Isn't it possible that she has or is interested in a girlfriend?" At other times, a discussion is called for, such as that illustrated at the end of the opening scenario of the section "The Important Role of Teachers and Schools" that appears earlier in this chapter.

Although the ultimate unequivocal message must be that certain comments and behaviors are completely unacceptable and will have consequences, simply telling students to stop and/or punishing them typically will not reach the ultimate goal of changing thinking and behavior and may in fact make things worse. Real change requires patience, caring, and honest discussion. Because digital means of communicating are prevalent among today's youth, it is also important to find ways to be attentive to "cyberbullying" that might occur via social media, texting, and so forth.

Develop Inclusive and Nondiscriminatory School and Classroom Policies and Norms

Initiate efforts to develop school policies, if they are not already in place, that safeguard all students and have consequences for inappropriate behavior. Help ensure that faculty know and enforce the school's anti-bullying/harassment and other policies that support student well-being. Sexual orientation, gender identity, and gender expression should be explicitly protected within these policies. Besides establishing policy in writing, policies and norms should be stated orally at times, as in a school principal giving a welcome speech to parents in which he or she says, "At Fairview Middle School, we are proud to have students from a diverse group of families … families from different racial and ethnic backgrounds … families who speak different languages … families with a mother and father or two mothers or two fathers. …" Displaying pictures of different kinds of families on posters in the school lobby or hallways or on school brochures, newsletters, and web pages are other ways to reinforce this message, which needs to explicitly reflect sexual-minority families and students.

School norms and practices that are inclusive and nondiscriminatory should also be established. For example, the school dress code should not be restrictive according to traditional gender roles, and school dances and proms should allow students to attend and dance with same-sex partners. Schools will also have to determine policies related to restroom use, as male and female restrooms can be problematic for transgender and intersex students, and they will have to decide what sports teams students may play on (e.g., consistent with one's self-identified gender). Other examples of equitable practices are having senior "who's who" categories where "cutest couple" may be male-female or same-sex, not having students line up or group by gender for school activities, and setting and enforcing expectations related to displays of affection between students in a manner that is consistent for male-female and same-sex couples.

Create a Culture of Learning and Communication among Key Adults

School personnel, including administrators, counselors, and teachers, as well as higher education faculty who conduct programs and courses for these individuals, should engage in ongoing professional development individually and jointly to increase their awareness and knowledge of sexual-minority issues. This learning should include attention to examining personal beliefs and attitudes, potential stereotypes and biases, and educational practices. Effort should be put into gathering and discussing relevant facts and information, learning appropriate language (e.g., preferred terms such as "sexual orientation" instead of "sexual preference," "gay life" instead of "gay lifestyle," and "intersex" rather than "hermaphrodite"), locating useful resources, and determining how to handle pressure from parents and others who resist attention to sexual diversity at school. (For information about the "two-spirit" terminology used in the Native American community, see "The 'Two-Spirit' People of Indigenous North Americans" by Walter L. Williams at http://www.firstpeople.us/articles/the-two-spirit-people-of-indigenous-north-americans.html.) School personnel can further pursue professional development through such means as having guest speakers and workshops, engaging in regular discussions, and holding a book and film study group that includes a mix of different types of books and films. (See sample suggestions in the curricula section above.)

Berg (2013) suggests having students create an online identity that differs from their own (e.g., gay or transgender) in order to experience what another person's life might be like. This idea might also be considered for adults seeking to further their own growth. In efforts to develop a strong network of adults to support sexual-minority youth, it would be worthwhile to build collaborative relationships with parents and community members as well (e.g., those who provide youth services). The strategy detailed in this section is an expanded version of what Kalantzis and Cope (2012) envision within their multiliteracies approach to teaching and learning: that teachers are "immersed in a professional culture of mutual support and sharing" (p. 12). These endeavors can take place face-to-face and/or online.

Make Sexual-Diversity Resources Available to School Staff, Students, and Parents

Actively seek and provide high-quality/reputable sexual-diversity resources in each classroom, in the school library, in central school spaces (e.g., the lobby, office, hallways, student lounges, cafeteria), and via the Internet. Resources should be a mix of various types of literature, news media, and films, as well as brochures that provide useful information and services, such as community resources and a list of websites similar to that which appears next in this chapter. Inspirational material might be included, such as a list of famous historical and/or contemporary gay, lesbian, bisexual, and transgender people. Resources such as these should be available for students as well as for teachers (e.g., curricular materials and a guest speaker list) and parents (e.g., PFLAG brochures).

Conclusion

Increasingly nuanced understandings are required to learn how to serve sexual-minority youth, who are a diverse group of people. For example, some populations suffer more than others at the hands of societal and school discrimination, ignorance, and ill feelings, and they have less access to helpful resources and services (e.g., Kosciw et al., 2012; Schmidt et al., 2012). Transgender students and gender-nonconforming students (e.g., those who express themselves in gender-atypical ways) are among these, as are students in rural and small towns. Sexual-minority individuals have greater challenges in the South and Midwest than in the Northeast and West. The younger the school grade level, the lower the likelihood of attention to sexual-minority issues and topics or availability of resources. Finally, it is important to consider intersections of student identities in working with sexual-minority youth (e.g., Blackburn & Smith, 2010; Dilg, 2010). For example, how do gender, race/ethnicity, and social class mediate a sexual-minority individual's experiences and perspectives? Life and school experiences can differ among the subgroups that fall within those and other identity-related categories. All people have multiple, complex, and evolving identities that vary according to social context (e.g., Berg, 2013).

Keeping up with needed knowledge and skills requires continual learning on the part of school administrators, counselors, and teachers, as well as higher education faculty who teach them. Further, it is in the best interest of schools and the students they serve to find ways to help educate parents and the community. Straight allies from both the school and the community should be solicited and enlisted to participate in efforts to support sexual-minority youth. Sexual-minority faculty and staff, a topic not addressed here, also deserve a concerted effort to support them. The resources listed in the next section can provide a strong start for pursuing the multifaceted areas indicated here.

Dilg (2010) notes, "Most important in our work is support for each of the students before us" (p. 74). This is what a multiliteracies approach, the foundation for this chapter, advocates: concerted and continued efforts to achieve greater parity in student outcomes (Kalantzis & Cope, 2012). This is what I call for in relation to sexual-minority youth who fall within our charge. After all, we educators sign on for the role of championing the welfare and growth of all students.

Selected Sexual-Diversity Resources

Listed below are a dozen of the many good resources that provide useful information on sexual-minority issues and topics. These resources, all of which may be found on the Web, are ones that are particularly useful to school personnel, parents, and youth themselves. In the descriptions, LGBT (lesbian, gay, bisexual, transgender) is used interchangeably with GLBT as per the website's language. However, the resources should be considered to address sexual-minority individuals in a wider sense (including queer, questioning, intersex, etc.).

- The Gay, Lesbian and Straight Education Network (GLSEN): http://www.glsen.org
  GLSEN is a leading national education organization focused on ensuring safe schools for all students.
- Gay-Straight Alliance Network: http://www.gsanetwork.org
  Gay-Straight Alliance Network is a national youth leadership organization that connects school-based Gay-Straight Alliances (GSAs) to each other and community resources through peer support, leadership development, and training.
- Intersex Society of North America (ISNA): http://isna.org
  ISNA, a resource for clinicians, parents, and affected individuals, provides information about sex-development disorders and how to improve affected individuals' health care and well-being.
- It Gets Better Project: http://www.itgetsbetter.org
  The purpose of this project is to communicate to LGBT youth around the world that it gets better and to create and inspire the changes needed to make it better for them.
- National Center for Transgender Equality (NCTE): http://transequality.org
  The NCTE is a nonprofit social justice organization dedicated to advancing the equality of transgender people through advocacy, collaboration, and empowerment.
- Parents, Families and Friends of Lesbians and Gays (PFLAG): http://community.pflag.org
  PFLAG is the nation's largest family and ally organization committed to advancing equality and societal acceptance of LGBT people through support, education, and advocacy.

- Rainbow Books—GLBTQ Books for Children & Teens: http://glbtrt.ala.
  org/rainbowbooks/rainbow-books-lists
  This set of booklists is released in January of each year by the American
  Library Association.
- Safe Schools Coalition: http://www.safeschoolscoalition.org/safe.html
  The Safe Schools Coalition is an international public-private partnership in
  support of GLBT youth that works to help schools become safe places where
  every family can belong, where every educator can teach, and where every
  child can learn.
- Stonewall Book Awards: http://www.ala.org/glbtrt/award
  Sponsored by the American Library Association's Gay, Lesbian, Bisexual, and
  Transgender Round Table, these GLBT book awards are announced each
  January in the areas of adult fiction and nonfiction and children's and young
  adult literature.
- Teaching Tolerance School Leader Guide: http://www.tolerance.org/sites/
  default/files/general/LGBT%20Best%20Practices_0.pdf
  This is a 2013 document titled *Best Practices: Creating an LGBT-Inclusive School
  Climate: A Teaching Tolerance Guide for School Leaders.*
- TransYouth Family Allies (TYFA): http://www.imatyfa.org
  TYFA empowers children and families by partnering with educators, service
  providers, and communities to develop supportive environments where gen-
  der may be expressed and respected.
- The Williams Institute: williamsinstitute.law.ucla.edu
  Housed at the University of California, Los Angeles (UCLA) School of Law,
  the institute conducts rigorous, independent research on sexual orientation
  and gender identity law and public policy.

References

Berg, M. (2013). Tolerance to alliance: Deconstructing dichotomies to advocate for all
students. *Voices from the Middle*, 20(3), 32–36.

Bidell, M. P. (2012). Examining school counseling students' multicultural and sexual orientation competencies through a cross-specialization comparison. *Journal of Counseling
and Development*, 90(2), 200–207.

Blackburn, M. V., & Smith, J. M. (2010). Moving beyond the inclusion of LGBT-
themed literature in English language arts classrooms: Interrogating heteronormativity and exploring intersectionality. *Journal of Adolescent and Adult Literacy*, 53(8),
625–634.

Bouley, T. M. (2011). Speaking up: Opening dialogue with pre-service and in-service
teachers about reading children's books inclusive of lesbian and gay families. *Journal of
Praxis in Multicultural Education*, 6(1), 1–19.

Cummins, J. (2009). Transformative multiliteracies pedagogy: School-based strategies for
closing the achievement gap. *Multiple Voices for Ethnically Diverse Exceptional Learners*,
11(2), 38–56.

Darwich, L., Hymel, S., & Waterhouse, T. (2012). School avoidance and substance use among lesbian, gay, bisexual, and questioning youths: The impact of peer victimization and adult support. *Journal of Educational Psychology*, 104(2), 381–392.

Dilg, M. (2010). *Our worlds in our words: Exploring race, class, gender, and sexual orientation in multicultural classrooms*. New York, NY: Teachers College Press.

Durso, L. E., & Gates, G. J. (2012). *Serving our youth: Findings from a national survey of service providers working with lesbian, gay, bisexual, and transgender youth who are homeless or at risk of becoming homeless*. Los Angeles, CA: The Williams Institute with True Colors Fund and The Palette Fund.

Gates, G. J. (2013). *LGBT parenting in the United States*. Los Angeles, CA: The Williams Institute.

Gates, G. J. (2014). *Food insecurity and SNAP (food stamps) participation in LGBT communities*. Los Angeles, CA: The Williams Institute, UCLA School of Law.

Intersex Society of North America (ISNA). (2008) How common is intersex? http://www.isna.org/faq/frequency

Jennings, T. (2012). Sexual orientation topics in educational leadership programmes across the USA. *International Journal of Inclusive Education*, 16(1), 1–23.

Kalantzis, M., & Cope, B. (2012). *Literacies*. New York, NY: Cambridge University Press.

Kitchen, J., & Bellini, C. (2012). Addressing lesbian, gay, bisexual, transgender, and queer (LGBTQ) issues in teacher education: Teacher candidates' perceptions. *Alberta Journal of Educational Research*, 58(3), 444–460.

Kosciw, J. G., Greytak, E. A., Bartkiewicz, M. J., Boesen, M. J., & Palmer, N. A. (2012). *The 2011 National School Climate Survey: The experiences of lesbian, gay, bisexual and transgender youth in our nation's schools*. New York, NY: Gay, Lesbian & Straight Education Network.

New London Group. (1996). A pedagogy of multiliteracies: Designing social futures. *Harvard Educational Review*, 66(1), 60–92.

Pearson, J., & Wilkinson, L. (2013). Family relationships and adolescent well-being: Are families equally protective for same-sex attracted youth? *Journal of Youth and Adolescence*, 42, 376–393.

Puchner, L., & Klein, N. A. (2011). The right time and place? Middle school language arts teachers talk about not talking about sexual orientation. *Equity and Excellence in Education*, 44(2), 233–248.

Quart, A. (2008, March 16). When girls will be boys. *New York Times*. Retrieved from http://www.nytimes.com/2008/03/16/magazine/16students-t.html?_r=0

Sadowski, M. (2013). *In a queer voice: Journeys of resilience from adolescence to adulthood*. Philadelphia, PA: Temple University Press.

Schmidt, S. J., Change, S. P., Carolan-Silva, A., Lockhart, J., & Anagnostopoulous. (2012). Recognition, responsibility, and risk: Pre-service teachers' framing and reframing of lesbian, gay, and bisexual social justice issues. *Teaching and Teacher Education*, 28(8), 1175–1184.

7

DESIGNING SAFE PLACES TO TALK ABOUT CONTENTIOUS TOPICS

Fenice B. Boyd and Andrea L. Tochelli

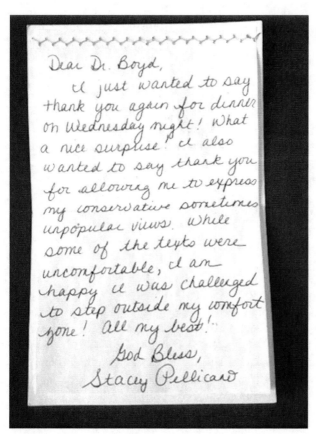

FIGURE 7.1 Stacey's Thank You Card.

Our opening vignette is a thank you card that Stacey (permission granted to use given name) sent Fenice after our class titled *Literature for Young Adults* ended May 2012. The class met on Wednesday evening from 7:00pm–9:40pm, a difficult time for graduate students to be interactive contributing members. A late evening class is especially difficult for graduate students who work full-time during the day and attend classes immediately after leaving work. Stacey was a practicing teacher working toward a master's degree by taking evening classes. Every Wednesday she attended class well-prepared and ready to participate. On the evening of the last class session, Fenice and Andrea had a local restaurant deliver pizza, chicken wings, and Sierra Mist for the students, which is what Stacey means when she refers to "dinner" in her thank you card.

We begin our chapter by highlighting Stacey's thank you card because her statement "I also wanted to say thank you for allowing me to express my conservative sometimes unpopular views" is an example of one major course goal: that students, preservice and in-service teachers, feel confident, comfortable, and free to respectfully express their thoughts with conviction. Stacey was one such student, as were several others who gradually flourished over the semester in expressing their beliefs and feelings about the multicultural literature and controversial issues we broached in the course. As Stacey notes, "While some of the texts were uncomfortable, I am happy I was challenged to step outside my comfort zone!"

Our approach for teaching a graduate young adult literature (YAL) course links well to what Kalantzis and Cope (2012) call a critical literacies pedagogy, which requires a positioning toward texts that compels and exemplifies critical thinking. This pedagogy involves students identifying questions that focus on personal and overarching human conditions and allows for learners to address challenging topics that do not have easy answers and may be contentious. Kalantzis and Cope (2012) argue that these discussions are not debating for the purpose of debate but instead are used to develop "purposeful and reflective habits of mind and action" (p. 149).

In a subsequent email almost two years later, Stacey said:

> Let me echo the sentiments in my note when I say that your class was pivotal for my thoughts about young adult literature. We live in a time when exposure to and discussion of social diversity through literature can create an empathy that may never exist for the individual without the platform that texts provide. I think that as an adult, most of the time I get in my own way when it comes to what I think is best for children. When I think of my experience in your classroom, the following quote always comes to mind. "Move out of your comfort zone. You can only *grow* if you are willing to feel *awkward* and *uncomfortable* when you try something new" (quote from Brian Tracy).
>
> *(Pellicano, personal communication, December 18, 2013)*

As Stacey suggests both in her own words and through Brian Tracy, educators need to support the idea of confronting their own prejudices and misconceptions before they can promote a positive classroom environment for all students (Stufft & Graff, 2011).

In this chapter, we convey how a multiliteracies pedagogy and practice were put into action in a graduate YAL course. We contextualize our description around a critical literacies framework (Kalantzis & Cope, 2012) and describe various course elements generated within *Situated Practice, Overt Instruction, Critical Framing* and *Transformed Practice* (New London Group [NLG], 1996). First, we provide a brief overview of the participants and the overall design of the course. Our aim was to use controversial YAL to help teachers understand the ways in which ideals and ideas are constructed based upon the values people hold and the actions they take. After we explain the overall course design, we focus on one class session that centered on literature written about Lesbian Gay Bisexual Transgender (LGBT) youth. We present excerpts from the class discussion and from students' written products to understand how they approached LGBT texts to think about their own beliefs, the ways in which authors developed the characters, and the story arc presented in the literature. We also convey how the students thought about the use of LGBT literature in their own classrooms. We end our chapter with the importance of designing safe spaces to talk about contentious topics and the significance of reading LGBT-themed literature for youth.

A Snapshot of Preservice and In-service Teachers

A total of fourteen students registered to take our course, and eleven agreed to participate in our project. Of the eleven participants, three were studying to become certified as Literacy Specialists, and eight were pursuing certification in English Education, Adolescence. Stacey, whom we introduced at the beginning of our chapter, had a full-time teaching position, and several others were substitute teaching. There was one European American male and one African American female participant; the remaining nine were European American females. In our next section, we present the class session where LGBT-themed literature was the focus. (See Figure 7.2 for a list of teachers and their majors. All names are pseudonyms.)

Designing a Multiliteracies Pedagogy

A multiliteracies pedagogy assumes the following: Learning is not simply a series of rules to be obeyed, facts to be learned, and knowledge authorities to be followed. We aimed for our students to be critically literate by identifying relevant and powerful topics from the literature, considering alternative points of

Name	Major
Vivienne	Literacy Specialist
Eleanor	Adolescence, English Education
Rylee	Adolescence, English Education
Stacey	Adolescence, English Education
Henry	Adolescence, English Education
Elizabeth	Adolescence, English Education
Lucy	Literacy Specialist

FIGURE 7.2 Students and Their Majors.

view, formulating possible solutions to problems, and then coming to their own conclusions to make well-reasoned arguments to support their ideas. Below, we convey how we structured the course and topics by situating our work within the NLG (1996) framework: Situated Practice, Overt Instruction, Critical Framing, and Transformed Practice.

Situated Practice

We ascribe to the principles of Situated Practice as defined by the NLG (1996): "Immersion in experience and the utilization of available discourses, including those from the students' lifeworlds and simulations of the relationships to be found in workplaces and public spaces" (p. 88). Moreover, it has been well documented that students learn best when they are motivated and when they believe what they are learning is useful (NLG, 1996). We had two immediate goals for our course: First, teachers in our course had to immerse themselves in reading, thinking about, and responding to a variety of YAL, and second, as they immersed themselves in the literature, they were expected to examine themes and issues, consider topics as related to diversity, raise questions and concerns, consider authors' intent and literary devices, and think about future trends of YAL. A broader goal was to better enable our teachers to enhance their understandings about literary theory and practices regarding reader response and its contribution to adolescents' reading development, including comprehension, writing, multimodal composing, critical thinking, and their overall learning and academic achievement.

We purposely did not design our course to be one for collecting "cute" activities or strategies to implement in the classroom. This did not mean that the literature we read and studied or the methods employed across the semester were not adaptable for secondary school students. Strictly speaking, our primary concern from a Situated Practice perspective was to work with the teachers as a community of learners to first immerse them in meaningful practices. It was important however, that they (a) engage in their own thoughtful and critical understandings, (b) explore the role of YAL in their own professional development, and (c) think about how they might teach adolescents to read and respond to the texts for personal as well as academic interests. Therefore, we informed our students that the course was designed to be an academic study of YAL and the success of the course was dependent, in part, upon their contributions: *What* ideas and thoughts they brought to the table and *how* they brought them was a contributing factor in *what* and *how* they learned.

The YAL we selected centered on a range of themes and controversial issues including:

- survival;
- heritage;
- teenaged parents;
- troubled teens;
- youth violence, including bullying;
- identity, including sexual identity; and
- challenged and banned books.

We chose a variety of genres such as realistic fiction, science fiction, nonfiction, graphic novels, poetry, and fantasy. Written responses such as blogs, journals, character reflections, and newsletters gave us insight into students' thinking about the literature they read. Additionally, students were required to develop multimodal representations in formats such as collages, digital video, and a small group project called "body biography."

The general format of the course was for the entire class to read one common text every week. Then they were given two to four options to read in addition to the common text around the theme of the week. The students were also expected to read a practitioner or research article focused on the topic. As an example, in the second week of the course, we began our ongoing discussion on censorship, noting challenged and banned books. All students read *Looking for Alaska* (Green, 2005). They could then choose to read either *Briar Rose* (Yolen, 1992) or *I Know Why the Caged Bird Sings* (Angelou, 1969). Before attending class, all students composed a written response to the texts they read and explored the ideas of censorship in middle and high school classrooms. In designing the class discussion, we developed focal questions for whole group discussion about *Looking for Alaska*. Students then broke into small groups based on one of the other texts they read. To facilitate the small group discussion, we provided them with guiding questions but also encouraged them to bring their own questions and comments to the group. At the end of class, we gathered again as a group and discussed the challenging and banning of YAL in relation to the books they had read. With the exception of one or two class sessions, this is the basic format that we used each week, but the focus shifted depending on the theme, genre, and topic.

Overt Instruction

Overt Instruction pertains to each of the steps we engaged in as instructors to scaffold learning activities for our community of learners (NLG, 1996). This is likened to the teacher assisting learners in activating their background knowledge, building on and developing what they may already know and have accomplished. To focus our graduate students on significant features of their own reading experiences and to assemble them as a community of learners, Overt Instruction was initiated to assist them in bringing forth topics and issues with which they wrestled. To illustrate this point, we explain why it was important to include LGBT YAL literature and the strategic placement of this topic.

The strongest positive influences for LGBT students in schools are to have supportive educators in their school building who form positive relationships with students (Kosciw, Greytak, Bartkiewicz, Boesen, & Palmer, 2012; Kosciw, Palmer, Kull, & Greytak, 2013). Rarely do teachers receive training on addressing sexual orientation and/or gender identity (Whitman, Horn, & Boyd, 2007). However, the process of becoming a supportive staff member generally begins with examining one's own biases and developing a knowledge base about the LGBT population (Graybill, Vargas, Meyers, & Watson, 2009). Examining one's attitude toward LGBT-identified students is important because, without doing so, educators may unknowingly be creating and perpetuating homophobia in schools (Aragon, Poteat, Espelage, & Koenig, 2014). Our decisions around the LGBT literature were framed with these understandings in mind.

We purposefully placed LGBT-themed literature over halfway through the semester because we believed that we needed to send the message and set the tone that our course was designed to be a safe place for students to comfortably share their thoughts about literature on topics that are not commonly discussed in college or secondary classrooms. Based on Fenice's prior experiences in teaching a YAL course, we think this was a wise decision. In these previous iterations of the course, many students either identified as LGBT or acknowledged a family member or a friend who identified as LGBT. Some of these students were concerned with sharing this information for fear of safety as well as their careers.

Approximately seventeen years ago, while teaching a multicultural literature course at a university in the Southeast, Fenice remembers a student telling her that she thought it was interesting that the LGBT literature selections were the last to be read and discussed on the very last class session of the semester. From Fenice's prior experience, we knew it was important to think about how we positioned the LGBT-themed literature: not at the beginning of the course, before a safe community was established, and not at the end, where students might perceive it as unimportant or an afterthought. We wanted our students to know that they could express their experiences and connections about relatives and friends who are members of the LGBT community, just as students who are members or have experiences with diverse ethnic, cultural, and linguistic communities have opportunities to express their views and make connections.

Critical Framing

Critical Framing is goal-oriented, and its purpose is to guide students in "standing back from what they are studying and viewing it critically in relation to its context" (NLG, 1996, p. 88). We had the responsibility to assist our students in deconstructing their understandings about what adolescents should and should not read in order to make strange what they had learned and mastered in the past and then reconstruct new meanings about the contemporary and non-canonical YAL read in the course. Stacey's acknowledgment is an example of how she grew in relation to her social, cultural, and value-laden beliefs; she stepped out of her comfort zone to allow herself to view critically the topics and issues that emerged from the novels and class discussions.

After teaching this course for several years, it is not uncommon to hear students initiate conversations about whether or not they would use certain literature selections with secondary students while discussing the novel with their peers. The most common reasons given not to use a book is because they want to avoid conflict, and they fear parents may confront them about certain content of a book (e.g., suicide, swear words). This conversation often evolves without thoughtful consideration about why a particular book may be educationally sound and purposeful to use in the classroom and that several swear words in a 200-page book may not be the best reason to exclude it from the classroom library. From these experiences, Fenice noticed that "self-censoring" was rampant and therefore decided students needed to see themselves as part of the ongoing problem of denying adolescents access to high-quality, contemporary YAL.

One way that we put Critical Framing into practice is by having teachers conduct a small research project on censorship, noting challenged and banned literature written for adolescents. For this inquiry project, they gathered information on ten books that were challenged or banned within a ten-year time period from the year of the course (e.g., 2002–2012). One requirement is to develop an annotated bibliography of the YAL books they research and include reasons for the controversy around the book. A request was that students pay close attention to whether or not they find any books used in our course as officially reported challenged or banned. Often they may find one or two. In this case, students identified both *Looking for Alaska* (Green, 2005) and *I Know Why the Caged Bird Sings* (Angelou, 1969) as frequently challenged novels. But more often than not, they do not come across as many books on the reading list for the course as they anticipated and they wonder why not. This revelation spirals a discussion about "self-censorship" and that in order for YAL to be challenged or banned in schools, teachers first have to be willing to move beyond the familiar stories or those with "happily ever after" endings and do what Stacey says: move out of their comfort zones. They must be willing to take risks.

LGBT YAL: Tenth Class Session

We address our LGBT YAL class session through a Critical Framing lens. In order to have the teachers stand back to view LGBT issues critically in relation to schools and society as a whole class discussion, we opened the session by high-lighting adolescents and adults who at some point and time had been thrust into the public arena because of their sexual identity and political ideologies (see Brock, Carter, and Boyd in this volume for a brief discussion of ideology).

We began by talking about Jamey Rodemeyer, a Western New York (WNY) openly bisexual teenager who committed suicide September 11, 2011, as a result of endless bullying and being called gay. Jamey's life was a particularly poignant way to begin as his suicide was still fresh in the minds of our students because it occurred only a few months before and the discussions around the bullying this student faced was a frequent topic on the local news through the end of the school year. We also discussed Tyler Clementi, a student at Rutgers University who jumped to his death from the George Washington Bridge on September 22, 2010, after learning that his roommate, Dharun Ravi, and a fellow hall mate, Molly Wei, had watched Clementi on a webcam (without his knowledge) while he was intimate with another boy in his dorm room; Matthew Shepherd, who in October 1998, was tortured and hung on a fence like a scarecrow and left to die; Harvey Milk, who became the first openly gay elected official in the country, held a public office in San Francisco, and was assassinated in 1978; and Bayard Rustin, an African American leader, who was active in civil and gay rights and instrumental in facilitating the 1968 March on Washington.

After this introduction, our students entered the discussion by sharing how they had gathered information or enhanced their background knowledge about the LGBT community. For instance, about four years previously, Elizabeth had attended a lecture presentation given by Matthew Shepherd's mother who talked about how her family's life had changed since his murder. Elizabeth told the class that Shepherd's mother was moving and powerful but also lighthearted. She believed that since Matthew was murdered in 1998, his mother had given herself time to heal and move on and that public speaking was one way in which she was helping herself and others. Elizabeth thought that including a video of excerpts of Shepherd's mother's talk would be one activity that she would use in her classroom to begin a discussion of LGBT-themed literature.

In addition to beginning the discussion about these public events, students watched two video vignettes from *Breaking the Silence* (National Center for Lesbian Rights, 2005). These vignettes were produced to give lesbian, gay, bisexual, and transgendered teenagers a chance to tell their stories. The youth's target audience was social workers. In one vignette, a youth who called himself Captain spoke about how he was multidimensional and that his identity was ever so complex. With music playing in the background, Captain said:

> There's not a word in the English language to describe me. Three sisters make up this man and without each other they cannot survive. How could you take a part of me and expect me to pass it away? What makes up me makes this man who he is. I am black, I am woman, I am queer. Those three sisters make me the man I am today … Remove one and I am incomplete. There is no word in the English language that describes Captain. I can never be a man for the sake that I am a woman. I can never be a woman for the sake that I am black. And I can never be black for the sake that I am queer.

From Captain's vignette a whole class discussion ensued. Eleanor said:

> I really like that story. I work with LGBT youth at a youth center in the city, and you see these kids come in and they try to fit themselves under a letter that is LGBT, and identify themselves … and people will ask them "Oh are you a butch lesbian? Are you fem? Are you a twink? Are you stud?" And they use all these titles as if people *have to* [emphasized in speech] fit in these categories. And it's complicated but … it's important to recognize how fluid it [identity] is? And Captain's story recognizes that fluidity, because I think like often if society or other people aren't willing to recognize that it can be more hurtful than helpful to put yourself in a box.

Other students brought up the fact that Captain's vignette was insightful in terms of being aware that identity is fluid. Elizabeth brought up the fact that we define gender based on social constructs, and for her, Captain's vignette defies that point of view. Captain did not purposefully identify with any one aspect of gender. Stacey also made a comment prompted by Captain's vignette:

> I just feel like, I mean obviously, I have a husband, I have four kids, so sexual orientation for me, I mean I know what my sexual orientation is. But I don't have to talk about it? You know what I mean? It doesn't define me

at all. And so, I just … I feel like … not that I'm saying we're talking about things that don't matter; I don't mean it like that. I mean that I think we place so much importance on like that's your most important role in life; like you know, how you align yourself; what your sexual preferences are. I think it's … it's not even important; not that it's not important, obviously it's important to the person. But I just feel like it doesn't define us.

A student chimed in to say that because our society is so "hetero-normative," anything that deviates from "the norm" is something that people talk about to define themselves. Eleanor challenged Stacey by first noting that it was easy for her to make this comment given that she will most likely not be critiqued for who she is, including her sexual identity. Eleanor explicated by saying that the vignettes from *Breaking the Silence* are pivotal educational tools because in our society, there are no equal social values or equal rights for the LGBT community. Therefore, the conversation that we were engaged in was important to have.

Often literature surrounding LGBT people focuses on the sexual identity aspect of the characters over the notion of intersecting identities and how the sexual identity of the character is intertwined and unable to be removed from race, class, gender, and other identities (Blackburn and Smith, 2010). Another student talked about an article that she read for another class where the participant attempted to raise children as gender neutral, even going so far as to change the gender of characters in the children's books that were read. We talked about how that would be a difficult endeavor bringing the point back to how people are influenced by societal constructs. Thus, Captain's vignette brought to the surface a discussion about the fluidity of identity and that people are multidimensional.

Students' Thoughts about Hard Love

For our course, there were opportunities for small and whole group discussions. Following the introduction and discussion of the public events and vignettes, we asked students to gather in small groups to discuss *Hard Love* (Wittlinger, 1999). The novel is about John, a protagonist, as he struggles to cope with his parents' divorce and their contentious relationship. He turns to writing for a zine (i.e., online self-published magazines featuring original work usually on a certain theme) and a friendship with Marisol, who identifies as a lesbian. John faces a challenge when he realizes he has fallen in love with Marisol. In order to frame the small group discussion, we provided several questions that covered a variety of topics. Within these conversations, students could talk about the prompts or they could speak from what they had written or created multimodally before the class session. For *Hard Love*, two students chose to write a character confession, two chose to compose a movie trailer, three chose to use songs to represent themes in the novel, one chose a movie clip, and two chose to compose a photographic essay. In our next section, we provide excerpts of seven students' blogs about *Hard Love*.

Written Responses

We coded students' written responses for emerging themes in *Hard Love* and their critique of Wittlinger's portrayal of the two main characters, Marisol and John. Three broad themes centered on sexual identity, relationships, and the author's style. Below we share excerpts from Amelia, Rylee, Elizabeth, Lucy, Henry, Vivienne, and Eleanor's blog.

Sexual Identity

The students had varied opinions on the characters' expressions of sexual identity in the novel *Hard Love*. Amelia felt positively about the book because of the way Wittlinger approached sexual identity:

> I spoke to one of my friends who had read this book many years ago, and she said she didn't like this book because it was kind of confusing. She didn't like that John appeared to be gay at some points of the book and didn't appear so at others. I could understand how that would be hard for a reader to follow, but I enjoy that disjointedness of his quest for sexual identity. Sexuality is fluid, and there's no perfect path to finding one's self in life. I liked that there were twists and turns in the narrative because it made the book more authentic. Furthermore, I like that his search for sexual identity was not at the forefront of the story. The book wasn't specifically about gayness. It was about characters and their sexuality [which] was one aspect of their rather profound connection.

Like Amelia, Eleanor viewed the focus on the fluidity of sexual identity positively:

> I did like how Wittlinger portrayed sexuality as something that was not always concrete. The fluidity of sexuality has been a part of gender theory for a really long time but society still has trouble trying to accept it. I appreciate any literature that contributes to that concept as being something true. Each character questioned their gender identity/sexual orientation at some point but also seemed to stay true to some categorical sexual identity, which I thought was interesting. Overall the book was decent but I probably would not read it again.

Both Amelia and Eleanor felt that Wittlinger's portrayal of sexual identity was a positive aspect of the novel because based on their understanding and experiences, sexual identity is not fixed but fluid. This perspective was an important part of their blog posts and became a discussion point during class.

Although both Amelia and Eleanor looked favorably on this questioning and fluidity of sexual identity in the novel, Rylee took a different position. She argued that the author portrayed Marisol as a "stereotypical lesbian" who questioned her sexual identity only after meeting John.

> I am going to be completely honest with my overall reaction to Ellen Wittlinger's *Hard Love* ... I realize it was a book about accepting your own identity and being okay with it, but I also had a hard time with Marisol's character. From a personal level, the book rubbed me wrong because of the way it illustrated Marisol's character in a questioning way when John (Gio) gave her attention. Although it was not exactly explicit, there was this lingering question if she liked Gio in the way he liked/developed feelings for her, even though he knew she was a lesbian before even meeting her, and she stressed this fact multiple times throughout the book. However, it was interesting (as a Lesbian myself) to see how these two characters formed a mutual bond that could not be explained, it echoed a similar bond that I have in my own life with my guy best friend. Yet, at the same time, I couldn't get passed [*sic*] the fact that Wittlinger seemed to give off this questionable message about teens still not understanding their sexual orientation. While I agree and disagree with the fact that teenagers may have a hard time understanding themselves while others around them for instance, are craving girlfriends, like Brian, I also think that teenagers can have a full understanding of themselves, too.

Rylee was open in her critique of how the author portrays the main character Marisol as questioning her sexual identity and why she found it objectionable as a stereotypical view of a lesbian. However, she acknowledged that she contradicted herself because while there were some angles that she did not like, she appreciated some aspects about major and minor characters. Rylee's identity as a lesbian seemed to shape her reading of the book, and while a member of the LGBT community, she seemed to distance herself from the notions of fluidity of sexual identity, as Amelia and Eleanor pointed out.

Lucy took a similar position to Rylee's in the portrayal of the relationship between John and Marisol and the questioning of sexual identity in the novel. In her blog she stated:

> Seeing John fall in love with Marisol knowing she is a lesbian was upsetting, since it was a doomed relationship to begin with. I know John had mentioned in the beginning of the novel that he was not sure if he even liked girls. That seemed to create a very brief moment in which John questioned whether he was gay or not, but that was quickly abandoned. If Wittlinger wanted to discuss more about questioning one's sexuality in this book, she should have gone more in depth with it. Then having him fall in love with Marisol and a seemingly quick love for Diana did not make this particular aspect of the novel believable.

While Lucy acknowledged the questioning of sexuality in this text, she recognized that it was not a point that Wittlinger delved into thoroughly. Vivienne's position regarding John and Marisol, bears likeness to Lucy's stating:

> I absolutely hated how he [John] fell in love with Marisol. It wasn't like she was hiding the fact that she was a lesbian. He literally had no chance with her, yet he somehow deluded himself into thinking he did. Throughout the book, I felt like hitting my head against the table because I just could not deal with John's stupidity.

These blogs share an inner struggle most of our students had with this novel: the portrayal of the characters' sexual identities and the relationship John wished he could have with Marisol. Their inner struggle led to a very spirited class discussion about these topics. While the students differed in their opinions of the text in relation to sexual identity, the opportunity to read the novel allowed them to explore opinions about sexual identity, and the class discussion was a safe place to share their perspectives.

Relationships

As stated above, while Rylee struggled with the novel in terms of how sexual identity was portrayed, she appreciated the relationship Wittlinger created between John and his mother: "The parts that went more in depth about Gio [John] and his mother's relationship were my favorite parts, especially her avoidance with touching Gio, because he inherited his father's looks." Her response to the story was not black or white, but she thoughtfully discussed the gray areas that she encountered to make meaning of the story.

Though Rylee was adamant about how she felt about the book, especially when Marisol questioned who she was, Elizabeth found Marisol to be a "free spirit," but she also found relationships in the novel confusing. Elizabeth makes visible ambivalent feelings:

> I don't know how I feel about *Hard Love* … Basically, John was cruel to everyone, until he met a girl that was cruel in her own way back to him, and then he was somehow better for it? I'm not sure how I feel about the ending and perhaps the author intended for it to be vague. I'm glad John finally told the truth to his parents, via letters, because his relationship with them was obviously eating away at him.

Henry's perspective differed from Elizabeth's as he looked more favorably on the relationships and John's home life as a center for this story. He also discusses how teenagers might find the story appealing:

> I found this book [*Hard Love*] to be very powerful and emotional. Its main theme in my opinion is that love does not always come in the most

conventional ways, and that we sometimes have to accept love in different forms and make the best of it. This would be very good read for teenagers. Many of the young adults in classrooms today have experiences with family that they have awkward relationships with and also many of them have feelings for peers that are not reciprocated in the same way. Reading this book might help them understand that it is important to discuss your feelings with those close to you in our life, as John does with his mother and father with the letters.

Amelia's family situation closely related to how she perceived the family relationships in the novel. She liked the fact that John's parents were divorced because she too came from a single-parent home; the story did not make one or the other parent at fault for the divorce but rather "both parents were given fault for the separation and aftermath." Amelia saw this family dynamic as a credit to Wittlinger's writing style because such relationships are more complex than often presented in some books.

Author's Style

Many students discussed Wittlinger's writing style as being important to their feelings about the novel. Wittlinger used zines as an anchor between the protagonist John and Marisol and these alternative forms of text were used throughout the novel.

In her blog, Lucy notes that the concept of zines was an intriguing way to bring John and Marisol together, but as seen in her comments above, her overall tone appears blasé about the novel. She stated, "It really took me a while to get interested in *Hard Love*. The premise of having a lesbian and a straight male bond over zines was really interesting." Eleanor felt that the use of zines was interesting and engaging. However she further explained that "I thought the characterizations were *okay* [Eleanor's emphasis], although I would never assign this book as the single story of LGBT literature in my classroom."

However, Vivienne held a different perspective of Wittlinger's style:

> I also thought the centering of the book around the concept of zines was off-putting. I was aware of the concept of zines, but I have never been part of the culture. I don't think I have ever seen a zine in person. The whole idea seems very nineties. I found it hard to relate to the characters that were so focused on something I knew so little about. To be honest it made the book seem outdated. Today's world is filled with blogs and websites that can be instantly accessed for free. Even the idea that the characters needed to go to the Virgin Record Store seemed archaic. Though I did not like how the book was centered around zines, I liked how some of the pages had what I imagine was a zine feel to them. It made it easier for me to imagine what a zine would look like.

Vivienne's concern certainly stems partially from the "dated" nature of reading a book published in 1999. At the time of publishing, zines and record stores were more likely a relevant social practice for some high school students. However, in 2012 when we read this novel, texting and listening to music on iPods was the most common form of social practice. This disconnect from the social practices in the novel to our students' social practices seemed, at times, to be insurmountable for some.

Amelia also touched on Wittlinger's style in her blog response:

> *Hard Love* by Ellen Wittlinger was a good read. I liked the protagonist John and felt like he was a real person. Often times we read stories and despite the fact that the characters are supposed to be relatable young adults dealing with real issues, I just don't find them to be. I guess this is a credit to the author Ellen Wittlinger. I grew to like and recognize John's voice throughout, and found myself rooting for him.

While Amelia did enjoy how Wittlinger framed the novel, she felt that the overall story was lacking and stated, "I just thought it was all right. I tried to keep the core audience of this book in mind while reading it, but still finished the book hoping for more." Amelia enjoyed the portrayal of John, but Vivienne had a different feeling about his character. She stated, "Part of my problem with the book was that I did not like John. As a protagonist, I found him really annoying. He whined and complained about his life, which wasn't perfect, but was not as bad as the lives of many of the characters we've read about this semester."

Eleanor also focused on the author's writing style and characters in her blog. She stated:

> I think that the characters in the book could exist in real life, but I also found them to be a little stereotypical for my taste, although I would argue that they were a decently developed stereotypical [*sic*]. Marisol in particular did not sit quite well [with] me. I know a lot of women that would be placed by other people into what her stereotype developed as but the "strong female feminist" who is usually an undereducated feminist latching on to a stereotype has been done many times before and Marisol was just another pretty poor example.

Throughout Eleanor's blog post, she acknowledged not only what she appreciated about the text, but also what her concerns were with the text. This stereotypical portrayal of Marisol was a challenge for Eleanor in reading and experiencing the novel. Cazden (2000) asserts, "Students of all ages should become sensitized to, and continuously critical of, how people are represented in whatever they hear, see and read, or which people are not presented at all" (p. 263). For our teachers, reading *Hard Love* (Wittlinger, 1999) was a challenging experience not because of the inclusion of LGBT characters, but in how these characters were portrayed as well as received by this audience. Overall, they responded favorably toward reading books with LGBT characters as seen in their discussion of the other novels read. However, *Hard Love* proved to be in opposition due to how the author portrayed characters.

Conclusion: Transformed Practice

Transformed Practice calls for "transfer in meaning-making practice which puts the transformed meaning to work in other contexts or cultural sites" (NLG, 1996, p. 88). It is not just that our students are teachers, but also that they are teachers who have to consider multiple identities when selecting literature. As they became absorbed in reading and responding to the YAL through written and multimodal composing as graduate students, it gave them a sense of what meaning-making is like and thus a sense of what their own students (e.g., current or future) might experience.

From a Transformed Practice point of view, our students have opportunities to transfer meaning-making applications they learned in our course to other contexts such as English language arts or social studies classrooms or cultural sites such as after-school programs (NLG, 1996). Miller, Thompson, Lauricella, Boyd, with McVee (2012) state, "To contribute to ... critical reframing of pedagogies, we as educators must attend to the identities of students, to critically consider how students' lifeworlds shape meaning-making and can re-shape literacy as meaningful in schools" (p. 126).

At the end of the course, we requested that students tell us their favorite and least favorite books from what they read. All but one student identified *Looking for Alaska* (Green, 2005) as one of their top five favorite books in the semester, with many of these students identifying it as their favorite text. We discussed the controversy around this text, especially considering a challenge attempt in the local area that occurred in 2008. The challenge attempt led Green (2008) to produce a blog and a short video defending himself. We watched the video in class and talked extensively about the challenge attempt, the text, and student opinions. While there are controversial topics within the book, no one believed that the challenge was warranted such that adolescents should not have access to the novel.

Similarly, while nearly everyone identified *Looking for Alaska* as a favorite text, nearly everyone identified *Hard Love* as one of his or her least favorite texts read in the course. The students did not object to reading about LGBT-identified people, as many students enjoyed the other texts we chose for the course and spoke positively about LGBT-identified people in our class discussions. Their main concern was stereotyped characters. Moreover, as Vivienne pointed out, the book now seems very dated, over ten years after it was published.

Designing Safe Spaces: Points to Consider

Listed below are some suggestions we found useful in designing safe places to talk about contentious YAL and topics within them. Our suggestions are all based on our experiences, designing and redesigning course content and listening to our students' voices and concerns:

- Select the YAL topics carefully and design an order to approach the topics during the semester to build a community before delving into novels.
- Encourage students to voice their opinions, comment about the texts and topics, and talk freely. However, also push their thinking to consider alternative perspectives that they may not have considered.
- Select the books carefully. Seek out online reviews and personal recommendations before selecting texts. As noted, *Hard Love* (Wittlinger, 1999) was a contentious book, not because of the focus on LGBT characters, but for the portrayal of characters and the stereotypes the novel seemed to reinforce. While we had an interesting discussion around the novel, there are many fantastic LGBT novels available today that work to break down stereotypes as opposed to reinforcing them.
- Seek out community resources. There are often LGBT organizations that are willing to talk with students. Talking with people who identify as LGBT can be powerful in changing attitudes about the community (Nelson & Krieger, 1997).
- Consider discussing local, state, and national events that are current and relevant to those who identify as LGBT. These events are useful to spark discussions to focus on LGBT students' experiences.
- Use educational resources available on websites such as Gay, Lesbian and Straight Education Network ([GLSEN], 2003–2012) to craft your discussions and focus on relevant topics. (See Wiest, chapter 6 in this volume for additional resources.)

References

Angelou, M. (1969). *I know why the caged bird sings.* New York, NY: Random House.

Aragon, S. R., Poteat, V. P., Espelage, D. L., & Koenig, B. W. (2014). The influence of peer victimization on educational outcomes for LGBTQ and non-LGBTQ high school students. *Journal of LGBT Youth*, 11(1), 1–19.

Blackburn, M. V., & Smith, J. M. (2010). Moving beyond the inclusion of LGBT-themed literature in English language arts classrooms: Interrogating heteronormativity and exploring intersectionality. *Journal of Adolescent & Adult Literacy*, 53(8), 625–634.

Cazden, C. B. (2000). Taking cultural differences into account. In B. C. Cope & M. Kalantzis (Eds.), *Multiliteracies: Literacy learning and the design of social futures* (pp. 249–266). New York, NY: Routledge.

Center for Digital Storytelling (Producer). (2005). *Breaking the silence: Lesbian, gay, bisexual, transgender, and queer foster youth tell their stories. A tool for training care providers on working effectively with LGBTQ youth.* [DVD]. San Francisco, CA: National Center for Lesbian Rights.

Gay, Lesbian and Straight Education Network [GLSEN], (2003–2012). *Gay, lesbian and straight education network.* Retrieved from: http://www.glsen.org/

Graybill, E. C., Varjas, K., Meyers, J., & Watson, L. B. (2009). Content-specific strategies to advocate for lesbian, gay, bisexual, and transgender youth: An exploratory study. *School Psychology Review*, 38(4), 570–584.

Green, J. (2005). *Looking for Alaska*. New York, NY: Penguin Group.

Green, J. (2008, January 30). *I am not a pornographer*. Retrieved from: http://johngreenbooks.com/i-am-not-a-pornographer/

Kalantzis, M., & Cope, B. (2012). *Literacies*. New York, NY: Cambridge University Press.

Kosciw, J. G., Greytak, E. A., Bartkiewicz, M. J., Boesen, M. J., & Palmer, N. A. (2012). *The 2011 national school climate survey: The experiences of lesbian, gay, bisexual and transgender youth in our nation's schools*. New York, NY: GLSEN.

Kosciw, J. G., Palmer, N. A., Kull, R. M., & Greytak, E. A. (2013). The effect of negative school climate on academic outcomes for LGBT youth and the role of in-school supports. *Journal of School Violence*, 12(1), 45–63.

Miller, S. M., Thompson, M. K., Lauricella, A. M., Boyd, F. B., & McVee, M. B. (2012). A literacy pedagogy for multimodal composing: Transforming learning and teaching. In S. M. Miller & M. B. McVee (Eds.), *Multimodal composing in classrooms: Learning and teaching for the digital world* (pp. 114–129). New York, NY: Routledge.

Nelson, E. S., & Krieger, S. L. (1997). Changes in attitudes toward homosexuality in college students: Implementation of a gay men and lesbian peer panel. *Journal of Homosexuality*, 33(2), 63–81.

New London Group (1996). A pedagogy of multiliteracies: Designing social futures. *Harvard Educational Review*, 66(1), 60–92.

Stufft, D. L., & Graff, C. M. (2011). Increasing visibility for LGBTQ students: What schools can do to create inclusive classroom communities. *Current Issues in Education*, 14(1), 1–26.

Whitman, J. S., Horn, S. S., & Boyd, C. J. (2007). Activism in the schools: Providing LGBTQ affirmative training to school counselors. *Journal of Gay & Lesbian Psychotherapy*, 11(3/4), 143–154.

Wittlinger, E. (1999). Hard Love. New York: Simon & Schuster Books for Young Readers.

Yolen, J. (1992). *Briar rose*. New York: A Tor Book.

PART II

Exploring Languages, Language Varieties, Culture, Ethnicity, and Identities in Classrooms and Communities

8

CODE-SWITCHING AND CONTRASTIVE ANALYSIS

Tools of Language and Culture Transform the Dialectally Diverse Classroom

Rebecca Wheeler and Rachel Swords

STUDENT: *Mrs. Swords, why you be teachin' maf in da aftanoon?*

MRS. SWORDS: *Why do I what?*

STUDENT: *Why you be teachin' maf in da aftanoon?*

MRS. SWORDS: *Why do I what?*

STUDENT: *Why* you be teachin' maf *in da aftanoon?*

MRS. SWORDS: *We don't say, "why you be teaching math in the afternoon. ..."*
We say, "Why are you teaching math in the afternoon?"

STUDENT: *Oh, OK.*

The next day the child would begin again, "Mrs. Swords, why do we be havin' maf in da aftanoon?" And Rachel would reply, "Why do we *what?*" It was always the same. She would attempt to "correct" the child's "error," but it was clear that no learning was taking place. Rachel Swords began her career in an urban elementary school by correcting every sentence she deemed incorrect. She noticed as time went on, however, that her students were asking significantly fewer questions. She would call for questions, and her students would begin: "Mrs. Swords, why you be ... ? Is you? Ain't you? Never mind." The students knew she was going to correct them. They tried to ask their questions in the form the school system wanted, but they didn't know how. Rather than risk the embarrassment of being corrected in front of the class, the students became silent.

After Rachel realized why the questions had stopped, she tried another, more passive approach. When a child asked, "Mrs. Swords, why you be teachin' maf afta lunch?" she would repeat their question in Mainstream American English ("Why do I teach math after lunch?"), and then answer it, also in the same language variety. While this method didn't embarrass the children or hinder their questioning, the children's language did not change. Even though Rachel consistently corrected their speech and writing, her students still did not learn the Standard English forms.

Concern with the vernacular dialects our children bring to school has been long-standing. Heath (1983) noted that school desegregation in the 1960s brought out these issues: "Academic questions about how children talk when they come to school and what educators should know and do about oral and written language were echoed in practical pleas of teachers who asked: 'What do I do in my classroom on Monday morning?'" (p. 1). Now, decades later, teachers remain concerned. Christenbury (2000) has observed that "[o]ne of the most controversial—and difficult—issues for English teachers is their responsibility to students who speak what is considered 'nonstandard' English, English that violates the usage rules we often mistakenly call 'grammar'" (p. 202).

Christenbury's comment sets the stage for the central focus of our chapter. English teachers routinely equate Standard English with "grammar," as if other language varieties and styles lack grammar, the systematic and rule-governed backbone of language. But this traditional literacy is a monoliteracy, reflecting dominant language ideology, the "ingrained, unquestioned beliefs about the way the world is, the way it should be, and the way it has to be with respect to language" (Rickford and Wolfram, 2009, p. 14). Dominant language ideology in the US "assume[s] that Standard [American] English [(SAE)] is the only legitimate dialect of English and view[s] other dialects such as African American English as incorrect" (Godley et al., 2007, p. 104; see also Gal, 1998; Schieffelin et al., 1998; Milroy, 2001; Alim, 2005).

Yet our world is no longer monocultural, grounded in monoliteracy, if it ever was. Ever more we are becoming, indeed have become, a multicultural, diverse society. With multiculturalism comes multilingualism and multidialectalism. That is, we inhabit a world of multiliteracies. Our classrooms, the ways we teach, how we understand our children, and their ways of speaking must come to reflect a linguistic understanding of our multidialectal world. And so, our work in the dialectally diverse classroom speaks from the conceptual framework of sociolinguistics; we foundationally presume the inherent equality, integrity, structure, and diversity of language and culture.

Thus, linguistics reveals that the child who speaks in a vernacular dialect is not making language errors; instead, she or he is speaking correctly in the language of the home discourse community. From a multiliteracy viewpoint, we can draw upon the language strengths of urban learners to help students code-switch— choose the language variety appropriate to the time, place, audience, and communicative purpose. In doing so, we honor linguistic and cultural diversity, all the while fostering students' mastery of the Language of Wider Communication, the de facto lingua franca of the United States.

The motivation for this chapter lies in our desire to bring the insights of linguistics to bear on the achievement gap, the "devastating rates at which schools fail African American students" (Rickford, 1999, p. 22; Barton & Coley, 2010; Wilkinson et al., 2011). Indeed, for fifty years we have observed: In "every measure of academic achievement black students lag behind their white counterparts" (Austen-Smith & Fryer, 2005, p. 551). Evidence in Figures 8.1 and 8.2 is just the most recent in a long, lamentable litany documented by the National Center for Education Statistics [NCES] (2011) in their National Assessment of Educational Progress [NAEP].

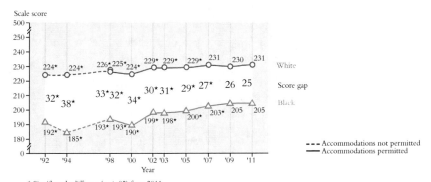

NCES, 2011, p. 11.

FIGURE 8.1 Trend in Fourth-grade Reading Average Scores and Score Gaps for White and Black Students from the NAEP.

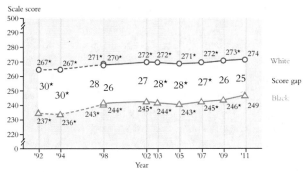

NCES, 2011, p. 40.

FIGURE 8.2 Trend in Eighth-grade Reading Average Scores and Score Gaps for White and Black Students from the NAEP.

In response, nearly 15 years ago, Rickford (1999) asserted that "the evidence that schools are failing massive numbers of African students with existing methods is so overwhelming that it would be counterproductive and offensive to continue using them uncritically" (p. 3).

Accordingly, we offer linguistically informed approaches for creating an accessible, research-based approach to language arts in the dialectally diverse, multicultural classroom.

We chart our course in two voices, that of a university professor and that of an urban elementary educator. Rachel shares her movement as a teacher from a monodialectal, monocultural model to a multidialectal, multicultural model of language arts in her classroom. Understanding the nature of language variation across region, ethnic identity, social class, language styles, and registers provides language arts teachers with a fertile ground from which to build a welcoming, multicultural language arts classroom.

Traditional Language Arts Methods Fail Many African American Students

Rachel became involved in this work because of her concern over how her students fared on statewide tests:

> When our disaggregated scores for the Virginia Standards of Learning tests (SOL) were put up on the board, in every case our Black children were performing much lower than our White children. It is very disheartening to say that I've taught the same way to all the children all year long and my White children are passing the tests and my Black children are not. Then our principal put up the scores for the entire district; it looked exactly the same. The children speaking African American vernacular are doing significantly worse on the writing test—not two or three points. In some schools, African American students scored 36 points lower than White children on average.

Such disparities of language performance are neither isolated nor restricted to Virginia. Rickford (1996) reported the results of a study of student writing performance across school districts contrasting in ethnicity and socioeconomic standing. The study revealed that

> third grade kids in the primarily white, middle class Palo Alto School District scored on the 94th percentile in writing; by the [sixth] grade, they had topped out at the 99th percentile. By contrast, third grade kids in primarily African American working class East Palo Alto (Ravenswood School District) scored on the 21st percentile in writing, but by the sixth grade, they had fallen to the 3rd percentile, almost to the very bottom (p. 1).

Similar statistics can be found in many other school districts and states. Minority language children seem to confront a brick wall when it comes to performance on standardized tests.

The question of why African American students struggle revolves around issues of language and culture, poverty, distribution of goods and resources, physical conditions of school buildings, training of teachers in urban schools, and ethnic and linguistic bias in standardized tests, just to name a few factors. While all of these issues need to be addressed, we focus here on approaches to language and culture in the linguistically diverse urban classroom.

We know that many urban African American children speak a language variety—African American Vernacular English (AAVE)—different from the language of the school (Craig & Washington, 2005; Delpit, 1995; Meier, 2008; Wolfram & Schilling-Estes, 2006). While speaking a vernacular dialect has been *correlated* with reading failure, scholars continue to debate whether dialectal contrasts *cause* failure.

As of the mid 1990s, "the conclusion of most sociolinguists was that the semantic and structural differences between AAVE and other dialects were not great enough to be the primary causes of reading failure" (Labov, 1995, pp. 48–49). Indeed, some educational researchers have found no particular dialectal intrusion in the reading process (Goodman & Goodman, 2000). Yet others demonstrated that "dialect *is* a source of reading interference" for speakers of AAVE and that the syntax of AAVE verb phrases resulted in African American students losing information regarding time structure of events in the test reading passage (Steffensen, Reynolds, McClure, & Guthrie, 1982, p. 296). And in an experiment on vernacular speakers' acquisition of consonant clusters, Labov and Baker (m.s.) found that "variability in speech is responsible in part for difficulties in decoding" standard English (p. 15).

Beyond linguistic structure, cultural conflict lies at the heart of why schools fail African Americans. Thus, in Harlem, the child's cultural system "opposed the values of the school system, which was seen as the particular possession and expression of the dominant white society" (Labov, 1995, p. 42). In turn, schools may ban literature reflecting African American language and culture. One Virginia librarian commented to us that "no children's books containing African American dialect are available in our school. This is a *very* controversial topic." As Smitherman observed, "[W]hen you lambast the home language that kids bring to school, you ain just dissin dem, you talkin bout they mommas" (Richardson, 2002, p. 677)!

Further, as teachers absorb "widespread, destructive myths about language variation" (Wolfram, 1999, p. 78), their cultural vantage turns to pedagogical damage. In other words, whether black or white, a teacher is likely to consider a child speaking African American Vernacular English as slower, less able, and less intelligent than the child who speaks standard English (Labov, 1995). Such dialect prejudice reduces teacher expectations for the child's abilities (Baugh, 2000; Lippi-Green, 2012). As teacher expectations are reduced, so potential child performance is diminished (Delpit & Dowdy, 2002; Nieto, 2000). No wonder that under these conditions, "the longer African American inner city kids stay in school, the worse they do" (Rickford, 1996, p. 1).

Traditional Responses to Language Varieties: Correction Does Not Work

It is not surprising that Rachel's initial attempts to "correct" her children's language did not produce change in their performance. As Gilyard (1991) shares in his account of his life as a black child in the American educational system, "Generations of Black English speakers have been subjected to 'correction' programs that haven't worked" (p. 114).

Teachers envision a single "right way" to construct a sentence (Birch, 2001) and so criticize student writing such as:

- I have two sister and two brother.
- Christopher family moved to Spain.
- Last year, he watch all the shows.

Teachers often view this kind of writing as error-filled, believing that the child does not know how to show plurality, possession, or tense. Believing that the student has left off the plural marker, the apostrophe '–s,' and '–ed,' teachers will respond, "That's not how you do it!" This approach seeks to eradicate the child's home language (Wheeler & Swords, 2006/2010).

Christenbury (2000) observes that "telling or teaching students that their language is *wrong* or *bad* is not only damaging, but *false*" (p. 203). Doing so presupposes that only one language form is "correct" in structure and that this form is "good" in all contexts. Joos (1961) comments:

> It is still our custom unhesitatingly and unthinkingly to demand that the clocks of language all be set to Central Standard time. ... But English, like national languages in general, has five clocks. And the times that they tell are not simply earlier and later; they differ sidewise, too, and in several directions. Naturally. A community has a complex structure, with variously differing needs and occasions. How could it scrape along with only one pattern of English usage? (pp. 4–5)

While the traditional approach attempts to correct, repress, eradicate, or subtract student language that differs from the standard written target, a different response to language becomes possible once we recognize that language comes in different varieties and styles, and each is systematic and rule-governed (Adger, Christian & Taylor, 1999; Adger, Wolfram & Christian, 2007; Delpit, 1995; Green, 2002/2011; Perry & Delpit, 1998; Smitherman, 1981; Wheeler, Cartwright, Swords, 2012).

Instead of seeking to correct or eradicate styles of language, we may add language varieties to the child's linguistic toolbox, bringing a pluralistic vantage to language in the classroom (Gilyard, 1991; McWhorter, 1998). We use the linguistic strategies of contrastive analysis and code-switching (or style-shifting). Such an approach allows us to maintain the language of the student's home community while adding the linguistic tools needed for success in our broader society—Mainstream American English (CCCC, 1974).

Key Notions from Applied Linguistics

A cluster of notions from applied linguistics underlies our work with language in the classroom: dialect, language variety, style, and register. Three insights about language serve as a foundation for all of these terms:

- Language is structured.
- Language varies by circumstance of use.
- Difference is distinct from deficiency.

A *dialect* is a "variety of the language associated with a particular regional or social group" (Wolfram & Schilling-Estes, 2006, p. 391). Since everyone is associated with a particular regional or social group, everyone speaks a dialect. Also known as *language varieties*, dialects vary in structure (sound, vocabulary, grammar, and social conventions for structuring conversations) on the basis of speakers' "age, socioeconomic status, gender, ethnic group membership, and geographic region" (Adger, Wolfram & Christian, 2007, p. 31). This means that so-called "standard" English is a dialect of English. Contrary to popular understanding, "'[d]ialect' does not mean a marginal, archaic, rustic, or degraded mode of speech" (Pullum, 1999, p. 44).

Register refers to the ways in which language varies by specific speech situations (e.g., newspaper headlines, rituals, recipes, technical writing, and even baby talk).

While variation in language structure is always present, a different kind of variation lies in the public's *attitudes* toward language. "Standard" English is often called "good" English while "nonstandard" English is considered "bad." These judgments are not based on linguistic grounds but on sociopolitical considerations. Thus, what we call the *standard* is a "widely socially accepted variety of English that is held to be the linguistic norm and that is relatively unmarked with respect to regional characteristics of English" (Wolfram & Schilling-Estes, 2006, p. 406). People regard this variety as good because they regard its speakers as meritorious, but this judgment has nothing to do with an inherent structural superiority of so-called "standard" English.

A *vernacular* is an "indigenous language or dialect of a speech community" (Wolfram & Schilling-Estes, 2006, p. 409). And a nonstandard dialect is a language variety "that differs from the standard dialects spoken by mainstream or socially favored population groups; usually it is socially disfavored" (Wolfram & Schilling-Estes, 2006, p. 401), containing socially stigmatized features such as the so-called English double negative ("I ain't got none") or irregular verb forms ("I seen it"). Just as the public holds standard varieties in high regard because of their high regard for their speakers, the public holds vernaculars in low regard and typically views its speakers with disregard. The judgment of badness is socio-political and has nothing to do with any structural inadequacy of vernacular dialects.

Finally, "standard" English is a misnomer, implying that only one standard exists. Yet, we can readily identify a range of standards from Formal Standard English, the Written Standard English of grammar books, reference works, and the most established mainstream authors, Informal Standard English, a spoken variety defined by the absence of socially stigmatized structures, and even Regional Standard English, the accepted dialect of English in a particular region (Wolfram & Schilling-Estes, 2006). Although the issues of language standardization and instruction are complex, our core point remains: Language is structured. Its structure varies by circumstance. But to perceive this we must let go of blinding conventional assumptions. Only then can we build upon the strengths of the language each child brings to school.

Discovering a New Vantage on Language in the Classroom

Rebecca teaches a class on language varieties in the schools and communities where graduate students explore how all language is structured and how the choice of language form is based on setting. This insight is actually quite hard to hear, so immersed is our culture in the view that standard English is the only real language and everything else is degraded. But when students examined their assumptions in the class, they came to perceive language structures and patterns they hadn't recognized before.

Classroom results reported from Chicago and Georgia were particularly revealing. In Chicago, Taylor (1991) studied student performance across two kinds of college writing classrooms. With one group, she used the traditional English techniques while in the other classroom, she led her students in explicit discovery by contrasting the grammatical patterns of AAVE and SE. The control group, using the correctionist model, showed an 8.5% *increase* in African American features in their writing after 11 weeks, but the experimental group, using a technique called contrastive analysis, showed a remarkable 59.3% *decrease* in African American vernacular features. Taylor observed that students had been neither aware of their dialect nor of "grammatical black English features that interfere in their writing" (p. 150). By contrasting the language varieties, students were able to learn the detailed differences between the two, thereby "limit[ing] AAVE intrusions into their SE usage" (Rickford, 1997, p. 4).

The same kind of approach was also implemented by teachers in DeKalb County, Georgia, who helped young speakers of minority dialects explicitly contrast their mother tongue with the standard dialect. Thus, when a fifth grader answered a question with a double negative ("not no more"), the teacher prompted the student to "code-switch," to which the student replied, "not any more." The children learned to switch from their home speech to school speech at appropriate times and places, and to recognize that "the dialect they might use at home is valuable and 'effective' in that setting, but not for school, for work—or for American democracy" (Cumming, 1997, p. B1). This program was designated a "center of excellence" by the National Council of Teachers of English.

Rachel Speaks of Her Classroom Journey: Moving from Correction to Contrast

In my third-grade classroom, I noticed that vernacular patterns intruded in many of my students' writings. As a correctionist, I would explain what we do and do not say. For example, when a student wrote, "The three friend went for a walk," my initial reaction was to correct my student's grammar by explaining the need for an '–s' on the end of plural nouns. But after Rebecca's class, I decided to use a contrastive approach.

The first notion students needed was that language varies (among other things) by formality of situation. To teach this concept, we discussed formal and informal clothing. First, I asked students what kind of clothes they wore to school. Since the school has a fairly strict dress code, the students named permitted clothing such as collared shirts, slacks, and belts. When I asked the students what they liked to wear at home on the weekends, they responded, "jeans, tee shirts, sweatpants, and swimsuits."

We brainstormed places or events that we might attend, aside from school, where more formal clothing was required. The students gave examples such as church, weddings, and graduations. They determined that informal clothing would be more appropriate for playing basketball, watching TV, and going to the pool.

I asked how their language might differ between formal and informal situations. The students explained that "yes, sir" and "excuse me" were formal and that "yo, wa's up?" and "he ain' nobody" were more informal. As we thought back on an exchange between two students in our class, I wrote the following on the board for group discussion:

STUDENT 1: *"Yo, Mz. Swords! Dat junk be tight!"*
STUDENT 2: *"McKinzie! You ain sposed ta talk t' Mrs. Swords dat way."*

Clearly, students come to school already having a good grasp of language style (the variation language shows in levels of formality) within their own variety, in this case, AAVE. In this way, my students were able to use their own prior knowledge to define formal and informal language.

We applied our understanding to the grammar of sentences. Using chart paper, I created two columns of sentences drawn from my students' own writing with the left one written in standard English ("I have two dogs"), and the right showing the same sentences written in the vernacular of many of my students ("I have two dog").

I labeled the SE examples as "formal" and the vernacular examples as "informal," terms that are readily understandable. We began with plural patterns because I knew that my students would immediately see the difference between the formal and informal usage.

We then compared and contrasted the sentences in each column. Immediately, one child said, "Oh, that's wrong. All the ones on that side [informal] are wrong and the ones on the other side [formal] are right." But another child said, "How is it wrong? Mrs. Swords wrote it!" Students were clearly confused. After all, since this was my second year of working with these children, and I had spent more than a year teaching them the right and wrong way to construct a sentence, they couldn't figure out why I would purposely write an incorrect sentence.

To address the students' confusion, I reminded them about our explorations of formal and informal styles of clothing and language. We looked at how language varies by region of the country, and I talked about how I switch my language to suit the setting. For example, I have a rather thick Southern accent. At home I might say, "I'm fixin' to go to the store. Ya'll need anything?" However, I certainly wouldn't ask my fellow Virginia teachers, "I'm fixin' to make copies. Ya'll need any?" I know this language variety is not appropriate at school. Instead, I might say, "I'm going to make some copies. Do you need any?" I talked to the students about how I change my language setting by setting and told them that when I make these language choices, I am code-switching.

To *code-switch* is to choose the pattern of language appropriate to the context. This is what I want my students to be able to do: choose the language form appropriate to the time, place, audience, and communicative purpose (Wheeler & Swords 2006/2010; Wheeler 2005/2008). I use a classroom technique called contrastive analysis to support children in learning how to code-switch between informal and formal language patterns (Baugh, 1999; Cumming, 1997; Rickford, 1998; Schierloh, 1991; Taylor, 1991; Wheeler, 2008).

Of course, the contrasts of formal/informal (or written/spoken, or home/school) are oversimplifications of the different ways that language is patterned by variety and style, but the key point I wanted to convey was one of contrast; different language patterns are appropriate to different contexts. Formal/informal was a rough and ready way to get that notion across with third graders.

Moving back to the chart, I asked the students if they understood what each sentence meant and if the informal sentence, "I have two dog," had the same meaning as the formal one, "I have two dogs." Again, the class agreed they did, so I asked, "If we can tell what they mean, what differences do you see between the two columns?"

Since we had previously talked about nouns and pronouns, the children were easily able to articulate responses. One child explained, "In this one [the formal form], the noun has an '–s' on it." I asked, "What does that mean? What is the '–s' doing there?" They said, "It's making it more than one." We talked about how the '–s' makes it more than one. I then explained that this is the way we show "more than one" in formal language. (See Figure 8.3.) To help the children, I created the heading of "Plural Patterns" for the patterns they were discovering and wrote the children's observations under the formal column.

Plural Patterns

Informal	*Formal*
I have two dog.	I have two dogs.
All the boy came home.	All the boys came home.
Taylor likes cat.	Taylor likes cats.
The Pattern	*The Pattern*
number words	-s
other words	
in the sentence	
in the paragraph	
common knowledge	

FIGURE 8.3 Plural Patterns.

Then we looked at the informal example, exploring its patterns. Reminding the children that the examples had the same meaning, I asked how the informal sentence showed us that the number is more than one. One child said, "You know it's more than one because it has the number 'two' in it." So I wrote "number words" under informal, commenting that "number words show there's more than one." Next we looked at "All the boy are here today." I asked, "What tells you there is more than one boy?" One child replied, "The other words in the sentence: 'all.'" So I wrote on our chart, "Other words in the sentence." Then we looked at "Taylor likes cat." This sentence was difficult because nothing in the sentence told the reader whether it was more than one cat. The children explained, "You have to look at the whole paragraph." So I wrote, "Other words in the paragraph," commenting that "other words in the paragraph show there's more than one." And then we noticed that we also just *knew*. The whole class knew Taylor and everyone knew she loved cats. So I wrote "common knowledge" on the chart. The children explored and named the contrasts in grammatical patterning between formal and informal language. Our plural chart (along with charts for possessive and tense) stayed up on our classroom walls for easy reference during the school day.

Students Discover Possessive Patterns across Language Varieties

For another lesson, I gave students a chart comparing sentences with formal and informal possessive structures. Figure 8.4 provides an example, but I always use sentences selected from students' writing.

Directions: Write three more Informal and three more Formal sentences that include possessive patterns. Then answer the question below.

Possessive Patterns

Informal	*Formal*
Taylor cat is black.	Taylor's cat is black.
The boy coat is torn.	The boy's coat is torn.
A giraffe neck is long.	A giraffe's neck is long.
Did you see the teacher pen?	Did you see the teacher's pen?

1)_____   _____

2)_____   _____

3)_____   _____

Question: What are the rules for using informal possessive patterns and formal possessive patterns? Write the informal rule under the informal column, and the formal rule under the column.

Informal possessive pattern   Formal possessive pattern

_____   _____

FIGURE 8.4 Discovering the Rules for Possessive Patterns across Language Varieties.

I wrote the term "possessive" on the board and asked if the students knew what it meant. When the children didn't know, I explained that possession means "someone owns something" and provided several examples.

Students looked closely at the underlined words on the chart and worked in small groups to find ways to describe how each language variety expresses ownership. When the entire class reconvened, students shared their responses and constructed a rule for using possessive patterns in the two language varieties. For example, in informal English, possession = owner + owned ("the boy coat"). However, in formal English, possession = owner + 's + owned ("the boy's coat"). Once this rule was determined, students made up additional examples. Through these instructional strategies, we discovered the grammatical rules of each language variety.

Language Varieties in Reading and Writing

Like most teachers, I integrate literature into the topics my class is currently studying. My interest in using contrastive analysis was reflected in many of my literary selections. One of the first linguistically enriched texts I introduced to my students was *Flossie and the Fox* by Patricia McKissack (1986). In this story, Flossie speaks in the patterns of AAVE while the fox speaks in standard English patterns. This book quickly became a favorite among my students, who chose it for every student-selected read-aloud. I was delighted when, at the third reading, without any prompting, the children all joined in the choral call of one particular line: "Shucks! You aine no fox. You a rabbit, all the time trying to fool me." Kids were *engaged* with this reading.

After contrasting several different grammatical patterns and reading literature reflecting differing language varieties, it was time for students to implement their new understandings of language varieties in dialogues within their own writing. I initiated a discussion about how different characters use different speech patterns, and several children mentioned their favorite book, *Flossie and the Fox*. We discussed how the different voices of Flossie and the fox made the book more interesting.

Following the discussion, the class created dialogue for a story we were writing together about a teacher and a giant cockroach. When I asked who would speak in what language style, the students decided the teacher would speak informal English while the cockroach would use formal speech.

After completing several lines of our story, I asked the students to think about the characters in their own stories and decide the speech style each would use. Some had each character speak with formal English, others chose to use informal English for each character, while other students mixed it up as we had done in our collective story.

I have seen tremendous growth in my students' command of language. Prior to teaching code-switching, my students simply guessed what language form was expected. One student explained, "It's because you don't know how to say it and you're just wondering how you're suppose to say it." My students are now becoming clear about the contrasts between formal and informal language. Students also understand that just as one tool doesn't suit all jobs, neither does one language style suit all communication tasks. Indeed, a well-stocked linguistic toolbox offers a diverse range of language forms to the mature speaker and writer.

Responding to Frequently Asked Questions

Crucially, in our work on code-switching between language varieties we are *not* saying, "anything goes." We are not ignoring language, and we are not "making allowances." We pay considerable attention to helping children command the intricacies of choosing the language appropriate to time, place, audience, and purpose. We are not implying that a child does not need to learn standard English. Indeed, in the broader American society, all children need to command Mainstream American English, the language variety often required in formal settings.

However, the issue of who learns what language is deeply political, rooted in the social and cultural structure of society (Wolfram & Schilling-Estes, 2006; Nieto, 2000). It can be a very damaging human experience for an AAVE-speaking child to learn Mainstream American English while the teacher dismisses AAVE as broken and error-filled.

With contrastive analysis, we move to break the cycle. Exercising their analytic eye, the teacher and all students, Black, White, Asian, Native American, and Hispanic alike, engage in critical thinking as they discover and analyze the patterns of diverse language varieties. In doing so, we take steps to unbind the "widespread, destructive myths about language variation" that underlie the dialect prejudice so rampant in society (Wolfram, 1999, p. 78).

Techniques of contrastive analysis also offer students tangible help in interpreting standardized test questions. Students come to understand that when the test asks whether a sentence is "correct" or "incorrect," it is asking for the patterns of the mainstream written language. This vantage helps students know to choose the formal English patterns on test questions. Indeed, as Rickford (1998) observes, "Teaching methods which *do* take vernacular dialects into account in teaching the standard work better than those which *do not*" (p. 1).

Code-switching and knowledge of language varieties serve children during the writing process. As children construct story narrative, they choose a range of language styles to enhance character. When the task is to produce formal English, we make editing into a game. After students have completed the substantive content of their reports, children highlight their successes in matching the patterns of standard English. If students find a sentence still in informal patterns, they change it to formal English, and then highlight the sentence. Students are enthusiastic about noting their grammar successes.

Further, students show an increased conscious command of standard English as well as the ability to code-switch. David, an African American student, wrote "Spy Mouse and the Broken Globe," a story in which Spy Mouse spoke informally ("I won't do nothin' to you"), while David's author's note used uniquely formal English patterns. By explaining that *he* knew formal English but Spy Mouse did not, David was able to independently articulate the reasons for his language choices, an impressive accomplishment for any student, let alone an urban third grader.

Conclusion

Our schools have long served a dialectally diverse population. We received a wake-up call 35 years ago when a northern school system was sued for educational malpractice. In 1979, "Michigan Legal services filed suit ... on behalf of fifteen black, economically deprived children residing in a low-income housing project" (Smitherman, 1981, p. 133). Their case, *Martin Luther King Junior Elementary School Children v. Ann Arbor School District Board*, resulted in a decision for the plaintiffs. The court found that the suit had merit since federal law directed that "no child should be deprived of equal educational opportunity because of the failure of an educational agency to take appropriate action to overcome linguistic barriers" (Labov, 1995, p. 46). The issue still before us today is *how* to take "appropriate action to overcome linguistic barriers."

Rachel has taken appropriate action. Her students have come alive. While their engagement and excitement with learning hold center stage, test results are also revealing. After just one year of using a contrastive approach, her Black and White children performed equally well on year-end benchmarks. Indeed, in math and science, African American children outperformed European American children.

We believe that a pluralist, multiliteracy response to language varieties holds promise for enhancing student performance and positively transforming the language arts classroom. The reasons for student productivity are complex. Not simply, or even perhaps primarily, a matter of fostering children's decoding and production of standard English, the crucial point may be that when we bring the child's language and culture into the classroom, we invite in the whole child. Doing so contributes signally to "the trellis of our profession—and the most crucial element of school culture ... —an ethos hospitable to the promotion of human learning" (Barth, 2002, p. 11). In this fashion, code-switching and contrastive analysis offer potent tools of language and culture for transforming language arts practice in America.

Authors' Note

We thank NCTE for permission to update and reprint this article published originally in *Language Arts*, *81*(6), July 2004, 470–480. Copyright 2004 by the National Council of Teachers of English. Reprinted with permission.

Children's Literature

Clinton, Catherine. *I, Too, Sing America: Three Centuries of African American Poetry*. Illus. S. Alcorn. (Houghton, 1998). Twenty-five poets are represented in 35 poems arranged chronologically from the 1700s to the present.

Giovanni, Nikki. *Shimmy Shimmy Shimmy Like My Sister Kate: Looking at the Harlem Rennaisance through Poems*. (Holt, 1996). A collection of poems is accompanied by a commentary about each poet and poem.

Hamilton, Virginia. *Bruh Rabbit and the Tar Baby Girl*. Illus. J. Ransome. (Scholastic, 2003). This version of the trickster tale was collected in the Gullah speech of the Sea Islands of South Carolina.

Hamilton, Virginia. *Her Stories: African American Folktales, Fairy Tales, and True Tales*. Illus. L. & D. Dillon. (Scholastic, 1995). Nineteen stories focus on African American women. Comments at the end of each tale explain the time period and the setting.

Hamilton, Virginia. *The People Could Fly: American Black Folktales*. Illus. L. & D. Dillon. (Knopf, 2000). Twenty-four tales are now accompanied by a CD narrated by both the author and James Earl Jones.

Hamilton, Virginia. *Tricksters: Animal Tales from America, the West Indies, and Africa*. Illus. B. Moser. (Scholastic, 1997). Eleven tales show the migration of African culture to America via the West Indies.

hooks, Bell. *Happy to Be Nappy*. Illus. C. Raschka. (Hyperion, 1999). hooks celebrates the joy and beauty of nappy hair. Also see *Be Boy Buzz* by hooks.

Lester, Julius. *To Be a Slave*. Illus. T. Feelings. (Puffin, 1968). In this compilation of oral histories, slaves and ex-slaves tell about their experiences.

Lester, Julius. *Uncle Remus: The Complete Tales*. Illus. J. Pinkney. (Dial, 1999). Lester uses "modified contemporary southern black English, a combination of standard English and black English" to bring these rollicking tales to a new generation of readers.

McKissack, Patricia. *Flossie & the Fox*. Illus R. Isadora. (Dial, 1986). A smooth talking, egg-stealing fox meets his match when he encounters Flossie, who is on an errand to deliver a basket of eggs.

Parks, Van Dyke (adapter). *Jump*. Illus. B. Moser. (Harcourt, 1989). Parks tells more lively adventures of Brer Rabbit. Two other books, *Jump On Over!* and *Jump Again* by the adapter and illustrator feature other stories about Brer Rabbit.

Smalls, Irene. *Don't Say Ain't*. Illus. C. Bootman. (Charlesbridge, 2003). In the 1950s when a Harlem girl gets the chance to go to an integrated school, her teacher singles her out for using "improper" speech.

Steptoe, John. *Creativity*. Illus. E. B. Lewis. (Clarion, 1997). Charlie helps a new boy adjust to school and learns about how people can speak differently and share a common ancestry. Also see *Stevie* by Steptoe.

References

Adger, C. T., Christian, D., & Taylor, O. (Eds.). (1999). *Making the connection: Language and academic achievement among African American students*. Washington, DC: Center for Applied Linguistics.

Adger, C. T., Wolfram, W., & Christian, D. (2007). *Dialects in schools and communities*. Mahwah, NJ: Erlbaum.

Alim, H. S. (2005). Critical language awareness in the United States: revisiting issues and revising pedagogies in a resegregated society. *Educational Researcher*, 34(7), 24–31.

Austen-Smith, D., & Fryer, Jr., R. G. (2005). An economic analysis of 'acting White.' *The Quarterly Journal of Economics*. May, 551–583. http://qje.oxfordjournals.org/content/120/2/551.full.pdf

Barth, R. (2002). The culture builder. *Education Leadership*, 59, 6–11.

Barton, P. E., & Coley, R. J. (2010). *The Black-White achievement gap: When progress stopped*. Policy Information Center. Princeton, NJ: Educational Testing Service.

Baugh, J. (1999). *Out of the mouths of slaves: African American language and educational malpractice*. Austin, TX: University of Texas Press.

Baugh, J. (2000). *Beyond Ebonics: Linguistic pride and racial prejudice*. New York, NY: Oxford University Press.

Birch, B. (2001). Grammar standards: It's all in your attitude. *Language Arts*, 78, 535–542.

CCCC. (1974). Students' right to their own language [Special issue]. *College Composition and Communication*, 25(3).

Christenbury, L. (2000). *Making the journey: Being and becoming a teacher of English language arts* (2nd Ed.). Portsmouth, NH: Boynton/Cook Heinemann.

Craig, H. K., & Washington, J. A. (2005). *Malik goes to school: Examining the language skills of African American students from preschool–5th Grade*. New York, NY: Lawrence Earlbaum.

Cumming, D. (1997, January 9). A different approach to teaching language. *The Atlanta Constitution*, p. B1.

Delpit, L. (1995). *Other people's children: Cultural conflict in the classroom.* New York, NY: New Press.

Delpit, L., & Dowdy, J. (2002). *The skin that we speak: Thoughts on language and culture in the classroom.* New York, NY: The New Press.

Gal, S. (1998). Multiplicity and Contention Among Language Ideologies. In B. Schieffelin, K. Woolard, & P. Kroskrity (Eds.), *Language Ideologies* (pp. 317–331). Oxford, England: Oxford University Press.

Gilyard, K. (1991). *Voices of the self: A study of language competence.* Detroit, MI: Wayne State Press.

Godley et al. (2007). "I'll speak in proper slang": Language ideologies in a daily editing activity. *Reading Research Quarterly* 42 (1). 100–31.

Goodman, Y., & Goodman, D. (2000). "I hate 'postrophe s": Issues of dialect and reading proficiency. In J. Peyton, P. Griffin, W. Wolfram, & R. Fasold (Eds.), *Language in action: New studies of language in society* (pp. 408–435). Cresskill, NJ: Hampton.

Green, L. (2002). *African American English: A linguistic introduction.* Cambridge, MA: Cambridge University Press.

Green, L. (2011). *Language and the African American child.* Cambridge, MA: Cambridge University Press.

Heath, S. B. (1983). *Ways with words: Language, life, and work in communities and classrooms.* Cambridge, MA: Cambridge University Press.

Joos, M. (1961). *The five clocks: A linguistic excursion into the five styles of English usage.* New York, NY: Harcourt, Brace & World.

Labov, W. (1995). Can reading failure be reversed? A linguistic approach to the question. In V. Gadsen & D. Wagner (Eds.), *Literacy among African-American youth* (pp. 39–68). Cresskill, NJ: Hampton.

Labov, W., & Baker, B. (m.s.). *Linguistic component, African American literacy and culture project.*

Lippi-Green, R. (2012). *English with an accent: Language, ideology and discrimination in the United States.* New York, NY: Routledge.

McKissack, P. (1986). *Flossie and the fox.* New York, NY: Dial.

McWhorter, J. (1998). *The word on the street: Debunking the myth of pure standard English.* New York, NY: Plenum.

Meier, T. (2008). *Black communications and learning to read: Building on children's linguistic and cultural strengths.* New York, NY: Lawrence Erlbaum.

Milroy, J. (2001). Language ideologies and the consequences of standardization. *Journal of Sociolinguistics*, 5/4, 530–555.

National Center for Education Statistics [NCES]. (2011). *The nation's report card: Reading 2011. National assessment of educational progress at grades 4 and 8.* (NCES 2012-457). Washington D.C.: Institute of Education Sciences, U.S. Department of Education. Retrieved from http://nationsreportcard.gov/reading_2011/reading_2011_tudareport/

Nieto, S. (2000). *Affirming diversity: The sociopolitical context of multicultural education* (3rd ed.). New York, NY: Longman.

Perry, T., & Delpit, L. (Eds.). (1998). *The real Ebonics debate: Power, language, and the education of African American children.* Boston, MA: Beacon.

Pullum, G. (1999). African American Vernacular English is not standard English with mistakes. In R. S. Wheeler (Ed.), *The workings of language: From prescriptions to perspectives* (pp. 59–66). Westport, CT: Praeger.

Richardson, E. (2002). "To protect and serve": African American female literacies. *College Composition and Communication*, 53, 675–704.

Rickford, J. R. (1996). The Oakland Ebonics decision: Commendable attack on the problem. *San Jose Mercury News*, December 26, 1996. Retrieved August 10, 2014 from http://www.johnrickford.com/Writings/PapersAvailableOnline/TheOaklandEbonicsDecision/tabid/1140/Default.aspx

Rickford, J. R. (1997, January 22). *Letter to Senator Specter, Chairman, U.S. Senate Subcommittee on Labor, Health and Human Services and Education*. Retrieved August 10, 2014, from http://www.johnrickford.com/Writings/PapersAvailableOnline/LettertoSenatorSpecter/tabid/1142/Default.aspx

Rickford, J. R. (1998, March 25). *Using the vernacular to teach the standard*. California State University Long Beach [CSULB] Conference on Ebonics. Retrieved August 10, 2014 from http://www.johnrickford.com/Writings/PapersAvailableOnline/UsingtheVernaculartoTeachTheStandard/tabid/1135/Default.aspx

Rickford, J. R. (1999). Language diversity and academic achievement in the education of African American students: An overview of the issues. In C. Adger, D. Christian, & O. Taylor (Eds.), *Making the connection: Language and academic achievement among African American students* (pp. 1–30). Washington, DC: Center for Applied Linguistics.

Rickford, J. R. and W. Wolfram. (unpublished ms.). Explicit formal instruction in oral language (as a second dialect). For: National Research Council Workshop on Language Development, Oct. 2009, semi-final draft of Sept. 27, 2009.

Schieffelin, B. B., K. A. Woolard, and P. V. Kroskrity. (eds) (1998). *Language ideologies: practice and theory*. New York, NY: Oxford University Press.

Schierloh, J. M. (1991). Teaching standard English usage: A dialect-based approach. *Adult Learning*, 2, 20–22.

Smitherman, G. (1981). "What go round come round": King in perspective. In G. Smitherman (Ed.), *Talkin that talk: Language, culture, and education in African America* (pp. 132–149). New York, NY: Routledge.

Steffensen, M., Reynolds, R., McClure, E., & Guthrie, L. (1982). Black English Vernacular and reading comprehension: A close study of third, sixth, and ninth graders. *Journal of Reading Behavior*, 3, 285–298.

Taylor, H. U. (1991). *Standard English, Black English, and bidialectalism: A controversy*. New York, NY: Peter Lang.

Wheeler, R., Cartwright, K., & Swords, R. (2012). Factoring dialect into reading assessment and instruction in the elementary classroom. *Reading Teacher* 65(5), 416–425.

Wheeler, R., & Swords, R. (2010). *Code-switching lessons: Grammar strategies for linguistically diverse writers*. Portsmouth, NH: Heinemann.

Wheeler, R. (2008). Becoming adept at code-switching. *Educational Leadership* 65(7), 54–58.

Wheeler, R. S., & Swords, R. (2006). *Code-switching: Teaching standard English in urban classrooms*. Urbana, IL: National Council of Teachers of English.

Wilkinson, C., Miciak, J., Alexander, C., Reyes, P., Brown, J., & Giani, M. (2011). *Recommended educational practices for standard English learners*. Austin, Texas: The University of Texas at Austin: Texas Education Research Center.

Wolfram, W. (1999). Repercussions from the Oakland Ebonics controversy—The critical role of dialect awareness programs. In C. T. Adger, D. Christian, & O. Taylor (Eds.), *Making the connection: Language and academic achievement among African American students* (pp. 61–80). McHenry, IL: Delta Systems.

Wolfram, W., & Schilling-Estes, N. (2006). *American English* (2nd Ed.). Malden, MA: Blackwell.

9

TANGLED IN *CHARLOTTE'S WEB*

Lessons Learned from English Learners

Claudia Christensen Haag and Margaret Compton

This chapter is about Claudia Christensen Haag's experiences learning from and with her students as an ESL teacher. For clarity, the chapter is written in Claudia's first person narrative even though both authors contributed to the writing.

> It was January, and all of my ESL [English as a Second Language] students' homeroom fourth-grade teachers were having their students create independent book report projects. I suggested helping my three fourth-grade ELs [English learners] with this project by reading aloud and discussing Charlotte's Web, one of the classic texts listed in the fourth grade curriculum. Sounded like a plan at the time … But it was a disaster in the making! None of my ELs appeared interested in the story, and all my dramatic voices and gestures during the read-alouds were doing little to get them engaged. Instead, the students were tangled in Charlotte's Web, and ultimately, so was I.
>
> *(January email from Claudia to Margaret)*

My own cultural identity is European American female. I spent my early years growing up in a farm community in Colorado, followed by a college experience at a small Protestant liberal arts university in Texas. After a decade of teaching experiences in three states that included working in a school district in Arizona with a population of over 90% Hispanic, I realized that I needed more understanding about cultural and linguistic dimensions of learning. This realization sent me back to school for an ESL certification followed by a master's and doctorate in literacy studies. Acquiring a doctorate only solidified the fact that through all this new learning, I was again aware of how much I still had to learn from my English learners (ELs). After my graduate work, I felt that I needed to go back into the ESL classroom to gain perspectives on how teachers and students come to negotiate this thing called learning.

I share my story from a personal perspective and in collaboration with Margaret, a colleague and the second author of this chapter. Margaret agreed to be my email pen pal and to interview me about my experiences throughout the year. I found the new realities of the ESL classroom to be disquieting. In the few years I had been away from ESL teaching, changes in program and policy demands had grown exponentially: new placement-testing paperwork, new time frame pull-out mandates for ESL students depending on their language levels, busing needs for satellite campuses, and the omnipresent statewide testing pressures. But one of the biggest changes was the new population of children who were dealing with more challenges than just learning a new language (Cummins, 2001; Garcia, Jensen, & Scribner, 2009). As we introduce my students below, we will elaborate on some of these challenges faced by ELs.

My beginning roster included 20 students. Over half of the children had just moved to the United States and scored at the newcomer level (Level 1) on our district language assessment test. Also, within the first few weeks, I had three separate family groups with children adopted from Russian orphanages, one student who had lived in the war-torn country of Pakistan, and a boy from India who had one day shared with one of his peers that he was going home to commit suicide. In one case, I was introduced to three newcomers from Russia: a trio of siblings who had been adopted by an American family and who actually came straight from the airport to the district's main office for language testing. By that afternoon, the siblings were enrolled and placed in classrooms. Just imagine coming to a new country and not only having to learn a new language and culture but also having new parents who had little understanding of your native language and your life. It is no wonder that all of my students had days when they ran out of classrooms, hid under tables, and refused to cross through new doorways. An interview in the first month of my teaching demonstrates my angst at trying to implement a new ESL program within the school along with understanding my new students' identities coupled with their social and emotional needs:

> So I guess during the first three weeks, between tears at home and trying to figure out how I coax this young child to even come see me or come in my doorway, I felt so much frustration because it didn't feel like teaching. It felt like social work, and it felt like trying to figure out, trying to get inside someone's head, and they couldn't tell you what they were feeling.
>
> *(September, Interview 1)*

My lack of understanding about how to bridge the social/emotional issues that came with my newly adopted students made my ESL teaching a *foreign* experience, and it took time to gain my footing in this new terrain. Although breaking through the affective issues to build trust and understanding was a yearlong process, I learned some key lessons across the year. This chapter is written around three of the most important lessons:

- Value English learners' identities and life experiences by bringing them in the door and into our instruction.
- Use multimodal pathways in instruction to help students build understandings and promote their sense of agency.
- Include student voices in problem solving when instructional practices are not meeting their needs.

You will see all three of these lessons interwoven in three scenarios; however, we have attempted to tease out and highlight each of these lessons separately in three sections below. The lessons we learned are presented in the form of vignettes from my classroom. Each vignette is couched within a multiliteracies perspective.

First Lesson: Value Students' Identities and Life Experiences by Bringing Them in the Door and into Our Instruction

> They all have come from other countries/cultures and in most cases, miss their "other lives."
>
> *(November email from Claudia to Margaret)*

As the email excerpt above reveals, I found that my students were not only dealing with new classes and new teachers, but also, for many entirely new lives, new cultures, and new families. This made our progress in the beginning months of the year a bit rocky.

Self-Portraits

Starting from day one, I needed to draw on a variety of modalities, including artistic response, since typical paper and pencil activities were often too limiting. Given that many of my students were at the beginning phases of acquiring both spoken and written English, the arts afforded a broader means for communication. The power of using drawing to express meaning in the ESL classroom paid big dividends by opening linguistic and academic roadways to learning and understanding one another.

One avenue of response that afforded a glimpse into my students' personalities and identities came in the form of self-portraits. I observed the students' serious concentration as they captured small details for their portraits. Bridging the "affect and the language barriers" through artistic response had worked well in previous ESL classes, and I found that each student worked on his/her drawing in distinct ways. For example, it was interesting to watch Sasha, one of my newcomers from Russia, who, after just three days in the United States, worked hard to read and copy the caption on his shirt. (See Figure 9.1.)

FIGURE 9.1 Sasha's Self-Portrait.

Several letters and numbers in Sasha's illustration are upside down because he was copying the letters from the shirt he was wearing, and visually they were literally upside down!

Joonas, a fifth grader from Finland who appeared to be shy, used his artistic prowess to share a bit of his true personality when he drew himself with his baseball cap on backwards, a style worn by many peers and sports figures. He drew his eyes crossed and tongue out, and he was sporting a fierce-looking Chicago Bulls shirt. (See Figure 9.2.)

FIGURE 9.2 Joonas's Self-Portrait.

Tae, from South Korea, was the only student who drew a huge frown on his face and also copied words from his shirt. (See Figure 9.3.)

FIGURE 9.3 Tae's Self-Portrait.

Tae was the trickster; the child who initially held so much behind the eyes that he could not or would not say aloud. However, through art, drama, and sharing his native language through writing and his Korean gaming books, his personality soon began to emerge.

Identity Charts

I was still missing information about each child's background that the cumulative records and first meetings with parents had not provided, so we launched into creating identity charts. Creating these charts gave students some freedom of expression to share the texts of their lives and to continue building understandings of one another as they also developed social and language skills (Cummins, Bismilla, Chow, Cohen, Giampapa, Leoni, Sandhu, & Sastri, 2005). Many of the students brought photographs for their identity charts, and one student brought a small, published booklet about his hometown. As we worked on these charts, the students informally talked to each other and to me, sharing photos or clip art they had found. Students pulled up websites with information about their countries and began to use the information to add captions and details to their charts. Several students used the art center supplies to make their country flags to adorn the boards. Peer mentoring and support was evident throughout the process as they showed each other photos; helped one another on their research outlines; and shared ideas, often through nonverbal gesturing. Once the identity charts were completed, the students shared them with the class. For those just learning English, much of this sharing took place through gestures such as pointing at the pictures and different sections of the chart.

I wanted to capture their language development throughout the school year, so I began to keep a video diary of many of our projects and dramatic enactments. These moments in our classroom life became a favorite avenue for students to view themselves because they always wanted me to play the videos so that they could watch and rewatch themselves and their peers. These screenings often led to informal discussions and self-critiques as students shared when they did not like the way they pronounced a word or realized they needed to understand a new word or a concept.

> In listening to the children share their posters [identity charts] in our small group today, the nonverbal cues spoke volumes. As Joonas asked Guilherme to hold his poster, his body posture changed; he was a different Joonas as he shared his "other life." He stopped and paused to take in the three flags, then smirked, turned to the camera, and said, "These are my three languages." And after a small amount of coaxing, shared by saying "Hello" in German, Finnish, and English.
>
> *(September, Claudia's Teacher Journal)*

Once the charts were displayed in the hallway, students saw that peers from their home base classes were interested in their lives, and they basked in this adulation.

Writing through Frustrations: The Stupid Book

This temporary adulation turned to the dark side as my English learners became frustrated with their peers because of their "stupid" misconceptions about their backgrounds and countries. One day Joonas came into the ESL classroom visibly frustrated. He stated that he hated our ESL sign plastered above the doorway and that English was not his second language but his *third* (italics added for emphasis) behind Finnish and German. Further, Joonas said the kids in his classroom were discouraging him by asking questions about his life in Finland. I could see this was a topic of great concern.

> Joonas was just blown away by his peers' "stupid" questions. When I asked what some of them were, he said, "Oh, like the kid that asked me, well, do you eat pizza in Finland?" He was looking at me like it's just the stupidest question that he's ever heard, and I asked, "Just what do you think about that?" and he's like, "Why not? You know we're closer to Italy than you are."
>
> *(April, Interview 3)*

This interview excerpt illustrates the frustration that Joonas felt about his peers' misconceptions and provided an authentic writing opportunity. I asked if he and Guilherme wanted to write about life in Finland and life in Brazil to help educate their peers. Since we were working on the writing process, we agreed that both boys would begin drafting their own *Silly Questions about Finland and Brazil* in question and answer format, a writing technique we had just explored from a mentor text. Both boys assured me that "silly" wasn't a strong enough word, and they wanted their titles to be *Stupid Questions about Finland/Brazil*. Writing ensued. (See Figure 9.4.)

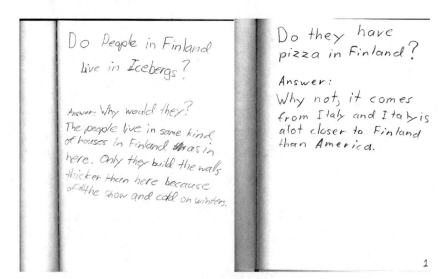

FIGURE 9.4 Excerpts from *Stupid Questions about Finland* by Joonas.

This question and answer format provided Joonas with an avenue to express his anger. The voice within his writing shows his sense of humor through moments when he felt his peers were underestimating and stereotyping his background experiences and his native country.

A multiliteracies lens assists in understanding the complexities of my year in the classroom (Kalantzis & Cope, 2012). I found that visual, tactile, and auditory activities helped all of us to develop deeper understandings of one another as well as the academic content. Our engagement in multimodal activities provided avenues for students' identities and personalities to be shared and valued in the context of life and work at school. Additionally, it opened up opportunities for my students to adapt, collaborate, problem-solve, and become flexible in their own learning.

Second Lesson: Use Multimodal Pathways in Instruction to Help Children Build Understandings and Promote Their Sense of Agency

The identity charts became a window into my students' home lives and also sparked the three siblings from Russia to ask their new parents if they could bring their video from the Russian orphanage for our class to view. As I watched Tonya on-screen with her class singing a Russian song replete with hand motions and dance steps, I became aware of my own skewed vision of what their life had been like in Russia.

> It was fascinating to watch them and they were very proud to show it—got more language out of Sasha than I have in weeks! Reminds me that we must start from their perspective and learn as much as we can about each other as we build this community.
>
> *(October email from Claudia to Margaret)*

I also caught a small glimpse into how school participant structures in Russia were very different from the classrooms they were now experiencing, which created a great dissonance in their knowing how to participate and "do school" in the United States. For example, Daniel, the youngest sibling, would often get up in the middle of our whole group time and start walking around the classroom. He didn't understand our whole group to small group lesson format where we would start in our reading center and share a read aloud or mini-lesson together and then move to small group. I realized that the participant structure during our whole group vs. small group was implicit and not explicit, and some of my students, including Daniel, needed more explicit guidance. Many students found these new ways of participating challenging as they were accustomed to a more traditional school participation format: sitting in rows during whole class discussions and raising hands to share their thoughts only when invited to do so.

Another insight from the video dealt with the inclusion of the arts in the curriculum. As noted scholar Marie Clay shared (personal communication, 1996), the arts play an integral part of academic learning in many countries including

New Zealand. This factor appeared to be mirrored in my Russian students' school experiences. I found that music would calm and help engage a frustrated Daniel and that art would be one of Sasha's favorite learning avenues and a precursor to other literacy activities. When I introduced our first story enactments in September, Tonya embraced this modality easily and often became a director for her peers on what actions and gestures to use in the dramatizations of predictable stories, poems, and songs. In the world of ESL teaching, I found that the use of different modes of meaning such as music and drama afforded greater learning opportunities (Haag, 1998).

Throughout the year, in my kindergarten through fifth-grade ESL lessons, we often used dramatic enactments to live through our read-alouds and content texts (Rosenblatt, 1978). For example, my second graders, Tanya from Russia and Tae from South Korea, were both in the same homeroom and their class was in the middle of a biographical study. Each student was assigned a famous historical character and was to bring this figure to life through a dramatic oral presentation. The children were encouraged to write their speeches in first person and to dress up as their characters for their presentations.

In working together with their teacher, we decided that I would begin pulling Tonya and Tae for additional time so we could study their characters together, and we would do our enactments through a pretaped video presentation. Tonya was assigned Eleanor Roosevelt, and Tae presented Thomas Edison. David Adler's picture book biographies (1995, 1990) were a good beginning for this assignment, but the Internet became one of our key resources for unpacking new vocabulary and developing an understanding of these two historical figures. On the Internet, we found videos and photos along with text and were able to experience, through these expanded modalities, what life looked like in each character's place in history. As a result of viewing sites that included videos of Thomas Edison's inventions, Tae became fascinated with his character. As we co-created our narration for the enactments, both Tae and Tonya became the directors of their scripts and problem-solved how to share their respective characters in the video presentations. Tae scoured his home and our classroom looking for items he could turn into props for his movie: A three-hole punch was pressed down to the rhythm of S-O-S for his scene on Edison's inventing the telegraph machine, and a glass science beaker was filled with particles of torn red, yellow, and orange construction paper which he swirled and tossed in the air to re-create explosions that occurred in Edison's lab as he worked on his inventions.

Tonya's foray into the world of Eleanor Roosevelt started out a bit rocky because she got lost in Adler's text and lost the meaning behind the story of Roosevelt's life. When I shared that she would become Eleanor in our video presentation, she became driven by her desire to wear a costume. Tonya problem-solved her own enactments more through gestures and spatial actions, making a scrunched up face in the beginning scene to show that Eleanor was considered an ugly child and including her ESL peers in scenes depicting how Eleanor taught dance. She used a small white board to write an explanation for each scene: "Scene 1–Eleanor goes to school," "Scene 2–Eleanor Teaching Dance." She instructed me to zoom in on this board before starting the narration for each scene. Tonya enlisted Tae who became a much-chagrined Franklin Roosevelt in Tanya's enactment. Tae showed serious emotional alarm when one scene called for him to marry Eleanor. The school nurse shared her wheelchair for the videotaping so Tonya could wheel an invalid Franklin, complete with spectacles, as he campaigned for another term as President. Tonya and Tae became directors of their respective videos, and when the final productions were shared with their peers in the homeroom biography presentations, both students' nonverbal behaviors included shy grins because they were able to show their peers that they could also participate fully and creatively.

Kalantzis and Cope (2012) contend that a multiliteracies conceptual framework asks us to see literacies more broadly; teachers engage students to become "active knowledge makers," and students are afforded more agency that will perhaps lead to greater equity (p. 12). Drama is an important multimodal avenue for broadening conceptions of literacies that can result in positive benefits for all students (Booth, 2005; Heath, 2004; Paley, 1981; Pellegrini & Galda, 1993; Martinez, Roser, & Strecker, 1999; Wolfe, 1994). For English learners, the benefits are magnified because drama provides alternate ways of showing and knowing the world. The ability to use their bodies and facial expressions to live through the stories or content being shared affords a deeper transaction with the text (Greenfader & Brouillette, 2013; Haag, 1998). Indeed, "The arts encircle learning with meaning and thereby make comprehension and engagement fundamental for participation" (Heath, 2004, p. 339). As Greenfader and Brouillette (2013) relate:

> Children possess a sense of dramatic narrative they can put to use in classroom arts lessons by acting out stories or discussing plot, character, and themes. This is especially valuable for ELs as it allows them to inject their own cultural understanding into the story, using other modes of communication to take part in a meaningful dialogue despite a limited English vocabulary. (p. 333)

Third Lesson: Include Student Voices in Problem Solving When Instructional Practices Are Not Meeting Their Needs

The *Tangled in Charlotte's Web* episode stands out as one of my biggest learning lessons and a turning point for my teaching. During this episode, I realized how much could be accomplished if we problem-solved together and if I listened to my students' voices when it came to meeting their affective and academic needs.

Since the ESL program was a pull-out model, I worked with the teachers at each grade level to address state-mandated time requirements. Initially, several different grade levels overlapped and met in the classroom at the same time. For example, early in the semester, the kindergarten students' time overlapped with the fourth-grade students. By January, the fourth graders' academic needs had changed, and all three complained about sharing the space with the younger students. They let me know that this arrangement was disrupting their journal writing, reading times, and interfering with their ability to concentrate.

Simultaneously, the fourth-grade teachers asked me to do a book report project with students, and they suggested *Charlotte's Web* (White, 1952). *Charlotte's Web* was on the state fourth-grade reading list, and it is a book with which most U.S. students were familiar. Talk about a disaster in the making! As an experienced teacher knows, a student's background knowledge, vocabulary, plus interest can make or break a book selected for read-aloud. I bombed on all three fronts with *Charlotte's Web*.

First, Sasha from Russia, Natalia from Brazil, and Hanna from Finland had little background knowledge about farms, much less a farm in the Midwest USA. Second, there were challenges with the language and vocabulary levels. Although E. B. White's wonderful format of placing academic words in context with their more familiar definitions often supported the reader, for an English learner, this format was doubly frustrating as none of the terms were familiar to my ELs. Third, interest. How could these students be interested when every other word was new and there were few pictures to support visualization? These problems notwithstanding, I continued to plod through the book with the children, increasing my use of gestures and dramatic character voices in a feeble attempt to engage them.

To address their initial concern, I had the brilliant idea that while I worked with the kindergarten students, Peg, my paraprofessional, could pull my fourth graders into an alcove in the hall to read aloud and discuss *Charlotte's Web* without any interference from the younger students. I then proceeded to work with my kindergarteners. A short time later, Peg appeared in my doorway followed by three fuming children, all with a countenance weighing in between anger and volatility.

> The two girls were almost in tears as they came in the room. Here I was trying to make their learning environment better but it flopped big time, and they were telling me with every fiber of their being, "This is too hard!"
>
> *(April, Interview 3)*

I felt as low as the children the day they proclaimed mutiny against my new plan. They slammed down into their seats and proceeded to lay their heads on the table. I looked around and asked if they wanted to talk about it. Violent head-shaking side to side was followed by a hearty chorus of "Nooo," so I got out the journals, mine included, and asked them to write about what had frustrated them. All three students indicated they were too angry to write in English, so I encouraged them to use their native languages. I could hear the pencils being lifted and returned with force to the paper with serious punctuation and exclamation marks being added. I truly didn't want to know what they were writing at that moment, but I did realize that the experience was allowing lots of anger and frustration to flow through the pencils. As the students continued their "anger management" writing episode, I also wrote in my journal, "What am I doing? Should I just call it a day, put this book away, and start over again" (March, Claudia's Teacher Journal)?

After we all calmed down and our writing postures began to lighten up, mine included, I asked if anyone wanted to share what they were feeling. Natalia related that she hated having her peers walk by them in the hall because they probably thought she was in trouble, and Hanna and Sasha agreed vigorously. Hanna shared that Ms. Peg's reading was different, and she was missing my voices for the different characters.

The next day I had the students read through their journal entries silently and then asked them to help me problem-solve. First, all agreed that they didn't want to be in the hallway again. Next, Hanna shared that she wanted me to go back to doing the reading again because she liked the different voices. Finally, Sasha provided a strong solution to help with comprehending the book. He checked his journal; looked up with his usual bored but mischievous smirk; and stated, "Show the movie!" It seemed that he had shared our debacle from yesterday with his mom, and she told him there was a movie of the book. So that's exactly what we did.

The movie allowed them to understand a farm, and seeing each character helped them build some much needed background knowledge about the context of the story. Sasha popped out of his chair each time Templeton appeared on-screen, pointing and yelling, "Templeton! Templeton!" as he laughed at his favorite character's antics. We then used this movie-viewing to support our continued reading of the book, but I also needed to change the reading climate. I worked with the kindergarten teachers to reschedule their ESL time so the fourth graders could have my undivided attention. Using my students' advice to change our learning experience paid off in a big way and became a learning experience for all of us.

The group book project included a huge mural with two of the key scenes from the book, one of the barnyard and one of the fairgrounds. Hanna suggested that we add captions to explain each scene and cleverly decided to put them on paper sacks, an idea she got from the movie when all the trash was flying around at the fairgrounds. Since Templeton was Sasha's favorite character, he illustrated Templeton's stash underneath the trash pile complete with a three-dimensional "rotten egg" that he concocted by using a Styrofoam ball that he split in half, then covered inside with some "smelly spices." Natalia, who did not see herself as the "artist," pulled pictures of carnivals and fairs from the Internet to add to the fair scene, and she also took the lead writing the group's summary that was placed at the bottom of the mural. We hung the mural in the hallway, and the three took turns approaching students in the hall to come take a survey they had developed about how Templeton's egg smelled. That is, survey participants voted for whether the egg smelled 'good' or 'bad' once they sniffed it. The group made a bar graph to share the results, and this was also posted on the mural.

In our video diary of this event, I asked all three students to identify their contributions to the mural and to talk about their learning experiences during the unit. Hanna shared that she enjoyed using her artistic expression to configure a 3-D Charlotte out of pipe cleaners and a small Styrofoam ball. She also created the spider web out of black yarn and actually wove the phrase "Some Pig" into it to mimic the book. She drew many of the farm scenes freehand and shared that she thought it was a great idea to put the captions on paper sacks. Natalia was very proud of all the clip art she contributed to the project and of her ability to help the group create the written summary to place on the mural. Sasha shared that his favorite parts were Templeton's "stinky egg" and the survey of his classmates to see what they thought of the smell. As I was about to switch off the camera, Natalia blurted out, "You know what? I know this book better than a boy in my class who used it for his book report!" (See Figure 9.5.)

FIGURE 9.5 *Charlotte's Web* Mural.

In our description here, it is evident that the students not only are active knowledge makers, but also draw from multiple sources of information, questioning to solve problems, and taking responsibility for their own learning. This level of student engagement reflects Kalantzis and Cope's (2012) concept for new learning. Due to our dynamically changing world, a new kind of learning and teaching must begin to transform our schools. Instead of the heavy concentration on passive learning where students sit back and view, listen, and take in new knowledge in a more formal context, new learning positions learners and teachers in more dynamic and interactive roles. English learners will be actively engaged in their own learning through researching information using a variety of sources and media; analyzing multiple perspectives; and tackling real-world problem-solving tasks. Taking more responsibility for their learning, includes self-assessing their own thinking and learning; and drawing from one another's collective intelligences through collaborations.

To initiate new learning, teaching must change and transform. Instead of delivering content, teachers will design new learning environments that support collaboration. Additionally, teachers will provide multiple pathways to learning that enlist the use of a variety of modalities where English learners are afforded opportunities to take responsibility for their own learning (Kalantzis & Cope, 2012). In this new teaching role, I had the opportunity to design a learning environment that offered more than one path to learning and incorporated more student collaboration and responsibility. Once I was finished with the turbulent side of *Charlotte's Web* (White, 1952), I found that the creative side to teaching, which continually gets pushed aside for high-stakes testing and new mandates, was also awakening in me. The students and I were feeling our sense of agency together.

Conclusion: Listening to and Learning from English Learners

As I reflect back on this year in the ESL classroom, I realize how important it was for me, as the teacher, to stay student-centered, to continuously question and reflect on my own practices so I could help my students negotiate their own learning through a broader lens of literacy learning opportunities. This journey together was never smooth and often filled with much turmoil as we figured out how to communicate and problem-solve together. We found that as our community solidified, we often had to push through not just the positive but also the negative learning experiences to untangle the webs in which we were initially caught.

As the literacy events shared in this chapter illustrate, the power of incorporating English learners' backgrounds and identities must be a central focus to bring the whole child in the classroom door in meaningful ways. Therefore, it is critical for teachers to use a widened scope of multimodal practices that value and incorporate students' backgrounds and home lives that provide a bridge into their new language and new world (Brock, Lapp, Salas, & Townsend, 2009). A teacher must understand not only issues of language acquisition, but also the intricacies of building a supportive learning community that values the identities and knowledge that each student brings to the classroom. By engaging English learners, we value the funds of knowledge they possess and draw from these funds to build new understandings (Moll, Amanti, Neff, & Gonzalez, 1992).

If we truly want to promote an authentic and effective learning environment, we must draw from the lessons our students share with us. Joonas helps us see how writing his book, *Stupid Questions about Finland*, allowed him to work through and alleviate some of his frustrations with peers who had skewed visions of his life in Finland. Tanya and Tae's dramatic video presentations remind us to broaden our views of what counts as literacy practices and to use a variety of modality pathways so all students can show what they know. And Sasha, Natalia, and Hanna teach us that often the best instructional resources, when our teaching lessons fail, reside in the learners and their abilities to problem-solve best solutions for their own paths to learning.

So, as teachers, what lessons can we all apply from my learning during this year back in the classroom? We ask teachers to:

- Recognize the power of bringing identity and affect into the teacher and student relationships that you are building in your classroom. "English language learners will engage academically to the extent that instruction affirms their identities and enables them to invest their identities in learning" (Cummins, et al., 2006, p. 40).
- Realize that the power of incorporating multimodal pathways in the classroom can bring rich results to teaching and learning. Through these pathways students are given the opportunities to share their knowledge and abilities that don't often translate within typical reading and writing activities (Pandya, 2012).
- Respect the power of using native language strengths and abilities not only to bridge to English, but also to develop cultural and linguistic understandings between students, peers, and teachers (Williams & Haag, 2009).

In sharing this research on Claudia's return to an ESL classroom, we invite you as the reader to ask yourself a similar question. How can you learn from your students, understand their perspectives about the learning process, and value what they bring to the classroom?

References

Adler, D. (1990). *Thomas Edison: Great inventor*. New York, NY: Holiday House.
Adler, D. (1995). *A picture book of Eleanor Roosevelt*. New York, NY: Holiday House.
Booth, D. (2005). *Storydrama: Creating stories through role playing, improvising, and reading aloud*. Portland, ME: Stenhouse.
Brock, C., Lapp, D., Salas, R., & Townsend, D. (2009). *Academic literacy for English learners*. New York, NY: Teachers College Press.
Cummins, J. (2001). *Negotiating identities: Education for empowerment in diverse society* (2nd Ed.). Los Angeles, CA: California Association for Bilingual Education.
Cummins, J., Bismilla, V., Chow, P., Cohen, S., Giampapa, F., Leoni, L., Sandhu, P., & Sastri, P. (2005). Affirming identity in multilingual classrooms. *Educational Leadership*, 63(1), 38–43.
Cummins, J., Chow, P., & Schecter, S. (2006). Community as curriculum. *Language Arts*, 83(4), 297–307.
Garcia, E. E., Jensen, B. T., & Scribner, K. P. (2009). The demographic imperative. *Educational Leadership*, 66(7), 8–13.
Greenfader, C. M., & Brouillette, L. (2013). Boosting language skills of English learners through dramatization and movement. *The Reading Teacher*, 67(3), 171–180.
Haag, C. (1998). *Exploring participation in a first grade multicultural classroom during two literacy events: The read-aloud and the literature dramatization*. Unpublished doctoral dissertation, Texas Woman's University, Denton, TX.
Heath, S. B. (2004). Learning language and strategic thinking through the arts. *Reading Research Quarterly*, 39(3), 347–366.

Kalantzis, M., & Cope, B. (2012). *Literacies*. New York, NY: Cambridge University Press.

Martinez, M., Roser, N., & Strecker, S. (1999). "I never thought I could be a star:" A readers theatre ticket to fluency. *The Reading Teacher*, 52(4), 326–334.

Moll, L., Amanti, C., Neff, D., & Gonzalez, N. (1992). Funds of knowledge for teaching: Using a qualitative approach to connect homes and classrooms. *Theory into Practice*, 31, 132–141.

Paley, V. G. (1981). Wally's stories. Cambridge, MA: Harvard University Press.

Pandya, J. Z. (2012). Unpacking Pandora's box: Issues in the assessment of English learners' literacy skill development in multimodal classrooms. *Journal of Adolescent & Adult Literacy*, 56(3), 181–185.

Pellegrini, A. D., & Galda, L. (1993). Ten years after: A reexamination of symbolic play and literacy research. *Reading Research Quarterly*, 28(2), 163–174.

Rosenblatt, L. (1978). *The reader, the text, the poem: The transactional theory of the literary work.* Carbondale, IL: Southern Illinois Press.

White, E. B. (1952). Charlotte's web. New York: NY: Harper & Row Publishers.

Williams, J., & Haag, C. (2009). Engaging English learners through effective classroom practices. In C. Rodriguez-Eagle (Ed.), *Achieving literacy success with English language learners* (pp. 159–174). Worthington, OH: Reading Recovery Council of North America.

Wolfe, S. A. (1994). Learning to act/acting to learn: Children as actors, critics, and characters in classroom theatre. *Research in the Teaching of English*, 28(1), 7–44.

10
CULTURE AND IDENTITY

Promoting the Literacies of a Sudanese
Father and Son

Doris Walker-Dalhouse and A. Derick Dalhouse

Immigrant and refugee students are often at risk of school failure in the United States (Virtue, 2007). Their out-of-school literacies, as represented in family and community literacy practices, can influence the development of their in-school literacies (Hull & Schultz, 2002). The literacies that refugees and immigrants participate in at home are often not transparent in school (Skilton-Sylvester, 2002). These literacies may be grounded in the realities of their lives, thereby allowing them to express their voices in ways that conflict with school-sanctioned means and forms of expression (Sze, Chapman, & Shi, 2009). Recognizing the importance of home and school literacies, we begin our chapter by sharing a community initiative to help Sudanese refugees and immigrants. We then tell you the story of Samuel (pseudonym), a Sudanese refugee father who migrated with his son Ethan (pseudonym) to our home state of North Dakota. After we present Samuel's story, we will tell you about the in- and out-of-school literacy practices of Samuel's son, Ethan. Finally, we end with implications for schools.

Journeying into Sudanese Culture

Sudanese families and adolescents without parents, known as "The Lost Boys," arrived in Fargo, North Dakota, with the assistance of a local service agency, local churches, and community agencies. These refugees came to a community of individuals who were white—predominantly Norwegian and German in descent—and who desired to help them become acclimated to their new home.

The Episcopal Cathedral in North Dakota was actively involved in the resettlement of Sudanese across the state. Initially, the parishioners supported them by collecting clothes and furniture, providing transportation, and helping them complete applications for employment. Parishioners also organized a daycare and preschool at the cathedral and held classes in English staffed by retired teachers at the church for the parents of the children. When one Sudanese refugee who was an Episcopal priest in Sudan arrived, the bishop appointed him as the rector for one of the parishes. As members of the cathedral, we (Doris and Derick) joined others in some of these efforts. As time went on, the Sudanese parents who attended our church came to know us as educators at the local university. They began to express to us their growing frustration about their children's adjustment to their local schools. They were unhappy about the fact that they were told that their children needed English as Second Language (ESL) instruction and were performing below grade level in reading and math. Although some of the parents and children were Arabic speakers, many of the families and children spoke both English and their tribal language (e.g., Uduk, Dinka, Nuer, Madi, Kuku). Yet, these children were placed in ESL classrooms for additional language arts instruction. The Sudanese parents felt that in general, teachers did not see their children or their children's parents as competent in one or more languages or able to help with homework.

Complicating this perception was the fact that heavy work schedules of the parents meant that they were not home in the afternoon, and their absence from parent-teacher conferences were perceived as a lack of the ability and/or interest in helping their children to be successful in school. A lack of teacher understanding of the Sudanese families and their home literacy practices became increasingly problematic for the families. We embraced the opportunity to share our experiences as members in the community and to help answer their school-related questions.

As a teacher educator (Doris) and psychologist (Derick), we wanted to find out about Samuel and Ethan's literacies to understand how they were connected to Ethan's literacy and identity development, as well as his school literacy. We were guided in our inquiry by three theoretical lenses: literacy as social practice, critical literacy, and multiliteracies. A literacy as social practice framework is based upon the following tenets:

- Literacy practices are purposeful and embedded in broader social goals and cultural practices.
- Literacy is situated in a historical context.
- Literacy practices are dynamic and constantly changing (Barton & Hamilton, 2001).

Critical literacy requires readers to be active, to read text from multiple perspectives, and to question text in an attempt to understand issues reflecting social change. Consequently, it frees readers to examine and to take action on past, present, and future events (McLaren, 1995; Van Sluys, Lewison, & Flint, 2006). According to Kalantzis and Cope (2012), "A multiliteracies approach attempts to explain what matters in traditional reading and writing, and what is new and distinctive about the ways in which people construct meanings in contemporary communication environments" (pp. 1–2). Accordingly, texts differ and meaning-making fluctuates according to the social context in which individuals deliberate, participate in life experiences, understand subject matter knowledge, construct specialist knowledge, function in a disciplinary domain area of employment, and understand one's own linguistic, cultural, gendered, sexual, and ethnic origins in relation to self and others.

Our Introduction to Samuel and Ethan

It was at the church and with the support of the Sudanese priest in recruiting children that we organized a reading clinic to help these families. To assist in the literacy skills improvement of the Sudanese children, we wrote grants to local and state foundations to secure funding to help us establish a community-based reading clinic in the local Episcopal Church. With the help of the Sudanese rector who served as a liaison to the Sudanese community, we were able to recruit children from grades K–6 to work with preservice teachers enrolled in a reading and language arts class. The community-based reading clinic began in the fall of 2006. It was there that we met Samuel and his adolescent son, Ethan.

In order to get to know Samuel and Ethan, we interviewed them separately in the fellowship hall of the church following the weekly Sudanese worship service. We talked to Samuel about his memories of his early literacy practices and his current literacy practices. During our interviews with Ethan, we asked him to talk about his reading and writing experiences at home and school.

Samuel and Ethan migrated to the United States in 2001. Samuel's wife and Ethan's mother, Rebecca, and the remaining four children, ranging in ages from one year to eight years old, arrived in the United States a year later. Samuel is multilingual, speaking Uduk, his native language, as well as Arabic and English. Currently, Samuel is a factory worker in North Dakota. He completed high school and earned a college degree to become a teacher and later headmaster in his village in Sudan before migrating to a Kenyan refugee camp and then to the United States.

Samuel's Literacies and Practices

Samuel was introduced to oral and print literacies primarily in cultural and school contexts in Sudan. According to Samuel:

> I grew up on a small rural farm in northern Sudan. Every morning, before going to school, it was my job to feed and milk our goats and light the fire my mother needed to prepare breakfast before I joined other boys in walking to school. As a boy, I learned many things by listening to what my father said about how to care for our goats and protect our small crop of

tomatoes and onions. I listened and learned as my father and the other men in our village talked about the fighting between Sudanese in the north and Sudanese in the south, and told stories about Africa that they heard from their parents and stories about important African leaders. It was through storytelling that I and other children in my village learned about the traditions of our people. That is how I began to know and understand the world both within and outside my village and country.

One of the lessons that I learned was the importance of family. My father used to say, "Family is the soil in which we grow. You must till the soil to keep family strong." It was through letter writing with family in other villages that we bridged time and distance between us and remained strong. I remember watching as my father wrote letters to family members in other villages and listening with great interest as we gathered around a fire to hear him read letters about the joys, sorrows, and concerns in our lives. I learned how important our religious faith was in our lives and how Bible verses memorized and shared in these letters contained messages to celebrate, encourage, and comfort.

It was at school that I developed a love for reading. I enjoyed reading *Tom Brown's School Days* [Hughes, 1999] very much and I still remember it. I cannot remember a book I read that I did not like. I wanted to get lots of education and do lots of things. There were no secondary schools in my village, so I had to travel to another village where there was a secondary school. If I were a girl, my parents would not have let me go since many parents feared for the safety of their daughters and were reluctant to send them to schools in other villages. I studied hard to become a teacher and later became the headmaster of the school in my village. School is harder for Sudanese youth who have come to the U.S. since the Civil War because they have had to transition from an oral to a reading culture.

Since I came to the USA, I read newspapers sometimes, but I am not able to read the newspapers regularly because I work long hours, and when I get home I am so tired that I just want to sleep. I can't just go to sleep though because my wife goes to work after I come home, and I have to watch our five kids. Back in Sudan I knew learning how to read and write would be an advantage. When I first came to the U.S. it helped that I already knew how to do both. However, my writing is not good now because I work hard and long hours, and when I get home I am too tired to call other family and friends in the community or to read or write letters to family in Sudan. Most of the writing that I do now is on Skype with friends or emails to my friends in the U.S. I feel it is important that I keep in contact with other Sudanese, especially those new to North Dakota, so that I can support them and help them adjust to their new lives here.

Getting to Know Ethan

Ethan was among the first group of children who attended the reading clinic. One of the first activities that we initiated was to have the children write about themselves. Ethan wrote:

> I was born in a little town called Kurmak in the changing continent of Africa. It was not safe to live there anymore with the war going on between the people in Sudan. When I was a little boy, I didn't know much. I was a boy that didn't know how to speak English that good, so when I moved to America I started to learn more English.

In our interviews with Ethan, he said:

> I made lots of friends. I love to write at home, and to have an audience with whom to share my writing. I like to add new things to tales that my father tells me about life in Sudan. I like it when he enjoys my tales as much as he does. I love to write fantasy, non-fiction, and fairytales using some of the things I see on television. I put a lot of details in my writing because I want it to be interesting.

According to Ethan:

> The thing I like most about writing at home is that I can choose my own topics to write about and can write as much as I like without worrying about the length of my writings. I put all of my writing on the computer so that I can share it with my Sudanese friends in North Dakota and my family in Sudan.

Ethan is also very interested in folktales, an interest undoubtedly generated by the folktales that his father often shared with him. One of his stories is a version of a Sudanese folktale that he entitled "Hyena, Lion, and the Baby."

> Hyena and Lion were sitting together in a village in Sudan. They were living together in the village. Hyena had a cow and Lion had a bull. One day, Hyena's cow had a baby, and he told Lion that his cow had a baby. Lion came and took Hyena's cow's baby and took it to his bull. Lion then told Hyena that his bull also had a baby. However, Hyena found out that his cow's baby was missing, so he and Lion got into an argument over the baby. Hyena was saying that the baby was his cow's baby, and Lion was saying that the baby was his bull's baby. While they were arguing Fox come by and heard them arguing. He asked them, "What are you guys arguing about?"

Hyena said "MY cow had a baby and Lion took my cow's baby to his bull and is claiming that my cow's baby is his bull's baby."

Lion said to Fox, "My bull also had a baby and the baby is not Hyena's cow's baby but my bull's baby."

Fox said to Hyena and Lion, "Why don't you guys go to the court to settle whose baby it is?"

Lion and Hyena agreed to go to court. When they arrived in court the judge was a Lion. Both Hyena and Lion started to talk at the same time, each claiming that the baby is theirs. The judge stopped them and asked, "Who wants to go first?"

Hyena said, "I want to go first, my father just had a baby this morning and I need to take him some medicine."

Lion immediately said, "You are a liar, who ever heard that a man can have babies?"

Hyena looked at Lion and said, "Then how is it that you claim that your bull had a baby?" Lion could not reply and the judge then ruled that the baby was Hyena's cow's baby.

Ethan's out-of-school literacies include books and other print material about Sudan, materials related to the content covered in school, and novels. He has access to a computer in his home, and it provides him with an opportunity to use the Internet to research writing topics assigned as homework.

He is also very interested in local and international news. He frequently uses the Internet to access websites focusing on news, including the BBC World News program (http://www.bbc.co.uk/news/world), Sudan Net (http://www.sudan.net/newslinks.php), South Sudan News Agency (http://www.southsudannewsagency.com), and Sudan Tribune (http://www.sudantribune.com). Ethan often shares what he learns with Samuel, which prompts both of them to engage in critical dialogue about the issues. Samuel admits that it makes him proud that his son has not "left the history of his people behind."

Ethan's School Literacy

Because Ethan likes to read, he routinely checks books out of the school library. During one of our interviews, he described his interest in reading about issues related to refugees. Among his favorite books on the topic are *When Elephants Fight* (Walters & Bradbury, 2008), personal narratives about the lives of children in Afghanistan, Bosnia, Sri Lanka, Sudan, and Uganda, along with factual information about each country; *Children of War: Voices of Iraqi Refugees* (Ellis, 2010); and *Inside Out and Back Again* (Lai, 2013), which focuses on a Vietnamese refugee family and their relocation and adjustment to life in the United States. Ethan also enjoys reading Shakespeare. Ethan said that books are displayed in his English class, and students are encouraged to read them when they complete their assignments. Although he likes that his teacher encourages students to respond in writing to the books they read, he does not like that time and page limits are placed on class writing assignments.

We learned that Samuel encouraged Ethan's development as a reader by sending him to the community-based reading clinic. He felt that because Ethan was able to get extra help at the clinic, he has become a more confident and better reader. Samuel said:

> I monitor Ethan's progress in school by attending parent-teacher conferences when I can and by reviewing Ethan's report cards. However, I am not able to attend every one of the parent-teacher conferences at Ethan's school because I do shift work and often have to work when conferences are held.

Nevertheless, when he can, he attends school programs and sports events in which Ethan participates. Samuel's statement helps us to understand the value he places on Ethan's learning and the importance of the social relationships between father, son, and the school in furthering Ethan's cultural identity and literacy development.

What We Have Learned

Samuel and Ethan's literacies were hidden from Ethan's teachers because their literacies had strong cultural roots that were not recognized in the larger predominantly white community in which they lived. It is significant to note that these literacies also occurred in contexts outside of school. By holding their cards close to their chests, these actions influenced the teachers' perceptions of Samuel's ability to promote Ethan's literacy development at home. That is, Ethan's teachers did not believe that Samuel and Ethan were proficient language users.

Both Samuel and Ethan are multilingual in their tribal language and in their understanding of English. Samuel's cultural history of storytelling, letter writing, and Bible reading were important social practices that were purposeful, embedded in social goals and cultural practices, and rooted in a historical context, as well as dynamic and ever changing (Barton & Hamilton, 2001).

Samuel's and Ethan's literacies reflected critical uses of literacy and multiliteracies as they both used the Internet to find information about life and events in Sudan and to question the practices and ideologies of Sudanese leaders as well as inequities and injustices in Sudan. For instance, both were interested in their readings and discussions about Sudanese politics and the lives of their relatives in Sudan. While emails have replaced the traditional practice of handwritten letters, the social and cultural practices of recording and sharing traditional tales are still communicated.

For Samuel, the social and economic realities of his early literacy experiences were connected to the availability of text, the type of text read, and the purpose of text both at home and in school. His home experiences centered on reading religious materials to meet spiritual needs. He also reads about Sudanese political and social issues in newspapers and writes letters to communicate with others about these issues. The political and social nature of literacy was evident in Samuel's current literacy practices of using technology (e.g., the Internet) to research information about the political turmoil in Sudan and to inquire about the well-being of family and friends in Sudan and in the United States. Clearly, Samuel used literacy critically to advocate for his people. He felt that the only way to do this was to examine all aspects of the war in Sudan and to question the injustices that he found. Ultimately he sought relief for his people.

Implications for Schools

It is important that schools provide classroom opportunities for refugee students to develop global literacy practices that emanate from interconnections made between their local (cultural and social) knowledge and their global academic experiences (Sarroub, 2008). To connect the in- and out-of-school literacies of adolescents, Alvermann (2002) recommends multiple literacies (i.e., digital literacies) to actively engage them in learning. The use of multiliteracies can also prompt students to make important connections between their cultural and linguistic backgrounds (Cope & Kalantzis, 2000), as well as provide opportunities for them to develop their literate identities (Skinner & Hagood, 2008; Sarroub, 2008).

The at-home and in-school literacy practices of Ethan and Samuel align to varying degrees with the school literacy practices of Ethan. We found that Samuel's home literacy practices supported Ethan's school literacy and that his current literacy practices are embedded in social goals and practices. Samuel supported Ethan's critical literacy as they investigated political and social issues related to Sudanese life and culture using multiple texts (oral, digital, and print). Samuel modeled the use of critical literacy by communicating with multiple audiences about social and economic problems encountered in adjusting to life in the United States. He wanted to improve the quality of the lives of his family members in the United States by reading about the issues that impact the lives of refugees. Samuel compared and contrasted information gained from media about the civil war in Sudan with the information that he learned about the social and political constraints affecting the lives of his extended family in Sudan. By writing autobiographical accounts of his life, Samuel was able to engage in critical thinking about whether their traditional values and attitudes were lost or maintained in the United States, thereby demonstrating his increased social awareness of life in a new country.

We believe that the home cultures of refugee students must be utilized in promoting their overall learning, including their literacy development, by sharing information, entertaining, and teaching life lessons. An examination of Samuel's data shows that his current literacy practices are embedded in social goals and practices. He communicated with a variety of audiences about issues related to problems encountered in the United States and issues related to social and political concerns in Sudan. He also shared experiences by writing emails and letters to friends and family members to convey information about his life.

The types of writing produced by Ethan included both narrative and informational writing and revealed his need to learn more about his family history and culture. Clearly, the school literacies of Sudanese and other refugee students may be improved by teaching practices that promote and make transcontinental connections (Sarroub, Pernicek, & Sweeney, 2007), practices that support the authentic purposes and literacies used in their homes.

Several implications can be drawn to help educators plan for and provide relevant literacy instruction for Sudanese and perhaps other refugee youth. Having teachers who acknowledge and value students' culture is important to increasing students' understanding of themselves and others and facilitating culturally responsive teaching (Anderson & Cowart, 2011). Children's home culture plays a critical role in developing and supporting their cognitive development (Nykiel-Herbert, 2010), and ethnic retention (i.e., immigrant families embracing their ethnic values and artifacts) is predictive of higher academic achievement (Akiba, 2007). However, incorporating the cultural experiences of adolescents is frequently ignored in literacy instruction in many secondary schools (Moje, Ciechanowski, Kramer, Ellis, Carrillo, & Collazo, 2004). Nykiel-Herbert (2010) believes that teachers who want to promote the academic achievement of minority, refugee, and/or immigrant students should use their home cultures as resources for learning. Teachers must recognize students' in- and out-of-school practices and think critically about how they inform school literacy instruction (Sarroub et al, 2007).

We believe that teachers need to create opportunities for students to design multimodal storytelling projects, as expressed by Schultz & Coleman-King (2012), in order for refugee students like Ethan to connect their home and school literacy practices, promote social diversity, and convey hopes and dreams about their lives in the United States while maintaining their ties to family and politics in their exiled homelands.

References

Akiba, D. (2007). Ethnic retention as a predictor of academic success: Lessons from the children of immigrant families and black children. *Ethnic Retention and School Performance*, 80(5), 223–225.

Alvermann, D. E. (2002). *Adolescents and literacies in a digital world.* New York, NY: Peter Lang.

Anderson, G., & Cowart, M. (2011). They are talking: Are we listening? Using student voice to enhance culturally responsive teaching. *Teacher Education and Practice*, 21(1), 10–23.

Barton, D., & Hamilton, M. (2001). Literacy practices. In D. Barton, M. Hamilton, & R. Ivantic (Eds.). *Situated literacies: Reading and writing in context* (pp. 7–15). London, UK: Routledge.

Cope, B., & Kalantzis, M. (Eds.). (2000). *Multiliteracies: Literacy learning and the design of social futures*. London, UK: Routledge.

Ellis, D. (2010). *Children of war: Voices of Iraqi refugees*. New York, NY: Groundwood Books.

Hughes, T. (1999). *Tom Brown's School Days*. Oxford, UK: Oxford University Press.

Hull, G., & Schultz, K. (2002). Connecting schools with out-of-school worlds: Insights from recent research on literacy in non-school settings. In G. Hull & K. Schultz (Eds.), *School's out: Bridging out-of-school literacies with classroom practice* (pp. 32–57). New York, NY: Teachers College Press.

Kalantzis, M., & Cope, B. (2012). *Literacies*. New York, NY: Cambridge University Press.

Lai, T. (2013). *Inside out and back again*. New York, NY: HarperCollins.

McLaren, P. (1995). *Critical pedagogy and predatory culture: Oppositional politics in a postmodern era*. New York, NY: Routledge.

Moje, E. B., Ciechanowski, E. M., Kramer, R., Ellis, L., Carrillo, R., & Collazo, T. (2004). Working toward third space in content area literacy: An examination of everyday funds of knowledge and discourse. *Reading Research Quarterly*, 39(1), 38–70.

Nykiel-Herbert, B. (2010). Iraqi refugee students: From a collection of aliens to a community of learners. *Multicultural Education*, 17(3), 2–14.

Sarroub, L. K. (2008). Living "glocally" with literacy success in the Midwest. *Theory into Practice*, 47, 59–66.

Sarroub, L. K., Pernicek, T., & Sweeney, T. (2007). "I was bitten by a scorpion": Reading in- and out-of-school in a refugee's life. *Journal of Adolescent & Adult Literacy*, 50(8), 868–879.

Schultz, K., & Coleman-King, C. (2012). Becoming visible: Shifting teacher practice to actively engage new immigrant students in urban classrooms. *Urban Review*, 44(4), 487–509. doi: 10.1007/s11256-012-0204-7

Skilton-Sylvester, E. (2002). Literate at home but not at school: A Cambodian girl's journey from playwright to struggling writer. In G. Hull & K. Schultz (Eds.), *School's out: Bridging out-of-school literacies with classroom practice* (pp. 61–90). New York, NY: Teachers College Press.

Skinner, E., & Hagood, M. C. (2008). Developing literate identities with English language learners through digital storytelling. *Reading Matrix*, 8(2), 12–38.

Sze, C., Chapman, M., & Shi, L. (2009). Functions and genres of ESL children's English writing at home and at school. *Journal of Asian Pacific Communication*, 19(1), 30–55.

Van Sluys, K., Lewison, M., & Flint, A. S. (2006). Researching critical literacy: A critical study of analysis of classroom discourse. *Journal of Literacy Research*, 38(2), 197–233.

Virtue, D. C. (2007). A glimpse into the school lives of young adolescent immigrant and refugee students: Implications for the middle level. In S. B. Mertens, V. A. Anfara, & M. F. M. Caskey (Eds.). *The young adolescent and the middle school* (pp. 237–254). Charlotte, NC: Information Age Publishing.

Walters, E., & Bradbury, A. (2008). *When elephants fight*. Hong Kong: Orca Books.

11

SOCIAL EQUITY TEACHING IN ACTION

My Community is My Classroom

Gwendolyn Thompson McMillon and
David Benjamin McMillon

> In order for the oppressed to be able to wage the struggle for their liberation, they must perceive the reality of oppression not as a closed world from which there is no exit, but as a limiting situation which they can transform.
>
> *(Freire, 1970, p. 31)*

The Midwestern neighborhood looked like many other neighborhoods invaded by "outsiders" when they decided to "upgrade" the area by building a highway in the middle of the community. Initially, there were two grocery stores, a laundromat, a drugstore, a record store, a movie theater, a swimming pool, a recreation center, four family-owned convenience stores (including one owned by a Hispanic family that sold freshly made taco bread), two beauty salons, a barbershop, a restaurant, and several churches in the community within a one-mile radius. But after the highway was finished, most of the downtown stores, which had been within walking distance, closed and moved to the suburban mall, and the self-sufficient community began to collapse, one business at a time. It was a common sequence of events—events that led to the emergence of a desolate inner-city area characterized by high crime rates, poverty, and failing schools.

It would be a travesty if the story ended here; fortunately, it did not. Several community advocates decided that liberation begins with the mindset presented by Freire in the introductory quote. Refusing to remain "oppressed," the community advocates decided to collaboratively transform their neighborhood. They realized that neighborhood children had nothing to do during the summer because they did not have transportation or enough money to get to parks, swimming pools, or recreation centers across town. Caring adult neighbors pooled community resources, bought and remodeled a vacant home across the street from the elementary school, and started a summer program for neighborhood children in what would be known as the Houghton-Jones Resource Center. These advocates included a minister, a city council member, a Catholic nun who chose to live in the inner-city neighborhood, and several parents.

The oppression in the neighborhood became the impetus for *All Around the Neighborhood*, an initiative plan consisting of many special projects housed in the neighborhood resource center, including a university-school collaborative literacy project on which I (Gwendolyn) served. The neighborhood resource center is located three blocks from my childhood home and two blocks from the church where my husband currently serves as pastor. I recruited my son David, the second author of this chapter, to become a student mentor and consultant on the project because of his success with science competitions and his willingness to share his experiences with younger students.

Similar to Friere's ideas, Lazar, Edwards, and McMillon (2012) discuss the need for teachers to understand the valuable ways that communities help children and families. They assert that there is a

> need for teachers to reexamine their assumptions about people who live in high-poverty communities to look beyond families' lack of economic capital, and to recognize the capital, strengths, or skills that are valued in local communities. To understand the struggles and recognize the varied forms of capital that exist in different high-poverty communities, teachers must position themselves as ethnographers and try to learn from those whom they wish to teach. (p. 27)

By asking teachers to "position themselves as ethnographers," Lazar et al. (2012) suggest that teachers seek to understand their students from an in-depth perspective. Teachers need to understand that what happens outside of the classroom may impact teaching and learning in their classrooms. Teachers need to investigate the ways in which students' out-of-school experiences affect their thinking, behavior, and quality of life. It is imperative that teachers understand the traditions, ways of communicating, and influential institutions of students and their families in order to effectively teach them (Heath, 1983; McMillon, 2001).

The site for this community literacy project was an impoverished Midwestern neighborhood where students were invited to participate in meaningful community activities. The teachers were participants of a larger six-year longitudinal study that included ninety-two teachers, administrators, and para-professionals from six elementary schools, two middle schools, and two K-8 schools, including a public school academy. The purpose of the broader six-year study was to improve literacy teaching and learning in urban schools, especially in the area of English language arts (ELA). Time constraints and changing curricular requirements during the academic year limited teachers' opportunities to implement new classroom strategies learned during the professional development sessions, and I realized that the teachers needed an opportunity to practice their strategies during the summer months. I met with Bakari McClendon, the executive director at the neighborhood resource center, to discuss the possibility of adding an academic component to the center's summer program. He was elated to incorporate our university-school literacy project into his summer program curriculum, and I was grateful to have children and a site for the teachers to implement and refine innovative instructional strategies that they learned during professional development sessions.

During the summer program described in this chapter, sixteen teachers from the literacy project improved their literacy teaching skills and spent their summer as ethnographers by becoming more familiar with students, learning about the neighborhood, and developing an understanding of the needs in the community. Moreover, teachers learned about the cultural capital offered by caring adults. The project included forty children: Thirty-two lived in the neighborhood, and eight were the children and grandchildren of teacher participants.

In this chapter, we examine the *Farm Stand Project*, an educational intervention born from the neighborhood initiative known as *All Around the Neighborhood*. The purpose of this chapter is to describe an educational intervention for children who live in a socioeconomically disadvantaged inner-city community. The chapter is structured as follows: First, we explain participatory cultures and multiliteracies, the conceptual lenses we use to frame our work. Next, we provide a brief overview of the *All Around the Neighborhood Farm Stand Project*, and we share specific information about the teachers who participated in the summer project. Then we highlight one participant's experiences on the *Farm Stand Project*. Finally, we discuss implications, and share ideas for developing similar community projects.

Participatory Cultures and Multiliteracies

Here, we discuss reciprocal learning and teaching using two theoretical frameworks: participatory cultures and multiliteracies. Jenkins (2006) defines participatory culture as:

> a culture with relatively low barriers to artistic expression and civic engagement, strong support for creating and sharing creations, and some type of informal mentorship whereby experienced participants pass along knowledge to novices. In a participatory culture, members also believe their contributions matter and feel some degree of social connection with one another (at the least, members care about others' opinions of what they have created). (p. xi)

Jenkins's forms of participatory cultures include affiliations, expressions, collaborative problem solving, and circulations. Affiliations are informal and formal memberships in online communities. Expressions are various representations that communicate a message, such as texts, art, and videos. Collaborative problem solving is teamwork that focuses on completing a task. Circulations are the ways in which information is disseminated.

Although participatory culture emphasizes digital literacy, its concepts are transferable to the discussion in this chapter concerning the acquisition and development of literacy skills that do not fit within traditional school subjects such as reading, writing, and arithmetic. Participatory cultures provide many benefits to participants. Specifically, students can learn school and workplace-valued skills, and they can develop a greater level of awareness concerning their responsibilities as citizens. One of the benefits of participatory cultures is that they bridge the gap between individualized ideas of digital learning and social learning by helping students develop important cultural competencies and social skills. Jenkins (2006) does not believe that schools are effectively teaching these competencies and skills. He asserts, "Schools as institutions have been slow to react to the emergence of this new participatory culture; the greatest opportunity for change is currently found in after-school programs and informal learning communities" (p. 14). More emphasis should be placed on literacies that focus on social skills that are authentically taught while students engage in collaboration and networking activities. These activities do not replace traditional forms of literacy (e.g., research, technical, and critical analysis skills), but use them as a foundation to build upon.

Similar to Jenkins's participatory cultures, a multiliteracies perspective emphasizes the various contexts in which literacy can be experienced, including community settings, social roles, interpersonal relations, and subject matter (Kalantzis & Cope, 2012). The learning that occurs in one setting can be utilized by participants across multiple settings. This perspective provides a rationale for placing great value on learning in out-of-school contexts. It also connects directly with Jenkins's participatory cultures' emphasis on collaboration and networking. Additionally, across these multiple contexts, meaning-making occurs through multimodal literacies, including written, visual, tactile, and oral expressions. Multimodal literacies move beyond reading and writing to include skills that prepare students for our changing world. Bearne (2009) also emphasizes the importance of examining the ways in which information is communicated and provides an example of multimodal literacies that prepare our students. She asserts that the switch from the page to the screen is a spatial dynamic that should be addressed in literacy teaching and learning. Students need to understand the organization of materials on pages and visual effects utilized in various representations, including communication sent via digital tools such as texting, Facebook, Twitter, Instagram, PowerPoint, and video recording, in addition to nondigital tools such as tri-fold boards, graphic organizers, and art.

Kalantzis and Cope provide an in-depth explanation of multiliteracies by discussing what they refer to as "old basics" and "new basics." They believe that "old basics" are the traditional forms of literacy and schooling that utilized specific bodies of knowledge, including a canonical set of materials that students learned and regurgitated when called upon to express their understanding. These old basics include the 3R's of reading, writing, and arithmetic; phonics rules; correct spelling and grammar; and a well-disciplined student. However, the "new basics" needed to matriculate in contemporary society include multiple literacies for a world of multimodal communications, many social languages, and variation in communication appropriate to settings; the kinds of people who can innovate, take risks, and negotiate diversity and uncertainty; a diverse range of texts, media, and text types; and people who can negotiate different human contexts and styles of communication. In contemporary society, students interface with numerous types of texts for multiple purposes; therefore, it is crucial that teachers understand that the traditional ways of teaching and learning are still important, but additional literacies must also be taught in order to effectively prepare students for the workplace and an improved quality of life.

Advocates from the Houghton-Jones neighborhood understood that students needed to learn "new basics" literacy skills. Our chapter shows how these community advocates and teachers collaboratively organized projects to meet the needs of students and families in their community.

All Around the Neighborhood Farm Stand Project

The *All Around the Neighborhood* initiative was developed over a period of several years. It began with a desire to provide recreational activities for children and families but eventually evolved into a program that met multiple needs in the community. For example, after much contemplation, the board of directors of the Houghton-Jones Resource Center decided to involve children in the development of a neighborhood garden. The area had become a food desert; the closest place to buy fresh fruit and vegetables was more than eight miles away. As is common in inner-city areas, obesity and other health problems were evident among neighborhood children and adults, and board members felt that a neighborhood garden could improve the quality of life in the community while teaching children valuable leadership and entrepreneurial skills.

Garden areas were chosen carefully, and Mr. Winbush, a senior citizen from the community, offered his tractors to clear and till the areas. The garden areas had to be cleaned up before planting could occur. Younger children helped by gathering up sticks and garbage, while older youth assisted with bagging and carrying loads of rubbish to a designated trash area. An artist became interested in the community project and helped students and volunteers draw a neighborhood mural of children and adults working in a community garden. (See Figure 11.1.)

One of the adult participants, Izetta, was the librarian assistant at the elementary school across the street from the area being prepared for the garden. She was hired to be the master gardener who would be responsible for managing gardening activities. Izetta took her job seriously; she understood the importance of teaching the students literacy skills and helping them develop a good work

FIGURE 11.1 Neighborhood Mural.

ethic. She had previously provided support for several students during science fair competitions, and when she learned about their lack of understanding of the scientific method, she incorporated this concept in her work with the children. She suggested that the children keep a journal of their daily garden activities. They followed the steps of the scientific method including making hypotheses concerning the growth of their plants.

Students conducted online research to identify the best types of plants to grow in their garden. They were allowed to plant in several spaces within a two-block radius. The gardens were located in two empty lots where houses had been torn down. They were also next to the highway that divided the neighborhood. Soil under old residential buildings and near highways is often contaminated with lead, zinc, and other chemicals. To cope with the soil contamination, the students used raised boxes for the crops, which allowed them to plant their garden above the ground in healthy soil. (See Figure 11.2.)

The Executive Director, Bakari McClendon, and board members contacted gardening stores in the area to request seed donations. They were elated that the stores willingly provided seeds for the community garden. Some seeds were free, and others were purchased at a discount. After Mr. Winbush and the students cleared and tilled the ground for a few weeks, the ground was ready for planting. Mr. Winbush constructed the boxes for the garden area and built a shed to store various gardening tools and materials. Additionally, he, along with other adults

FIGURE 11.2 Using Raised Boxes to Plant the Garden.

who were garden experts from the community, assisted the children with planting rows of tomatoes, peppers, beans, cucumbers, collards, cabbage, sweet potatoes, and squash.

Some of the students became impatient with the lengthy process. They began missing days and/or deciding to go home when it was time to work in the garden. Mrs. Cecil Reed, who was the treasurer of the board and a retired home economics teacher, decided it was time to reinforce the importance of having a good work ethic. Mr. Bakari McClendon and Mrs. Cecil Reed held a meeting to show students the entire vision for the neighborhood gardening project. This was an important step; students needed to take ownership in the project. Cecil created a "company" and divided the company into "shares." At the meeting, Bakari and Cecil explained how profit sharing would work. (See Figure 11.3.) Each shareholder had to participate in at least 51% of the designated activities sponsored by the center,

Name	Activities	Garden	Meetings	Market	Total
	15	30	10	15	70
Anna	10	22	8	10	50/ **$96.15**
Bill	5	19	8	10	42/ **$80.76**
John	8	28	7	8	51/ **$98.07**
Mary	7	26	9	7	49/ **$94.22**
Joe	3	15	6	12	36/ **$69.22**
Jenny	4	10	6	5	25
Tom	3	8	4	5	20
Total					273

FIGURE 11.3 Profit-Sharing Example That Was Shared during the Meeting.

which included club meetings and activities, work days, workshops, market days (e.g., harvesting, set-up/take down, sales), additional credits, and the Junior Master Gardener Program. The amount of their individual profits was determined after deducting expenses from revenue, and individual shares could not exceed 20% of the total profits.

Izetta, the master gardener responsible for managing gardening activities, created a chart with students' names. Every day the students checked in and out with Izetta to keep track of their work hours.

Interest and consistent work time increased exponentially; they began to take ownership, and they decided to give themselves a name. Students made suggestions for names. Then they voted for their favorite name, and "The Mighty Fresh Gardeners" won by a landslide. The students understood that products from the garden would be sold at the neighborhood garden stand during the months of August and September, and they would receive a return on their investment based on their number of shares.

Additional fruit and vegetables were purchased at a discount from the local farmer's market to increase the amount available to neighbors at the neighborhood stand. After harvesting, the students sold their produce. (See Figure 11.4.)

FIGURE 11.4 Preparing Produce at the Neighborhood Farm Stand.

At the end of the summer, the Houghton-Jones Resource Center sponsored a neighborhood festival with food, entertainment, and various vendors. One of the activities at the end of the Farm Stand Project was a science fair competition designed to engage student participants. Their projects were exhibited inside the center so the public could see their work, and awards were given during the festival. Kindergarten through second-grade students had class projects, while third- through eighth-grade students had individual projects. Each project entry included a data journal, a written report, an abstract that summarized the project for public viewers to take with them, an oral presentation, and a tri-fold board that identified each part of the scientific method. Judges for the projects were college students from the community who were math and science majors. Students were required to make oral presentations when the judges stopped at their station. Each judge completed a rubric that provided a score for oral presentations, the tri-fold board, written report, data journal, abstract, and the students' knowledge of their project based on their responses to questions from each judge. First-, second-, and third-place awards were given based on grade levels. Students also received awards for the best oral presentation, most creative tri-fold board, best-written report, and best data journal. In our next section, we describe the ways in which teachers positioned themselves as ethnographers to learn about their students and the community.

Teachers Learn That the Community Is Their Classroom

The initial purpose of the collaboration between the literacy project and the neighborhood summer program was to offer academic support to students and provide the sixteen teachers who worked on the summer project with an opportunity to practice and refine innovative instructional strategies without the distracting pressures they experience during the academic year. The project lasted ten weeks. I provided two weeks of training for the teachers. Then the teachers worked with the students for eight weeks. Academic sessions were Monday through Thursday from 9:00 A.M. to noon. They consisted of classroom sessions that included oral language development, reading, writing, and inquiry-based projects, followed by lunch from noon to 1:00 P.M. Each afternoon, students worked on the gardening project and participated in various recreational activities. Students and teachers also went on weekly field trips that included visiting a nature center and a hands-on science museum.

During afternoon sessions, we used a curriculum developed by the C.S. Mott Group for Sustainable Agriculture Systems to help the children learn about principles of gardening. In addition to reading and listening to lectures, the students also engaged in hands-on team-oriented activities, and they kept journals of their progress. All of the adults present during the summer project afternoon sessions, including teachers, representatives of the Mott Group, as well as Bakari, Cecil, Izetta, and other adult workers, focused on helping students learn about the importance of health and nutrition as well as gardening. Group activities helped students learn how to identify problems and utilize individual strengths to collaboratively solve problems. For example, one activity was for each student to write down what they ate for an entire day. Students were divided into groups, and they combined their meals to determine which group had the most healthy and unhealthy eating habits. They learned about the importance of making healthy food choices, and they became more aware of the connection between food choices and illnesses.

Keeping journals that included observational notes and drawings, students hypothesized what would happen, made observations, recorded data, analyzed the data, and wrote results. This process is an example of the ways in which "old basics" literacies still matter and should still be taught in addition to "new basic" literacies. Math, science, reading, and writing skills were taught and utilized during the project; however, team-building, collaborative problem solving, and other "new basics" were also addressed. Math, science, reading, and writing skills were important during the summer program, but collaboration and decision-making skills developed during the project were equally important. Students utilized both old and new basic skills to become more knowledgeable about health and nutrition, something that can improve their quality of life forever.

After about two weeks, we all realized that something miraculous was happening. Teachers were becoming familiar with the students in a different way. They learned about their neighborhood, who lived where, who could be trusted, and who needed to be watched. They learned who went on vacations and who had never gone anywhere beyond the city limits. Teachers developed special relationships with their students' parents, grandparents, siblings, and relatives who visited during the summer. Teachers became involved in the daily lives of their students. They began to understand the limitations of the environment where their students lived, but teachers also began to understand that their students had access to cultural capital in their neighborhood.

Students treated people like Sister Lois, a Catholic nun, as if she were a family member because she was always around. Students respected Mr. Winbush like a grandfather, because he took care of things for them and watched over them to ensure their safety. Teachers learned that the students knew how to use resources to help their families. For example, if extra snacks were available, the students asked to take snacks home to their younger siblings. Although they did not have much, most of the students had great compassion and tried to share with their loved ones.

Several teachers brought their children and grandchildren to the summer program. At the end of the program, they realized that their children and grandchildren learned from the students in the community gardening project. Their children became more appreciative of the sacrifices that their parents made for them, developed a greater understanding of the life of a teacher, and became more culturally competent because they spent the entire summer interacting with students from different backgrounds. Teachers and their children and grandchildren learned that an impoverished environment does not mean that students have limited mental capabilities.

During an interview at the end of the program, Mrs. Beyer, a first-grade teacher, stated:

> This summer I learned more about myself as a teacher and more about my students than all the years I've spent in the classroom. I can't wait for the school year to begin. My students will become awesome writers this year, because now I know how to teach them writing; and my confidence level is higher than ever. I know my students in a different way now. I know where they come from; I know what they do when they're not in school; I know what they're exposed to; and I even know what they are not exposed to. So now I can fill in those gaps. My students will be able to write from experiences, because I know how to talk to them about their experiences now, and I can teach them how to put it down on paper. This has been good for me. It was a big sacrifice, but I'm glad I did it. I worry about my students during the summer when I'm with my own kids, because I know my students don't get to go on vacations and stuff like that. This summer we stayed home and I brought my son James with me every day. He has matured so much! I know he's ready for school this year. He has a whole new attitude about school.

Although Mrs. Beyer had high expectations for her students before participating in the program, she realized that her relationship with her students was strengthened by spending time with them outside of the classroom and learning about their out-of-school experiences. The community became her classroom.

Mrs. Beyer used skills to gather information in ways similar to that of ethnographers, who locate themselves in the natural settings of others and observe daily phenomena to learn about a group of people. Teacher participants worked in the natural setting of the students and observed their daily lives. Based on Mrs. Beyer's comments, it is clear that teachers can improve instructional strategies in "old basic" skills such as writing by helping students utilize their "new basic" skills such as being able to communicate across contexts. In other words, teachers can help their students become better writers if they allow them to write about real-life experiences, rather than asking students to respond to writing prompts that are unrelated to their lifeworlds. For example, Mrs. Beyer stated that most of her students had never taken summer vacations; in fact, some of them had never been outside of the city limits. A writing prompt that asks students to write about their "best family vacation" would be inappropriate; however, a prompt that asks students to write about "a time when cooperation paid off" would be appropriate to ask any student.

Reflections on the Farm Stand Project through a Student's Eyes: Multiliteracies and Participatory Cultures in Action

Ashante Franklin is an eighth-grade student at Saint Lucious Preparatory Academy and the former Student President of the Farm Stand Project. He holds fond memories of the work he did three years ago. He recalls:

It wasn't so much about teaching us how to farm as teaching us how to be leaders. Team work was really important in order for us to get things done. So we learned how to share ideas and cooperate with other kids. The older kids had to take initiative to get things done. We were told we are only as strong as our weakest link, so we would show the younger kids what we learned. Then we were rewarded based on how much work we put in, just like in the real world.

Ashante's experiences clearly illustrate important aspects of participatory cultures and multiliteracies. Experienced fifth-grade participants learned how to pull weeds, till the soil, plant vegetables, and maintain the garden from adult mentors. They mentored novice third- and fourth-grade students and showed them everything they learned. Collaborative problem solving became the norm, and the children developed interpersonal skills by learning to settle disputes and work together to grow crops more efficiently. For example, the older students learned to be patient with the younger students. Some students were only allowed to gather and bag sticks, weeds, and trash, while others were responsible for watering and fertilizing the gardens. Everyone had to learn the importance of their individual contributions toward the collective success of the garden. Children were given profit shares based on how much time they worked in the garden and the number of activities in which they participated. Therefore, they learned workplace-valued skills and took more ownership in their responsibilities. Additionally, membership in The Mighty Fresh Gardeners Club emphasized the importance of affiliation. Students became more interested when they understood their personal value to the collective membership.

Besides scholastic achievement, Ashante has applied these principles on the basketball court. During a recent interview, he stated, "It's important that everyone on the team does his job. We're only as strong as our weakest link; just like in the Farm Stand Project. If there's any weakness in our formation, we all suffer." Ashante's team recently had an undefeated season. If he's not able to play basketball professionally, he intends to become a computer scientist/hacker for a government agency. As a participant in *All Around the Neighborhood*, he often heard adults emphasize the importance of having a Plan A and a Plan B, and based on the mature decision-making process that he currently uses to talk about his present experiences and future plans, it is apparent that he learned to transfer his multiliteracies and experiences.

Specific Ways to Implement Social Equity Teaching: A Call to Action

The neighborhood resource center provided a space that allowed students and teachers to connect in ways that benefited both. This space was a participatory culture that provided authentic opportunities to develop important literacy and life skills. These skills were multicontextual; they cut across community setting, social roles, interpersonal relations, and subject matter. They were also multimodal, including written, visual, tactile, and oral modes of communication. Additionally, the development of each skill was multileveled; students and teachers moved from novices to informed apprentices. The skills were multidirectional in that students and teachers learned from each other and engaged others in the community to assist with teaching and learning. Finally, the skills were also multigenerational; students, parents, grandparents, teachers, their children, and others in the community were members of the participatory culture at the neighborhood resource center.

The knowledge acquired by teachers during this time was valuable in their efforts to develop innovative teaching strategies for inner-city students. Additionally, student participants benefited by learning creative strategies from caring teachers who were passionate about their work. In this context, teaching and learning was reciprocal between students and teachers, and the community was their classroom.

We believe teachers need to make a special effort to implement social equity teaching in two very specific ways. First, assist with programs in the community where your students live. Teachers who spend time in their students' communities will learn about them from a deeper perspective. Similar to Mrs. Beyer, they will be able to identify the strengths of their students' environments and determine if there are gaps that they can fill that will help their students become better readers, writers, and thinkers. In other words, they will be able to better link students' out-of-school experiences and their in-school learning. By assisting in this way, teachers will help students acquire the ability to transfer knowledge from one context to another. Assisting with programs in the community will also improve home-school connections, because students and their parents will realize that the teacher has an invested interest in them. Teachers gained a new respect for the students in the project, and students also gained a new respect for teachers. As previously stated, teaching and learning were multidirectional.

Next, help students identify real problems and develop realistic solutions. It is vitally important that teachers help students learn the importance of getting involved in social justice activities. Community involvement can improve the quality of life for the entire community. The community advocates who cared about the children in the Houghton-Jones area have made a difference in the neighborhood for many years; however, the teachers did not get involved until the university-collaborative project was implemented. Teachers do not have to wait to be invited into the community. They can begin in their classroom by helping students identify a problem and working with them to develop a solution. For example, if students do not have computers at home, teachers can help organize "technology nights" for students. Parents can organize themselves and take groups of students to the public library once each week, or senior citizen mentors from the neighborhood may be willing to chaperone students. Also, some churches may have computers that are available for student use at certain times. If the public library is too far away, teachers might help students write letters to neighborhood churches and businesses to ask for computer access. The idea is that teachers must become more involved in the out-of-school lives of their students, especially students who need additional support. Involvement in out-of-school projects and activities can lead to improved academic achievement.

A famous Chinese proverb states: "If you give a man a fish, he will eat for a day, but if you teach him how to fish, he will eat for a lifetime." As teachers, it is our job to help students learn how to use their knowledge to improve their quality of life. The highest form of social equity teaching is helping students learn to help themselves. While teaching old and new basics skills, we must remember that education cannot be the great equalizer unless we teach students how to improve their own quality of life. In other words, teachers must help students and their families acquire knowledge and skills needed to liberate themselves. This process is most effectively realized when teachers understand that they are not bound by the four walls of the classroom of their school, but that the community is their classroom.

Authors' Note

We gratefully acknowledge Dow Corning Foundation, Dow Chemical Foundation, and the Michigan Department of Education—Improving Teacher Quality Grant as funding sources for this project.

References

Bearne, E. (2009). Multimodality, literacy and text: Developing a discourse. *Journal of Early Childhood Literacy*, 9(2), 156–187.

Freire, P. (1970). *Pedagogy of the oppressed*. New York, NY: Herder and Herder.

Heath, S. B. (1983). *Ways with words: Life and work in communities and classrooms*. Cambridge, UK: Cambridge University Press.

Jenkins, H. (2006). *Convergence culture: Where old and new media collide*. New York, NY: New York University Press.

Kalantzis, M., & Cope, B. (2012). *Literacies*. Cambridge, UK: Cambridge University Press.

Lazar, A. M., Edwards, P. A., & McMillon, G. M. T. (2012). *Bridging literacy and equity: The essential guide to social equity teaching*. New York, NY: Teachers College Press.

McMillon, G. M. T. (2001). *A tale of two settings: African American students' literacy experiences at church and at school*. Unpublished dissertation.

12

TRANSFORMING LOCKED DOORS

Using Multiliteracies to Recontextualize Identities and Learning for Youth Living on the Margins

Sean Turner

They hear me, but they don't listen / They see,
But they see through me / They never speak to me,
But down at me / They don't understand so they fear,
They hate/ I don't blame them / I don't blame them
Because it's our fault / We rob stores whenever
The income comes in shorthanded / Because
We're used to having everything handed to us.
If one hand cleans the other & both clean the face,
We're not short of hands / only in need of a clean one.
When the status quo ain't met we take / Burn hate
Into those we take from with bullets / Disguise our fears
And insecurities with black ski masks & Steal away dreams
& Hope & Faith / As we run with cash. Engraving just another
Footprint on the pavement / Like the seasons, the cycles repeated
Over, over, over, over & over again / But fuck it right, isn't that what everyone
says / Can't blame them /See we the ones snatching purses
Not caring how bad they might be doing / Couldn't make it in life
Because they ain't graduate school, no jobs, starving from the addictions that strips
their youth / We steal from the ones who told us to go to school
& get a job & do good & don't ever do drugs / I don't blame them / They see us as
what we appear to be / What for some reason
We imagine ourselves to be.

I open my chapter with a vignette written from the perspective of a 15-year-old male named Tek (pseudonym), who paints the vicious cycle of urban decay and its impact on youth at risk of failure. While the context of the monologue is situated around the dreams and thoughts of an incarcerated youth, Tek's perspective highlights the complexities that exist between youth living on the margins and mainstream society. This chapter provides a picture of the possibilities for teachers who wish to close this gap. Drawing on a multiliteracies conceptual framework, I provide a portrait of ways to shape a critical learning space in which the histories of youth living on the margins can be recontexualized and reimagined.

Taking on the Challenge

Over the course of one year, a group of six teachers working in a secure detention center that housed pre-adjudicated youth, ages 9 to 17, decided to take on a challenge and explore ways in which a new pedagogy for student identity and learning could be implemented within the classroom. The teachers who took part in the planning of these activities were certified in special education, English, and social studies but wanted to look specifically at ways in which the arts and technology could change the landscape that situated most of their students as antisocial, illiterate, or unmotivated. This was particularly significant for teachers and school administrators, as school data indicated the majority of the population was highly transitional, with over half reading below a fourth-grade level, being diagnosed with a mental disorder, and having experienced some form of past academic failure (Turner, McKenna, Scott, & Birzin, 2007; Turner & Scott, 2007).

At the time of this project, I was Director of Literacy Programs at the detention center and in the process of completing research for my doctoral degree. The teachers met with me once a week to reflect, discuss, and plan different activities and programs around the use of art and technology. Our initial work was centered on situating Shakespeare's *Hamlet* and Suzan Lori Park's *Top Dog Underdog* within multimedia adaptations of both narratives. The initial productions were well received by students as well as school and jail administrators and led to the development of a comprehensive eight-week summer performing and visual arts program. The structure of the summer program allowed incarcerated youth to share their insight and perspectives about the struggles of urban youth by writing original plays about their own struggles and then producing and performing those plays within a multimodal theatrical production entitled *Through Our Eyes*.

The design and production activities situated within the summer program were shaped by different pedagogical stances made by these teachers over the course of the year. These stances are illuminated within Video 12.1, entitled *History of the g*. Within this digital narrative, the teachers posit two motivating factors for student learning, even among those who identified as a "gangsta" or a "g": "everyone want(ed) to be heard" and "everyone want(ed) history to remember them." The teachers elaborate further on the importance of these factors by arguing that the literacy process can be redefined, reestablishing the students' own sense of inertia when they interact with text, allowing their stories to write new histories. The factors are exemplified in the following stance taken by the teachers:

> If we were to compare the enormity of text to the vast expanse of the universe, we could view both as the constant colliding and toppling of an infinite number of objects struggling to exist in an ever changing history of context. Therefore, when a text collides with a student, the text appears as an object in a new context and must adapt and evolve to survive in the new perspective so that the appropriation of this text by a student rearranges a moment in the universe.

According to the teachers, there were four critical principles involved within this process:

- Teachers and students were expected to work collectively wherein everyone in the room was looked upon equally and lines of hierarchy between teacher and student were blurred.
- A safe space to create must be developed so that everyone was viewed as a creator and could do their utmost with expressing a greater sense of self.
- Students should design a framework where insights into their battles would be produced and distributed.
- Students should take ownership over the means of production and must be given multimodal tools necessary to enact their creative vision.

These principles provided a framework in which the teachers and I would discuss how elements of multimodality could be incorporated into the curriculum during our weekly meetings. Over the course of the year, the teachers discussed connections between their own work and the dialogic and collaborative construction of knowledge, inquiry based learning, guided participation, and multimodal consumption and production of text. According to Bailey (2012), this type of positioning and dialogue is important as "how, specifically, teachers should teach new literacies is not entirely clear" (p.44).

Video 12.1: *History of the g.*
Note: To view video, insert the following link into an Internet browser.
https://vimeo.com/85150358

A Transforming Narrative

In my chapter, I narrate the stories of one teacher, Michael, and three students, Lucky, LA, and Homicide, who participated in three events around the design and production of a theatrical set (all names are pseudonyms). Within this narrative, I highlight the possibilities for multimodal design and production activities to lead to social diversity through notions of hypertexuality and interactivity, as illustrated within the recontextualization of student-written plays and the identities of youth who participated in the activities, as well as the classroom spaces in which the activities occurred.

I compose my narrative in three ways. First, I focus on each of the three events as I highlight the purpose of different activities involved and what types of knowledge were recontextualized within each. Second, I use notions of hyper-textuality and interactivity to discuss the intersection of all three events and in particular how the plays, student identity, and classroom spaces were recontextualized through the design and production of a hypervisual set. Third, I discuss the implications for teachers who wish to shape a critical learning space that fosters social diversity.

Introducing Michael, Lucky, LA, and Homicide

At the time that this work was implemented, Michael was a white 24-year-old second-year special education teacher, who, in his spare time, also enjoyed being a visual artist and painter. Lucky was a lean 14-year-old African-American male, who read at a fifth-grade level and had been retained one year in seventh grade. LA was a 13-year-old Haitian male who had been retained for two straight years due to ongoing attendance programs and failure to meet promotional criteria. Homicide was a 16-year-old African-American male. He read at a fourth-grade level and had not earned any high school credits despite being in high school for two years.

Michael lead the activities around the design and production of the theatrical set in part because he had taken a leading role in the earlier adaptations of *Hamlet* and *Top Dog Underdog* as well as the weekly teacher discussions around how to integrate art and technology into the classroom. As a result, Michael's approach to his own artwork influenced some of the pedagogical underpinnings of the design/layout of the summer performing and visual arts program. Although Michael had never received any formal art training, his work intertwined symbols of pop culture, religion, philosophy, politics, and history into his visual narratives as a means for social critique and change.

Through Our Eyes

The production *Through Our Eyes* was based on five student-written plays. Revolving around real experiences of incarcerated youth, the themes of death, poverty, hustling, and abuse were prominent. Students used elements of symbolic expression, resistance, and reversal to develop figurative worlds whereby the hero of each play, in spite of his good intentions, makes a tragic error leading to a reversal of fortune (events out of his control). Below, I provide a brief description of each play.

In *Mega/August*, the main character, August, attempts to save his younger brother, Mega, from selling drugs. Mega does not listen and eventually becomes wanted by the police. In order to save Mega from a parole violation, August tells the police that he sold the drugs and is arrested. While in jail, August becomes an official gangster, while his brother gives up hustling and starts to go to school.

The second play, *Mexico/Brooklyn*, portrays two teenagers, one from Mexico and the other from Brooklyn, who take turns narrating their own personal experiences as they wrestle with the poverty, death, and hustling that lead to incarceration.

In *Mommy Dearest*—the title borrowed from the motion picture about the actress Joan Crawford—a young girl named Monique recalls life events that led to her being put into a foster home, including being raped by her mother's boyfriend who was a drug dealer and pimp, and her mother selling and using crack.

Within *Birds of a Feather*, Miguel, a main character in the play, confronts Pops, his abusive father, and events within his life that tore his family apart and led him to become a gang member.

The fifth play, *Oranges*, portrays a 15-year-old boy named James who is seduced by money and power offered by a character named Fear. Oranges, a metaphor for crack, is what James enjoys selling, especially the rewards. Much too late, however, he realizes the consequences of his actions.

Incarcerated Youths' Multimodal Composing Events

Event One

During preproduction activities, students read and discussed each of the five chosen plays and then drew pictures on sheets of white paper that represented either lines, scenes, or what they thought each of the plays meant. LA shared his thoughts about this process:

> First we drew pictures for each line of the play and then [as we were drawing] we would discuss the plays. Michael told us to visualize what we thought the play represented. That's where we brought up a lot of ideas about pictures and what we thought the play meant. Like if we read it [a play] and it tell us about selling drugs, then we drew about selling drugs.

While the activities situated around Event One lasted only one week, Michael and the students proposed them as being part of a larger event tied to the production of the set. Lucky expanded on this by describing how the process of "drawing all the pictures" included multiple social actors (i.e., teachers, artists, incarcerated youth) and multiple social practices (i.e., reading the script, acting out parts, recording scenes, drawing pictures, and discussing the play) for the purpose of making background scenes "that were used as another set":

I had to draw little background pictures because we knew we were going to have the door and a big picture on it and little background scenes, stapled little parts of my play. I remember the whole play. So like that's another set, drawing all the pictures for the background.

And then I would meet—me and LA, 'Marvin' (pseudonym) on the recorder—in Marvin's room. We would play all the lines. I did Mega, and LA—August did August. And after that, LA and other kids drew the pictures in Michael's room.

In comparison to how a teacher might traditionally approach the analysis of a play within her or his class, such as using close reading strategies to identify literary devices or theatrical conventions, both reflections highlight ways in which students and their teachers interacted and in effect analyzed text through their collective work and use of multimodal tools to visualize and construct meanings of texts.

Within the drawings produced, recontextualizations took place in the following ways: The plays characters were abstracted as semiotic images, representing a shift from an emphasis on dialogue to an emphasis on the visual. Behavior and mental reactions were depicted more than the verbal actions. The chronological sequence of events found within the plays was disrupted at times, placing a larger emphasis on the actual settings.

Examples of these are illustrated within Video 12.2, a montage of 28 different scenes from the five plays. While all of the scenes use semiotic images to represent social actors and actions, scenes 13, 17, 18, 19, 23, and 25 include dialogue and scenes 1–9, 12, 13, 20, and 21–24 include words and phrases that label the social actors. Scene 19 uses a concrete image of a broom as a symbol of the main characters of *Birds of a Feather* sweeping floors within a jail and also as a metaphor for being able to sweep away one's problems. Scene 4 depicts a contrast between the good and bad sides of the main character in the play *Mega/August* and in the process attempts to disrupt the chronological order of events taking place in the play. Scene 2, also from the play *Mega/August*, shows the action of the scene outside a crack house although there is no explicit reference to a crack house within the play.

Video 12.2: Video depicting drawings made during event one.
Note: To view video, insert the following link into an Internet browser.
https://vimeo.com/48375244

These examples were particularly significant to the students and Michael as they believed that this event allowed them not only to make personal connections to the scenes, but also to add details from their own lives into the narratives. This was exemplified in scene 12, which compares life and death through the semiotic representations of a funeral home and a bodega. Within the scene, LA associates himself with the main character through the action of passing money, while life is represented within the line "we is cool." LA shed light on this by noting how he drew himself within the action of the scene: "We started doing a lot of pictures. And like when it tell us about, like, basketball, anything, we did it [drew pictures]. Or when they were selling drugs, we drew when we was selling drugs."

Event Two

Within the second event, student groups worked with Michael, LA, and Lucky on the design and production of five doors, each depicting one of the five plays. According to Michael, the overarching idea behind the design and production of the doors "was to have students deconstruct symbols from the play and turn them [symbols] on their heads." Michael's idea followed a basic principle of multimodality, which is that meanings are made, distributed, received, interpreted, and remade in interpretation through many representational and communicative modes—not just through language—whether as speech or as writing (Burn, 2008; Jewitt & Kress, 2003; Kress, 2003; Kress & van Leeuwen, 2001). Further, the notion of multimodality has often been used to denote the hypertextualization of representation, also known as recontextualization (Bernstein, 1990, as cited in van Leeuwen, 2008, p. vii). Below, I offer examples of what these principles looked like in the second event.

First, students took the drawings representing each of the plays and pasted them to the door that would be used to represent a specific play. Then students discussed with Michael what they thought the characters were trying to say and what they thought the play meant and came up with ideas to draw and paint on top of the pictures. In some instances, the students came up with ideas; Michael drew an outline and then colored the picture using paintbrushes. In other instances, students worked with Lucky and LA and gave each other ideas and then drew parts on their own if they thought they could draw. Lucky notes, "Me and Homicide were sitting and reading scripts, and just for some reason, I saw a part, where I thought I could draw it, and Homicide say a part he thought he could draw it, and so we just drew it and helped [another student] out on his door."

These activities were situated within a safe classroom space where everyone was viewed as a creator and could express himself while continuing to work on the design and production of the set. Lucky explicated this process by stating:

> The paintings of the door relate to the plays because ... when we read it, we think what the character is trying to say. How he feel? Like you know, how he act? How his face would look? Like this picture [points to the door representing the play *Mommy Dearest*] everyone know how crackheads are. They always want to smoke crack 24-7. That's why we draw the missing tooth. And crackheads always laugh. They scratch their heads. And all that. (See Figure 12.1.)

FIGURE 12.1 Picture of Door Representing *Mommy Dearest*.

The notion of using symbols to represent critical views and perspectives of the plays was also supported by LA, who noted:

> We drew funny faces to show you how he looked … like this one [points to the door representing the play *Birds of a Feather*]. His tongue is always out.

And has a bottle in his hand. Because he was always thirsty to drink—you know liquor. He's got little things on top of his head because he is like the devil. When people get drunk, they don't know what is going on. (See Figure 12.2.)

FIGURE 12.2 Picture of Door Representing *Birds of a Feather*.

Lucky and LA's reflections show how the action sequence, or social practices that were used within the design and production of doors, were connected to the comprehension, critique, and production of the plays. Their reflections support the idea that the design and production of the doors were part of a literacy event, as the processes involved are consistent with Heath's (1983) definition of an event being "any action sequence, involving one or more persons, in which the production and/or comprehension of print plays a role" (p. 386). It is also consistent with Kress (2003), who notes when events occur, understanding is first communicated through speech and then through a framework of multimodal design, where the active consciousness is both stimulated and expressed.

Within the design and production of the doors, knowledge about the plays was recontextualized in the following ways: First, compositions of symbolic and contradictory images depicting the overarching hostilities between the protagonist and antagonist of each play were painted on the front of each door. The teeth and belly of a pregnant woman are used in the door representing *Mommy Dearest* and symbolize the affect of drug use upon both a mother and her child. Ribs are depicted within the door representing *Birds of a Feather* and symbolize the effect of physical abuse, and a serpent is used as a paradoxical combination of wisdom and evil within the door representing the play *Oranges*. In Video 12.3, a montage of pictures and video footage of the five doors made during event two are exhibited.

Second, each playwright is objectified and abstracted on the back of each door (Video 12.3). Michael provides insight: "Drawings on the front of the doors were represented as being in the head of the writer, and his memories no longer controlled his reality." This concept was illustrated primarily through exposing the drawings that were pasted underneath the paintings within the open head of a stick figure, or as Lucky-August said, "the mind of the whole play." This was embellished through the abstraction of the figures having full bodies frozen in a state of dance as well as having each figure hold an instrument that represented the antagonist from their play. The latter showed that the social figure had become powerful and had control over the antagonist.

Video 12.3: A montage of pictures and video footage of the five doors made during event two.
Note: To view video, insert the following link into an Internet browser.
https://vimeo.com/46199752

Event Three

The third event comprises five activities that were simultaneously taking place while the doors were being produced. For activity one, students were working with Michael to build columns made from 330 cardboard boxes and which ranged from 4 feet to 14 feet in height. Activity two consisted of students working with Michael and Homicide to paint the outside of different buildings, including two housing development projects, a bodega, a jail, a courthouse, and a liquor store. Each building was depicted through sketches and paintings on sheets of brown roll paper that would be placed on the columns of cardboard boxes. Activity three entailed students working to paint brick walls on sheets of styrofoam. The brick walls were to be used as bookends on a mural that was suspended above the set. Activity four was situated around the painting of a 40-foot mural depicting the transcendence of past, present, and future incarcerated youth, and activity five involved assembling different parts of the set in the gymnasium.

Within event three, changes in knowledge took place through what Kress (2003) notes as a shift of semiotic material across modes—where new resources are produced out of existing resources. The five simultaneous activities are represented through what Kress (2003) calls the matter of materiality, wherein affordances of media, and in particular new media, allow for both notions of interactivity and hypertextuality to transpire. The interactivity of new media allowed the students to "write back to the producer of a text with no difficulty" and in turn directly to effect the social power of the user while developing new texts (Kress, 2003, p. 5).

The different activities that I described above allowed students to perform a range of literacy skills, including reading scale drawings, analyzing plays for given circumstances, and engaging in discussions around design concepts, drawing scenes, painting, measuring, cutting, pasting, gluing, taping, and assembling. In the following reflection, Homicide explained how these activities overlapped:

> First, we took the boxes and put glue on them, stacked them together, then put tape on them to preserve in one pile (column). Then we would paint scenes on paper. Painting in like the window, making sketches, drawing, and then filling in the boxes for the projects. Sometimes we would paint other things that we thought should be added, like the NYPD, parking pictures, and FDNY. Sometimes we discussed what we thought you would see in the windows: Guy working out. Someone coming out of the shower. Then we would paint more windows. Then we continued to put the boxes together and tape them.

Homicide's reflection conveys both the overlap of the different activities as well as how students made connections between the given circumstances of the play and their own lifeworlds. The former was further explicated by Homicide, who noted that in one of the projects, he drew the "house where they said a character use to live and where his mother died" and made it look like "every time it rain, water would go through it, just like the play said." The latter was supported by Michael, who when asked by Homicide what should be painted inside the windows of the projects, told him "to imagine what you would see in the projects and draw that." Within such a process, students were able to infuse images that were symbolic of their own lifeworlds into the given circumstances of the play.

Although it appeared that some of the activities such as cutting, pasting, and gluing boxes together were mundane, it was clear that student investment increased through embodied social practices. Homicide's reflection supports this assertion as he noted:

> When I first started painting, I just did it to just make time pass [while in jail]. First, I put away materials, measured paper, taped down the brown paper to the wall, and painted on the doors. Then I realized how serious this was, and Michael gave me a chance to be a leader. At first, I thought this was just because I was one of the few people who could draw. Then I saw that it was because people believed in me. After that, I made sure that everything was done right, the boxes, the painting, drawings, everything. And Michael kept giving me more important things to do. For a thug like me, all I be doing is smoking weed and get money and be on the streets. Now I was doing something that I was proud of. Nobody had ever given me that chance before.

Event three allowed for a larger number of students to participate in different activities situated around the creation of media-based texts that were going to be used as part of a theatrical set and gave students multiple opportunities to recontextualize text of the plays as well as gain a sense that they were taking part in something bigger. Michael elaborates on this further:

> The last couple of weeks were really intense. Everything that was taking place was about the play. Kids knew that they were part of something big and everyone in the jail was begging to come to school to be part of it. We probably had over 100 students each day doing one or more activities. You had LA and Lucky supervising a few kids working on the doors. You had different groups of kids working on the mural, others working painting different scenes. I think every classroom on the school floor had five or six kids working on different parts of the set at the same time. Even the guards who usually just sit and watch us were getting involved. What was crazy was that no one really had any idea what everything would look like when it was all put together in the gym—they just knew that they were taking part of something really important and that their work was going to be part of the final production.

Hypervisual

While the three events delineated separate practices around the design and production of a set, it was the affordance of hypertextuality that allowed the different media texts created within each event to interact as part of one larger hypervisual set or a "multiplicity of semiotic resources" (Kress, 2003, p. 5). Below, I provide a brief description of how the functionality and redistribution of semiotic resources allowed the individual media-based texts created in the first three events to take on new meaning when they were situated within one larger, hypervisual set.

The functionality of the set is represented in Video 12.4, which shows five doors created from event two being rolled onto the stage and rotated from front to back in front of the various buildings created from event three. Initially, the doors served as a metaphor linking the worlds of incarcerated youth, realized by a door being rolled on stage before the play began, and then placed upstage on the platforms. As such, the door served as a window between inside jail (audience) and outside jail (buildings of the set).

> Video 12.4: Video footage of the completed set: Scale drawings, pan of set, doors, and mural.
> *Note: To view video, insert the following link into an Internet browser.*
> https://vimeo.com/48381413

The redistribution of media texts is represented in a comparison of Figures 12.3 and 12.4. Within Figure 12.3, the components of the set, including the mural, scrim (lightweight cloth used for theatrical special effects), doors, platforms, boxes, painted scenes of a jail, cardboard boxes representing buildings, etc., are situated as parts of a theatrical set all while within the gymnasium of a jail. Figure 12.4 reveals an implosion of these individual components through the distribution of electricity,

FIGURE 12.3 Individual Parts of the Set within the Jail's Gymnasium.

FIGURE 12.4 The Set Becomes Hypervisual through the Multiplicity of Semiotic Resources.

light, and digital media. The picture shows the actor on stage as no longer situated within a jail, but transformed within the electric distribution of the hypervisual.

Student Identity

During the design and production activities, over one hundred students completed journal entries (N=514). Within these entries, social practices associated with design and production of the set were validated in 71% (N=359) of journal entries, while the construction of purpose around the activities were represented in 51% (N=262). Through their abstractions of learning and school, students illustrated examples of validation. For instance, within many journal entries, students used phrases such as "I learned something new today" or "This was something I never experienced before." Students placed value on the activities in which they participated using statements such as "I liked painting the doors" or "Today was really cool." In other instances, students wrote about school from a positive perspective. Examples from their journals include statements such as "School was fun," "I look forward to coming to school," or "I work hard today at school." Students' statements about their teachers such as "The teachers were helpful" or "The teachers were good" also supported the notion that learning and school were of some benefit. Additionally, students offered positive associations about other students, as in "I worked with ..." or "We built boxes."

Examples of construction of purpose were situated around the belief that students were involved in something significant. This finding was supported by students nominating themselves as leaders (N=103), writers (N=68), painters (N=62), and performers (N=78), who all had the autonomy to assist others by showing people alternative behaviors acceptable to society so that they would not end up "in jail or even worse dead." Students' construction of purpose conveys that they believed that the stories being told were important and could help others enact change. This assertion supports van Leeuwen's (2008) view that validation is "conveyed through narratives whose outcomes reward legitimate actions and punish nonlegitimate actions" (p. 106).

For students such as Lucky, LA, and Homicide, this legitimization allowed for a shift in social power to take place during the summer program. For example, all three students had long histories of school failure and experiences that mirrored the struggles of the protagonists within the plays, including identifying themselves as prisoners, hustlers, fiends, and gang members. By the time the production was completed, it was clear that all three students had undergone identity transformations. For example, at the end of the summer, Lucky nominated himself as a writer, lead dancer, and painter and saw his participation in the production as a means for "letting everybody know jail is not the place to go." LA nominated himself as a lead painter, actor, and writer who wanted "to continue to write and tell stories to show people the way it is," including helping "Blacks and Hispanics change their ways, and stop robbing and killing each other." Likewise, Homicide nominated himself as an artist and actor and "learned that if you put your mind to something that you can accomplish anything and make great paths for yourself."

Classroom

Within all three events, a sense of community was created and shared by students and teachers wherein the lifeworlds of marginalized youth, including non-sanctioned social practices, were valued within the classroom and included within the design and production of the set. The following classroom observation was included in a journal reflection by Homicide, where he discussed how activities in the classroom included non-sanctioned social practices, such as talking about "gang shit" or "rocking new fresh chicks," and were incorporated within the shared sense of purpose that Michael and the other students had, while embodying social practices such as painting, drawing, working on billboards, and supervising others:

> Five kids painting, one drawing on paper. Michael working on billboards supervising everything. One kid is working for the first time in his whole life. Michael's rocking new fresh chicks. ['Russ' (pseudonym)] is taking attendance. ['Derrick' (pseudonym)] just looks dumb, but he's working.

Kids are farting. Other kids are talking a bunch of gang shit. Michael joins in. But it is cool, as the plays are all about gang stuff anyways. [Kids are] drawing drips on the doors. Not a drop falls on the floor all day.

The classroom observation supports the notion that non-sanctioned social practices that were an integral part of the identities of marginalized youth can be incorporated within sanctioned learning activities. LA's comment supports this perspective as he noted that the dialogue around gangs "helped influence the paintings, as the plays were about gang stuff anyways." Further, Homicide acknowledges, "Most of the time we were painting we would just talk about stuff going on in our lives, like whatever was happening on the [dorm] halls, girls, what we hoped to be doing when we got out [of prison]."

The social arrangement and functionality of classroom space was recontextualized to become meaningful, purposeful, and a place of value to the students. This change in perspective is a result of the social semiotic representation of the social practices of the community. Video 12.5 provides a montage of different pictures of what the classrooms looked like before and during the six weeks of design and production. The pictures depicting design and production activities show a redistribution of power within the spatial reconfiguration of the classroom as well as the potential for the semiotic power of the mediums used within the production to reshape the form of the classroom. Within this context, the space becomes shaped as an extension of the hypertextual relationship between the different mediums and the legitimate use and purpose around the form and content of the recontexualization of the plays.

Video 12.5: Montage of pictures of the recontextualization of a literacy classroom.
Note: To view video, insert the following link into an Internet browser.
https://vimeo.com/46200777

In addition, it is important to note that this reshaping of the classroom aesthetic was influenced by the creation and legitimization of a shared sense of community that valued the lifeworlds of incarcerated youth and integrated the resources of school and society for the purpose of design and production of new texts. Video 12.5 (images 8–15) shows semiotic representations of student identities, including gang literacy. That is, non-sanctioned literacy practices were shown as being integrated into recontextualizing space that was used in the production of these texts. The transformations represented a process of deconstructing the value stances of the primary discourses that had shaped the identities of the incarcerated youth in this project, including their lifeworlds and mainstream society.

What Have We Learned?

In my chapter, I have highlighted the possibilities for multimodal design and production activities that lead to social diversity through notions of hypertextuality and interactivity, as illustrated within the recontextualization of student-written plays, the identities of the youth who participated in the activities, as well as the classroom spaces in which the activities occurred. The events portrayed in this chapter show that the question at stake does not ask whether marginalized students are willing to participate in such spaces that lead to transformation and social change. Clearly within this program, incarcerated youth were motivated to participate in activities that were meaningful and purposeful to their lives. Rather, the larger question being asked is whether educational stakeholders of marginalized youth are willing to support such types of learning and be open to thinking differently about the possibilities of their students' multiliteracies. Within such a context, this project offers the following for future consideration.

First, the relationship between youth living on the margins and their teachers was reshaped through their collective effort within an affinity space. Instead of LA, Lucky, and Homicide being perceived as antisocial, delinquent, unmotivated, or academically deficient, they were situated as working in consonance with teachers, collaborating and problem-solving around the design and production of media-based texts used in a hypervisual theatrical set. The underlying principle of this effort was that the meaning of the collective was created from the meanings and talent of individuals. Within such a context, every student, regardless of background, academic deficit or behavior disorder, every student contributed to and had a shared purpose in the design and production of the final product.

Second, the result of this collective effort led to the histories of incarcerated youth being rewritten and futures reimagined within the design and production of media-based texts. The mutliliteracies of these youth were valued and used to shape both a critically reflective performative space and works of art. The students' literacy practices offer a strong counterperspective and the potential for open dialogue. The circumstances suggest that leadership and teaching will transform students' lives and open up possibilities for future teachers to consider how the multimodal design and production of media-based texts should not only be situated within their classrooms, but also used by their students to think about themselves and the world in which they live.

Below are some principles drawn from what we learned by working with Michael, Lucky, Homicide, and LA. You may find these ideas helpful in designing your own instruction that addresses the mutliliteracies and needs of students living on the margins:

- Situate your classroom as a safe space for students. Within such a context, students should be allowed to choose the multimodal tools they want to work with and to express themselves without fear of judgment.
- Develop and support a felt or embodied sense of purpose and ownership around design and production activities. Within such a context, the collective effort of every person in the class, including the teacher, should be valued and tied to a final product or production that is shared with others.

- Learning should be situated around the repackaging and recontexualizing of texts. Within such a context, as texts are reproduced, knowledge will increase, shedding new light on student perspectives of themselves and the worlds in which they live.
- Be flexible and open to ideas from students. By doing so, you will be participating in critical dialogue with them.

References

Bailey, N. M. (2012). The importance of a new literacies stance in teaching English language arts. In S. M. Miller & M. B. McVee (Eds.), *Multimodal composing in classrooms: Learning and teaching for the digital world* (pp. 44–62). New York, NY: Routledge.

Bernstein, B. (1990). *The structuring of pedagogic discourse*. London, UK: Routledge.

Burn, A. (2008). The case of rebellion: Researching multimodal texts. In J. Coiro, M. Knobel, C. Lankshear, & D. Leu (Eds.), *Handbook of research on new literacies* (pp. 151–178). New York, NY: Lawrence Erlbaum Associates.

Heath, S. B. (1983). *Ways with words*. Cambridge, UK: Cambridge University Press.

Jewitt, C., & Kress, G. (Eds.). (2003). *Multimodal literacy*. New York, NY: Peter Lang.

Kress, G. (2003). *Literacy in the new media age*. London, UK: Routledge.

Kress, G. & van Leeuwen, T. (2001). *Multimodal discourse: The modes and media of contemporary communication*. London, UK: Arnold.

Turner, S., McKenna, T., Scott, J., & Birzin, E. (2007, May 2). *Exploring professional learning communities across alternative spaces: An action research project examining literacy within GED and incarcerated programs in New York City*. Paper presented at the New York State Association of Incarcerated Education Programs Conference. Saratoga Springs, NY.

Turner, S., & Scott, J. (2007, February 12). *Exploring literacy within a three-tier approach to instruction: A statistical analysis of literacy gains for pre-adjudicated youth in New York City*. Paper presented at the New Jersey State Association of Incarcerated Education Programs Conference. Seawall, NJ.

van Leeuwen, T. (2008). *Discourse and practice: New tools for critical discourse analysis (Oxford studies in sociolinquistics)*. New York, NY: Oxford University Press.

13

"THAT TEACHER JUST USES HER MOUTH"

Inviting Linguistically Diverse Students to Learn

Zaline M. Roy-Campbell

> One day, while I was talking with 11th grader Afron about her failing science grade on her report card, she asserted, "That teacher she just uses her mouth." Afron observed that unlike her other teachers, the science teacher did not write anything on the board.

I begin my chapter with this comment because I recognize it as an indication of how numerous English learners (ELs) experience language overload when sitting in subject-specific classrooms. Afron was born in a refugee camp in Kenya and entered third grade when she arrived in the United States. I started mentoring Afron when she entered ninth grade; I had previously mentored her sister, Mumina, when she was in tenth and eleventh grades (Roy-Campbell, 2012). At the time I began mentoring Afron, she was no longer receiving English language support services. In my interactions with her, however, I found that she continued to struggle with her English language skills. Mumina entered fifth grade when she arrived in the United States and continued to receive English language support services into her junior year in high school. In New York State where they attended school, the stipulation is that students designated as English learners can receive English language support services up to six years. During the time that I mentored the sisters, I visited them weekly to see how they were doing and to check up on their schoolwork.

In my chapter, I contextualize Afron's and Mumina's experiences as a case to highlight challenges some ELs encounter in teacher-centered classrooms. I consider alternative ways teachers can communicate with and teach linguistically diverse students to actively include them in the learning process, and I draw on research literature to illustrate the affordances a multiliteracies approach offers in this respect. My impetus to center my chapter on the two sisters' experiences emanates from comments they made that manifested the frustration they were experiencing in some of their classes. Aside from Afron's remark quoted in the title of this chapter, Mumina once exclaimed to me, "I just feel like crying" (Roy-Campbell, 2012) as she described her experiences of feeling unable to participate in class discussions in her English language arts class.

As an educator who prepares teachers to teach English learners, I was challenged by the sisters' comments to consider how teachers can invite students who continue to struggle with English language proficiency to learn in their classes. As I contemplated Afron and Mumina's statements, I reflected on my own observations in classrooms and conversations with teachers over the years where I have often witnessed middle and high school teachers complain about students who cannot speak English being placed in their classroom. A coordinator for EL support services in an urban school district in New York State recently told me that many teachers do not want EL students in their classrooms because they are concerned that the students will bring down their scores on the state tests.

I recognize the necessity for teachers to have an awareness of ways to purposefully engage all students in their classroom, including English learners. There are increasing numbers of students from diverse linguistic backgrounds entering U.S. schools; for example, by 2020, more than a quarter of the student population will come from a wide diversity of language backgrounds other than English (NCELA, 2011; Payán & Nettles, 2006). Additionally, many teachers will have students in their classroom who are at different stages of developing English proficiency. Some students may enter their classroom speaking very little English and in some cases have had interrupted or very little prior education (Freeman, Freeman, & Mercuri, 2002). Many teachers, however, have not received preparation for working with ELs (Abbate-Vaughn, 2007; Lucas, Villegas, & Freedson-Gonzalez, 2008; Roy-Campbell, 2013). These teachers are often at a loss as to how to teach ELs; they believe they are unable to address the students' needs (Freeman, Freeman, & Mercuri, 2002). Yet, the changing demographics of schools in the United States signals the necessity for all teachers to acquire pedagogical skills to effectively teach ELs. How can teachers draw on a multiliteracies perspective to envision and enact effective instruction for English learners? The remainder of this chapter addresses this question.

Envisioning a Multiliteracies Pedagogy for English Learners

In the absence of preparation for working with students who speak languages other than English, some secondary schoolteachers proceed with the implicit assumption that all students can follow instruction in English, simply because they have been placed in their classroom. Such teachers may be oblivious to the struggles of students in the class, such as Afron and Mumina, who experience cognitive overload while trying to understand "teacher talk" delivered in English (Mayer & Moreno, 2003). The processing demands required for ELs in teacher-centered classrooms can induce negative emotions that cause frustration and anxiety (Mayer & Moreno, 2003). Thus, English learners like Afron might perceive that "the teacher just uses her mouth," or they might be like Mumina, who "just feel[s] like crying."

Afron's assertion that the teacher just uses her mouth was an indication that the teacher-centered approach of "stand and deliver," common in high school classes, was not working for her. She commented that the teacher sometimes told jokes that she did not understand, and this increased her feeling of exclusion from the class. She requested that I speak with her counselor about dropping the class. I observed that much of the work she was required to complete outside of many classes included packets of worksheets with assigned readings related to the topic and sets of exercises ranging from labeling diagrams to filling in the blanks and answering short-answer questions. When Afron shared with me the notes she had taken in class, I found them difficult to understand, as she had not recorded the information clearly or accurately. The notes were a reflection of her lack of understanding of the lecture combined with her lack of proficiency in expressing herself in English.

Teachers' beliefs about what students can do are often intertwined with their notions of what the students should know and be able to do given their grade level. This impression, which contributes to their expectations of students, is invariably derived from a culturally laden perception of what it means to know and how that knowledge is represented and received (Wells, 2000). The teacher-centered pedagogy that Afron and Mumina described, lecturing and teacher-led class discussion, is based on the assumption that all secondary students are able to receive academic content through the auditory and oral modes. This approach to teaching privileges some approaches to learning while excluding others (Cope & Kalantzis, 2009). It also discounts students like Afron and Mumina, who are still developing English proficiency and have difficulty processing large amounts of oral language in the classroom. A multiliteracies approach to teaching appreciates where students are in the process of acquiring English as well as where teachers want to take students conceptually in their learning. I address each of these central issues in the remainder of this section.

Appreciating Where Students Are

Although English learners represent a wide diversity of languages, cultures, and educational backgrounds, they all struggle with accessing the academic content of their school subjects and negotiating the cultural nuances of their new school environment. While some ELs may appear fluent in English when observed in social interaction with their peers, they experience difficulty when the teacher presents academic content either in a text or as a lecture. Cummins (1980) characterizes this as a distinction between Basic Interpersonal Communication Skills (BICS), which students develop through interacting with their peers, and Cognitive Academic Language Proficiency (CALP), which students need to understand academic content. Although there are critiques of Cummins' distinction (Edelsky, 1990; Valdés, 2004), I find it a useful way of framing the different forms of English proficiency that ELs need to be successful in school. Research shows that students generally develop BICS within two to four years, while it may take seven to ten years to develop CALP (Cummins, 2000; Thomas & Collier, 2002). Many general education teachers, unaware of this difference, believe that ELs should be able to learn English in two years (Reeves, 2004). They do not realize that the academic language they utilize presents difficulty for most English learners. Afron and Mumina are good examples of this distinction, as they both express themselves fluently in general conversations yet struggle with the academic language of their content area subjects. Teachers can only begin to address this discrepancy when they recognize it.

Another dimension of students' struggle with academic language is the teachers' view that students cannot begin learning content until they have developed English proficiency and that they should not be in their class until they understand English (Yoon, 2008). The expressed sentiment of Mumina's and Afron's English language arts teacher is an illustration of this view. English language arts have discursive features that differ from everyday language. Some of this discourse is introduced in earlier grades, where students also develop background knowledge. So when ELs enter the United States in middle or high school or arrive with limited or interrupted formal education, they may not have this prior knowledge, which includes some of the basic discourse for expressing that knowledge. An example of this would be the difference between literal and figurative language prevalent in literary texts. Awareness of the BICS and CALP distinction enables teachers to consider ways of utilizing multimodal channels for helping students develop and increase academic English proficiency skills.

Getting Students Where We Want Them to Be

In my interactions with Mumina, I found her to be very talkative, inquisitive, and outgoing, rarely at a loss for words. I was therefore surprised when she revealed that she felt like crying as she sat in the class, feeling unable to participate. The classroom environment she described was not conducive to her active engagement, leading to her frustration. Had the teacher utilized a pedagogy that actively engaged all students in processing and representing the information in different forms, Mumina would have had a greater opportunity to participate and feel included in the class. Similarly, had Afron's teacher used more than her mouth and actively engaged the students with the content, Afron would have been able to connect with the class. Once teachers have an awareness and appreciation of the types of struggles English learners have in their content classroom, they can begin to actively develop ways of scaffolding instruction for them by making the information they want students to learn available in multiple modes.

Effective pedagogy for English learners invites them to learn rather than distances them (Yoon, 2008). For students to become invested in learning (Norton & Toohey, 2001), they must have some agency in the process and be "an active designer of meaning" (Cope & Kalantzis, 2009, p. 175). Engaging students in gathering different types of information from a variety of sources helps them actively construct meaning. The next section will consider some ways of engaging English learners through a multiliteracies approach.

Enacting a Multiliteracies Perspective with English Learners

A multiliteracies lens provides a frame for conceptualizing literacy beyond the traditional "read the text and answer questions" format used in many classrooms (Anstèy & Bull, 2006). Students need to develop advanced oral, listening, reading, and writing skills to be able to access and produce a variety of genres. But developing these skills need not be limited to printed texts received from "more knowledgeable" others (Cope & Kalantzis, 2009). Multimodal pedagogy exposes English learners to different types of texts and offers diverse ways of exploring and interpreting information (Ajayi, 2008, 2009). It also enables ELs to integrate their prior leaning and understandings into the accessing of new knowledge (Ajayi, 2009). In interacting with Afron and Mumina, I observed that the assignments they found most exciting were those that required them to locate information and images on the Internet and prepare a visual presentation. I draw on the work of Rea and Mecuria (2006), as well as other scholars, to illustrate how teachers can design meaningful instruction for English learners that:

- activates or builds on background knowledge.
- provides comprehensible input.
- offers alternative ways for students to demonstrate what they have learned (Echevarría, Vogt, & Short, 2013).

Activating and Building Background Knowledge

When introducing a new theme to adolescent students, teachers often assume that the students have some prior knowledge of the subject since many of the topics covered in secondary school were introduced in earlier grades. Students gain more complex and abstract understandings of these topics in the higher grades. It is important, therefore, when working with ELs that teachers consider what prior knowledge they expect students to have. Many English learners, especially those with an interrupted prior education, may not have that knowledge or may have different understandings derived from their cultural and linguistic backgrounds. It is important, therefore, that teachers activate English learners' prior knowledge of the new topic and, where students do not have prior knowledge, help them to build the background knowledge the teachers deem necessary to understand the topic.

In their description of ways to build and activate English learners' background knowledge in the Sheltered Instructional Observation Protocol (SIOP), Echevarría, Vogt, and Short (2013) emphasize the importance of visuals such as realia, pictures, video clips, and sound media in making content comprehensible to English learners. SIOP is a research-based model for teaching academic content to English learners while they develop English proficiency (Echevarría, Vogt, & Short, 2013). Rea and Mecuri (2006) describe how a classroom teacher, Denise, activated students' background knowledge by bringing a butterfly to the class to get students discussing what they knew about butterflies and what more they would have liked to have known. After activating their background knowledge and eliciting from students other things they would like to know about butterflies, she listed additional questions they could investigate to increase their understanding of the content. In this instance, the teacher incorporated realia in introducing her topic; she could have alternatively used pictures or video clips of butterflies to provide a visual representation. Many adolescent English learners may be familiar with a butterfly, so they recognize it when they see it, though some may not know the English name "butterfly."

Once teachers have introduced the new concept in a meaningful way, to help students make connections or construct an image in their minds, teachers then need to ensure that they provide means of extending the students' understanding of the new information in a way that is accessible to them and provide comprehensible input.

Providing Comprehensible Input

There are a variety of ways through which teachers can provide comprehensible input to students using multimodalities. They can use pictures and other visual images in addition to multimodal texts, both print-based (e.g., comics, picture storybooks, and graphic novels, as well as posters, newspapers, and brochures) and digital (e.g., slide presentations, animation, book trailers, digital storytelling, live-action filmmaking, and music videos, in addition to various Web texts and social media). Teachers can also engage students in kinesthetic activities such as dramatizations and role play. Although these are not new tools and activities for many teachers, I highlight them here as strategies that employ multimodalities.

In Denise's lesson, when teaching the students the stages of the butterfly's life cycle, she engaged her students in observing the process through a variety of reading materials, pictures, and video clips. There are numerous picture books and Internet sites that provide at varied literacy levels vivid images of all types of butterflies and their life cycle. The life cycle of the butterfly is a topic many students in the United States learn about in their early years of school through

Eric Carle's *The Very Hungry Caterpillar*. Adolescent English learners who may not have been introduced to this topic in their country can access information about butterflies in multiple formats at various proficiency levels.

Utilizing multimodal texts offers the possibility of engaging all students, as these texts provide diverse ways of exploring and interpreting information (Ajayi, 2009). Knowledge is made available in multidimensional ways, including languages other than English, by combining and integrating language, images, graphics, and layouts to enable students to make connections to their own social-cultural experiences and perspectives (Ajayi, 2008). Exposure to information in multiple modalities increases the possibilities for students to comprehend new information and concepts as it provides message abundancy (Gibbons, 2003), which is the provision of multiple semiotic systems to make information available to students. This is an important component of multiliteracies, as the repetition of information through different modalities and the interactivity between these varied representations (Guichon & McLornan, 2008) reinforces the material being taught and thereby improves comprehension. The multisensory experiences engage students in higher-order thinking (Anstèy & Bull, 2006) and enable them to draw on multiple intelligences to bring more meaning to the oral and written texts they typically encounter in the classroom (Armstrong, 2003). Providing comprehensible input for students by activating students' auditory and visual channels fully engages students in constructing their understanding of the content. In the classes that Afron and Mumina described, message abundancy was nonexistent as they were unable to make connections or fully follow the teachers' lessons, factors that contributed to their frustration.

Demonstrating New Knowledge

As students construct knowledge about the topic, there are a variety of means for them to demonstrate what they have learned. After gaining an understanding of the life cycle of the butterfly, students in Denise's class shared their findings orally, using visual representations, and in written form (Rea & Mecuri, 2006). This involved engaging in research to gather additional information for their presentation. There is a range of possibilities for presenting information through multiple channels. I will briefly focus on two methods that have been used with adolescent English learners: digital stories (Danzak, 2011; Ranker, 2008; Skinner & Hagood, 2008) and comics (Chun, 2009; Derrick, 2008; Schwarz, 2002).

Through digital stories, English learners can link their foundation literacies in English with digital literacies, as Skinner and Hagood (2008) demonstrated in their study. They helped ELs scaffold their linguistic development as they engaged in the process of locating and uploading images and background music to produce visual text. Ranker (2008) extended this exemplification in his portrayal of how struggling students in a language arts class built their knowledge base on the selected topics through digital and print-based resources in preparation for producing a video. The students then utilized the video production process to organize and understand their subject matter, using multiple modes of representation: text, images, and sounds. Rather than passively receiving information from the teacher, the students were engaged in actively locating information to construct their knowledge of the topic. This entailed selecting relevant information and deciding on the best modes for presenting it.

In describing the students' process of gathering information from the Web, Ranker observed that the students followed a nonlinear path as they negotiated the online texts. After reading through several texts together and identifying useful information, the students began a web search for images related to the reading. He highlighted the process in which students who were researching baseball and music in the Dominican Republic engaged in locating images and assembling their digital story (Ranker, 2008). The students engaged in a dialogic process of locating additional images to go along with text and narratives they decided to include in their video and creating text to annotate images they had selected.

Digital storytelling offers a means of reaching invisible students in classrooms, as it gives a voice to struggling students (Bull & Kajder, 2004) as they construct meaning using photos and graphics, video clips, audio narration, and supporting written text. They can also create documentary films, multimedia poetry, and multimedia posters to demonstrate learning (Danzak, 2011). Students acquire and demonstrate learning in different ways, so teachers should provide opportunities for multiple forms of exposure to and production of content to support optimal learning for all students in content classes (Egbert, 2002). Egbert outlines several ways of assisting students in gathering data, including identifying websites that are accessible to English learners, some of which may be in their native language or dual languages. I observed a high school technology class of English learners where the students were instructed to locate images on the Internet and import them into a PowerPoint with a brief description. As I walked around the class observing students at work, I noted that some of them went to sites in their native language. For students who are literate in their first language, such sites can be helpful for them to make connections between what they understand and know in their native language and what they are learning in English. Egbert emphasizes the importance of student collaboration when working on projects, mixing native speakers with English learners, and assigning students different roles so that they can all make a contribution in producing knowledge on the topic.

Comics and graphic novels provide a medium for students to access as well as produce knowledge as they provide comprehensible input for English learners (Danzak, 2011) and can deepen English learners' engagement with reading (Chun 2009). Schwartz (2002) provides numerous examples of how graphic novels can be used across the curriculum. They engage students in reading and writing as students must use words to describe the images, and they stimulate inquiry-based talk as students clarify their stories and seek clarification of their classmates' stories (Daud, 2011). Danzak (2011) suggests three ways teachers could use comics in their classroom: "(a) having students create titles for untitled comic strips, (b) asking students to fill in written dialogue for a comic strip presented in pictures only, and (c) inviting students to draw pictures to illustrate a written dialogue" (p. 191).

A multiliteracies approach enables teachers to draw on students' preferred intelligences using the multiple channels through which they can access and produce knowledge (Haley, 2004). Receiving information through the auditory mode was insufficient for both Afron and Mumina and caused them frustration. Students' lack of or insufficient response to the teachers in Afron's and Mumina's classes also created frustration for the teacher as she publicly berated the English learners by wondering aloud why they were placed in her class. Both sisters on separate occasions recounted to me such comments from their teachers. A more interactive way of engaging the students, such as using a multimodal pedagogy to include them, may have lessened the frustration of Afron, Mumina, and their teachers.

Implications for Teachers

Comprehensible input, both to activate prior knowledge and as part of the process of presenting new concepts and information throughout a lesson, is an important component of effective instruction for English learners. A multiliteracies approach that draws on multimodalities, using strategies such as digital stories or comics, offers a platform for presenting information in a comprehensible manner as well as guiding students in constructing their understanding of the content. Although multiliteracies entails more than providing text in multiple modalities, awareness of the affordances of presenting texts that activate varied dimensions of the auditory and visual channels and draw upon students' multiple intelligences can be a first step for teachers who are not familiar with multiliteracies. In-service teachers will require professional development to engage them in an understanding of the full potential of multiliteracies and how to implement such an approach in their classrooms. Preservice teachers can gain an understanding of a multiliteracies pedagogy in their program courses. Thompson (2008) described a method that she models in her teacher education class for the students to use within their teaching. She requires her students to assume different roles and approach the assigned text from that perspective. As the students made their presentations on the reading, one group made a CD of songs representing the story and another bringing in a video clip from a film to exemplify part of the book, they were able to gain a deeper meaning of the texts as they considered it from different vantage points.

Teachers must develop pedagogical skills where they use more than their mouths in teaching ELs like Afron and Mumina. Effective engagement of all the students requires a positive attitude toward culturally and linguistically diverse students, acknowledging that they have ideas and experiences that teachers might tap into through digital storytelling, comics, and other multimodal strategies. This entails a shift from viewing ELs as a burden that will bring down teachers' scores to recognizing that they have assets teachers can build upon to benefit all the students in the classroom. Considering how to actively engage linguistically diverse students in authentic active learning by utilizing a range of literacies is inviting the students to learn.

Selected Resources for Enacting Multiliteracies with English Learners

Listed below are some valuable resources that provide useful information for engaging adolescent English learners' multiliteracies. These resources, all of which may be found on the Web, are ones that are particularly useful for classroom teachers and professional developers.

- Colorín Colorado, a website that provides a wide range of information, articles, and resources for working with English, addresses multiliteracies for English learners in Kristina Robertson (2008), Preparing ELLs to be 21st-Century Learners, http://www.colorincolorado.org/article/21431/
- Educational Technology and Mobile Learning: A resource for educational webtools and mobile apps for teachers and educators provides a list of the best digital storytelling tools for teachers at http://www.educatorstechnology.com/2012/06/list-of-best-free-digital-storytelling.html
- Educational Uses of Digital Storytelling website offers a range of resources for teachers, including lessons plans for digital lessons: http://digitalstorytelling.coe.uh.edu/
- Kathy Schrock's website provides a wide range of resources for using digital storytelling to teach common core standards: http://www.schrockguide.net/digital-storytelling.html
- Life Academy Instructors and the Bay Area Writing Project present a You-Tube video clip that describes how teachers led adolescent English learners in a digital storytelling project that was grounded in literacy. Literacy, ELL, and Digital Storytelling: 21st Century Learning in Action, Life Academy, Oakland, CA: http://www.youtube.com/watch?v=Hrw66BL-Izo
- ReadWriteThink website of the International Reading Association has a student interactive comic creator: http://www.readwritethink.org/classroom-resources/student-interactives/comic-creator-30021.html?tab=5
- William Zimmerman has a website the enables students to create their own comics at http://www.makebeliefscomix.com. He discusses with a high school teacher success she has witnessed using *MakeBeliefsComix* in a YouTube video: http://www.youTube.com/watch?xl_blazer&v=qRblhYvDhEU

References

Abbate-Vaughn, J. (2007). Highly qualified teachers for our schools: Developing knowledge, skills, and dispositions to teach culturally and linguistically diverse students. In M. E. Brisk (Ed.), *Language, culture and community in teacher education* (pp. 175–202). New York, NY: Lawrence Erlbaum.

Ajayi, L. (2008). Meaning-making, multimodal representations, and transformative pedagogy: An exploration of meaning construction practices in an ESL high school classroom. *Journal of Language, Identity, and Education*, 7(3–4), 206–229.

Ajayi, L. (2009). English as a second language learners' explanation of multimodal texts in a junior high school. *Journal of Adolescent and Adult Literacy*, 52(7), 585–595.

Anstèy, M., & Bull, G. (2006). *Teaching and learning multiliteracies: Changing times, changing literacies*. Newark, DE: International Reading Association.

Armstrong, T. (2003). *The multiple intelligences of reading and writing: Making the words come alive*. Alexandria, VA: Association for Supervision and Curriculum Development.

Cope, B., & Kalantzis, M. (2009). "Multiliteracies": New literacies, new learning. *Pedagogies: An International Journal*, 4(3), 164–195.

Chun, C.W. (2009, October). Critical literacies and graphic novels for English-language learners: Teaching *Maus. Journal of Adolescent & Adult Literacy*, 53(2), 144–153

Cummins, J. (1980). Psychological assessment of immigrant children: Logic or intuition? *Journal of Multilingual and Multicultural Development*, 1, 97–lll.

Cummins, J. (2000). Academic language learning, transformative pedagogy and information technology: Towards a critical balance. *TESOL Quarterly*, 34(3), 537–548.

Danzak, R. L. (2011). Defining identities through multiliteracies: ELL teens narrate their immigration experiences as graphic stories. *Journal of Adolescent and Adult Literacy*, 55, 187–196.

Daud, F. (2011). Pictures speak: Graphic novels for English language learners. *Engaging Cultures and Voices*, 2, 18–40.

Derrick, J. (2008, July). Using Comics with TESL/TEFL Students. *The Internet TESL Journal*. 14(7). Retrieved from http://iteslj.org/Techniques/Derrick-UsingComics.html

Echevarría, J., Vogt, M. E., & Short, D. (2013). *Making content comprehensible for English learners: The SIOP model* (4th Ed.) Upper Saddle River, NJ: Pearson.

Edelsky, C. (1990). *With literacy and justice for all: Rethinking the social in language and education*. London, UK: The Falmer Press.

Egbert, J. (2002). A project for everyone: English language learners and technology in content area classrooms. *Learning & Leading with Technology*, 29(8), 36–39.

Freeman, D. E., Freeman, Y. S., & Mercuri, S. P. (2002). Closing the achievement gap: How to reach limited-formal-schooling and long-term English learners. Chicago, IL: Heinemann.

Gibbons, P. (2003). Mediating language learning: Teacher interactions with ESL students in a content-based classroom, *TESOL Quarterly*, 37(2), 247–273.

Guichon, N., & McLornan, S. (2008). The effects of multimodality on L2 learners: Implications for CALL resource design. *System*, 36(1), 85–93.

Haley, M. H. (2004). Learner-centered instruction and the theory of multiple intelligences with second language learners, *Teachers College Record*, 106(1), 163–180.

Lucas, T., Villegas, A. M., & Freedson-González, M. (2008). Linguistically responsive teacher education: Preparing classroom teachers to teach English language learners. *Journal of Teacher Education*, 59(4), 361–373.

Mayer, R., & Moreno, R. (2003). Nine ways to reduce cognitive load in multimedia learning. *Educational Psychologist*, 38(1), 43–52.

National Clearing House for English Language Acquisition (NCELA) (2011). The growing numbers of English learner students, 1998/99–2008/09. Retrieved from http://www.ncela.us/files/uploads/9/growingLEP_0809.pdf

Norton, B., & Toohey, K. (2001). Changing perspectives on good language learners. *TESOL Quarterly*, 35(2), 307–322.

Payán, R., & Nettles, M. (2006). *Current state of English-language learners in the U.S. K–12 student population.* Retrieved September 14, 2011 from http://www.ets.org/Media/Conferences_and_Events/pdf/ELLsympsium/ELL_factsheet.pdf

Ranker, J. (2008). Making meaning on the screen: Digital video production about the Dominican Republic. *Journal of Adolescent and Adult Literacy,* 51(8), 410–422.

Rea, D. M., & Mecuria, S. P. (2006). *Research-based strategies for English language learners: How to reach goals and meet standards, K–8.* Portsmouth, NH: Heinemann.

Reeves, J. (2004). 'Like everybody else': Equalizing educational opportunity for English language learners. *TESOL Quarterly,* 38(1), 43–66.

Roy-Campbell, Z. (2012). Meeting the needs of English learners. *Journal of Adolescent and Adult Literacies,* 56(3), 86–88.

Roy-Campbell, Z. M. (2013) Who educates teacher educators about English language learners? *Reading Horizons,* 52(3), 255–280.

Schwarz, G. E. (2002). Graphic novels for multiple literacies. *Journal of Adolescent & Adult Literacy* 46(3), 262–265.

Skinner, E. N., & Hagood, M. C. (2008). Developing literate identities with English language learners through digital storytelling. *The Reading Matrix,* 8(2), 12–38.

Thomas, W. P., & Collier, V. P. (2002). *A national study of school effectiveness for language minority students' long-term academic achievement.* Santa Cruz, CA: Center for Research on Education, Diversity and Excellence, University of California-Santa Cruz. Retrieved from http://repositories.cdlib.org/crede/finalrpts/1_1_final/

Thompson, M. (2008). Multimodal teaching and learning: Creating spaces for content teachers. *Journal of Adolescent & Adult Literacy,* 52(2), 144–153.

Valdés, G. (2004). Between support and marginalization: The development of academic language in linguistic minority children. *International Journal of Bilingual Education and Bilingualism,* 7(1–2), 102–132.

Wells, G. (2000). Dialogic inquiry in the classroom: Building on the legacy of Vygotsky. In C. Lee and P. Smagorinsky (Eds.), *Vygotskian perspectives on language and research* (pp. 51–85). New York, NY: Cambridge University Press.

Yoon, B. (2008). Uninvited guests: The influence of teachers' roles and pedagogies on the positioning of English language learners in the regular classroom. *American Educational Research Journal,* 45(2), 495–522.

PART III

Lessons Learned about Social Diversities within Multiliteracies

14
TRANSFORMING PRACTICE IN ACTION

Cynthia H. Brock and Fenice B. Boyd

If there is no struggle, there is no progress.

(Frederick Douglass)

We began our book by reminding readers that it has been almost two decades since the New London Group's (NLG) original 1996 article on a multiliteracies pedagogy was published. Along with many colleagues, we argued that the article has been pivotal in changing the way we think about literacy teaching and learning; moreover, the field has benefited from two additional decades of multiliteracies theory and research (Leander & Boldt, 2012). However, many educators have struggled to engage in innovative multiliteracies research and practices in the face of difficult, if not repressive, institutional structures. Since 1996, researchers, teacher educators, teachers, and pre-K–12 students have faced evolving educational policy mandates (e.g., NCLB, 2001) and pedagogical practices (e.g., scripted literacy programs in urban schools) that are counterproductive to innovative twenty-first-century teaching and learning practices suggested by the NLG. As we bring our book to a close, we are reminded of Frederick Douglass's admonition: "If there is no struggle, there is no progress." Drawing on the wisdom of Douglass we emphasize that the important work conducted by scholars who contributed to this book represents struggles on many fronts, including but not limited to internal struggles as educators searched for new and different ideas, materials, and perspectives; classroom struggles as educators worked toward shifting classroom practices in meaningful ways to capture the minds and hearts of their students; struggles at the school and community levels as educators were intent on helping preservice teachers understand the communities where their students lived; and struggles to engage in innovative practices in the face of high-handed policy mandates.

In this final chapter, we address ways that the ideas presented here rest on and extend a multiliteracies framework (NLG, 1996). We explore lessons learned within and across chapters as well as implications of these lessons for our work as a field. We address two questions: First, how does this work instantiate a multiliteracies perspective that focuses on transformative literacy practices? And second, how does a multiliteracies perspective help us, as a field, to transform conceptions of social diversity?

Multiliteracies and Transformative Pedagogy

As we come full circle to examine the implications of our work, we review ways that it instantiates a multiliteracies perspective with respect to social diversity. Exley and Luke (2010) write persuasively that a multiliteracies perspective in practice must (a) foreground inquiry and be situated in the lifeworlds of learners, (b) provide overt instruction that extends to new knowledge, (c) include critical framing of problems and issues that address real audiences for real purposes, and (d) result in transformed literacy practices. Taken together, these four criteria can result in transformative pedagogy (Cope & Kalantzis, 2009). We borrow these criteria from the work of Exley and Luke (2010) and Cope and Kalantzis (2009) to serve as a litmus test to illustrate how the chapters in this book epitomize a multiliteracies perspective.

Inquiry and Learners' Lifeworlds

All of the chapters coalesced around inquiry and learners' lifeworlds in four different contexts. Three chapters were situated in university classrooms whereby preservice and in-service teachers inquired about their own lifeworlds. They considered the implications of their inquiries for their work as literacy teachers. In chapter 2, Goodman's university students explored their own dialects and considered the implications of their learning for their work with students. In chapter 5, McVee guided her coauthors, three European American males, in a self-study of their own significant learning experiences as well as their troubling insights about diversity in a university course. Finally, Boyd and Tochelli (chapter 7) enabled their university students to engage in meaningful dialogue around contentious topics and issues that arise in young adult literature (YAL).

The writers in two chapters drew on cases or vignettes to help readers inquire into the lifeworlds of students with respect to dialect and sexual identity. In chapter 3, Brock, Carter, and Boyd discussed the Oakland, California Ebonics case and the case of bi-dialectical teaching and learning in Western Australia to invite readers to interrogate ideological conceptions of different language varieties. Wiest, in chapter 6, presented composite vignettes of LGBT youth, asking readers to consider what it may be like to enter into the lifeworlds of gay youth.

Three chapters combined work in university classrooms with community literacy projects whereby pre- and/or in-service teachers inquire into the lifeworlds of children and their families. Salas and Pennington introduced a community literacy course into their university students' programs (chapter 4). An important aspect of the course included teaching preservice teachers to inquire into the life-worlds of children and their families served by the schools in which the preservice teachers work. After learning about the difficulties that refugee children faced in their local schools, Walker-Dalhouse and Dalhouse (chapter 10) described their work with a local church to start a community-based reading clinic. Learning firsthand from the children and their parents at the community reading clinic and under the scaffolded guidance of Walker-Dalhouse, university students "turned around" from deficient views of Sudanese children and their families (Comber & Kamler, 2004); the university students learned to recognize the valuable lifeworlds the children brought to their study of literacy in the United States.

Finally, three chapters chronicled how teachers in public school classrooms can draw on their students' lifeworlds to provide meaningful contexts for literacy teaching and learning. In chapter 8, Wheeler and Swords explored how they might build on Swords' students' dialects to improve their school success. Haag and Compton (chapter 9) discussed how Claudia and her English learners engaged in authentic inquiry to craft meaningful literacy instruction. Drawing on her experience tutoring two high-school English learners from Kenya, Roy-Campbell (chapter 13) provided insights into effective literacy practices to educate English learners at the secondary level.

Overt Instruction Extended to New Knowledge

Overt instruction refers to the specific ways that teachers scaffold students' learning to build new knowledge (NLG, 1996). As we studied the ways that chapter authors scaffolded learning about diversity, we noticed that they typically used a two-pronged approach to foster a deeper understanding of some aspect of diversity. First, authors deftly crafted arguments or experiences that got readers to question their understandings of some aspect of diversity. Second, authors then used relevant literacy research, as well as research in their respective categories of social diversity, to inform readers' thinking about effective instructional practices. We present three examples that vary with respect to the nature of diversity, age of students, and nature of context to illustrate this scaffolded approach to instruction.

In chapter 2, Goodman scaffolded her university students' study of language through class experiences and field projects that engaged them in close, systematic study of language-in-use. Once her students realized that they, as well as their families and friends, spoke different viable dialects, they began to study linguists' work on dialects and language variation. Goodman then prompted the students to consider how their own instruction might be modified in meaningful ways to address their new learning about language. As a result of their work, the teachers gained powerful insights into the role that language can play in pedagogical practices. This learning empowered Goodman's university students to be professional agents of change in their classrooms rather than customers of programs and practices that did not meet their students' learning needs.

Wiest, in chapter 6, drew the reader into the complex lives and experiences of sexual minority youth in public schools, and she crafted a compelling argument for why teachers should understand and embrace sexual diversity in their classroom teaching. Once the reader was invited to explore her beliefs and understandings about sexual minority youth, Wiest skillfully drew on relevant literature and student experiences to educate readers. She then offered myriad suggestions for concrete ways that teachers could enact their understandings about sexual minority youth in their instruction.

In chapter 10, Walker-Dalhouse and Dalhouse narrated their experiences helping to organize a community reading clinic at a local church to assist the children of Sudanese families who sought refuge in their community. This setting provided a powerful context for the authors to scaffold students' learning, and by extension, readers learn about the unique and rich literacy backgrounds that Sudanese children bring to U.S. classrooms. As a result of their concrete experiences, Walker-Dalhouse's university students learned that they can draw on the backgrounds and experiences of refugee children and their families to design meaningful literacy instruction in their classrooms.

Critical Framing for Real Audiences

Critical framing refers to "standing back" from what one is studying and viewing a situation "critically in relation to its context" (NLG, 1996, p. 8). Every chapter in this book is framed critically around an issue that mattered for those locally involved in the work. Moreover, authors applied content and different modes of representation to the issues with which they grappled. Two central themes reflect the manner in which critical issues were framed across chapters. First, the authors, the students in their care (including school-aged children as well as pre- and in-service teachers), and in some cases other educators, *interrogated together* their own understandings of some aspect of diversity. That is, in each chapter, participants worked together using a joint problem-solving approach to frame and address important issues. For example, in chapter 7, Boyd and Tochelli worked with their graduate students to explore ways to create a discursive classroom space where they could meaningfully and openly discuss contentious topics and issues represented in YAL. The authors highlighted one class where instructors and students worked together to explore ways to effectively use multicultural literature that addressed LGBT-themed literature with adolescents.

Similarly, Wheeler and Swords worked collaboratively in Swords's elementary classroom to sort through a thorny problem of practice: How could Swords, a white, monolingual teacher, provide meaningful instruction to African American students who spoke African American Vernacular English (AAVE) and were not scoring as high on standardized tests as their white counterparts? Recognizing that traditional language arts methods typically fail African American children (Barton & Coley, 2010), Wheeler and Swords worked side by side to bring insights from linguistics to bear on Swords's literacy instruction. Their joint problem solving resulted in the creation of accessible and research-based approaches to language arts instruction that fostered student learning in a dialectically diverse, multicultural classroom.

A second theme relative to critical framing cut across each chapter: The interrogation process involved embodied experiences or the analysis of embodied examples. That is, the interrogation process was not merely conceptual; it also involved studying corporeal and circumstantial ways of knowing and understanding (Cope & Kalantzis, 2009; McVee, Dunsmore, & Gavelek, 2005). For example, in chapter 11, McMillon and McMillon shared their experiences working with community advocates to develop a neighborhood initiative, *All Around the Neighborhood*, for children from a disadvantaged community. One component of the project involved creating a community garden. When the project participants discovered that the soil at the garden location was contaminated, they built raised boxes and filled them with uncontaminated soil to plant their garden. In the neighborhood setting described by McMillon and McMillon, community advocates enabled the students to turn around (or reframe) their own situation and use it to their advantage. Not only did the students learn about planting and growing vegetables, they learned to build devices that would allow them to plant the vegetables; they learned not to be deterred by obstacles that might seem insurmountable, but rather to work around the obstacles.

Similarly, Turner, in chapter 12, shared a complex dilemma that he and his colleagues at a youth detention center framed and studied together: How could meaningful and engaging arts-based literacy learning experiences be enacted for, by, and with incarcerated youth? Told through the experiences of three incarcerated students, Lucky, LA, and Homicide, Turner illustrated how these students used multimodal representations to engage in meaning-filled literacy experiences that involved crafting and sharing authentic representations of urban living, as well as their own lives and experiences.

Transformed Literacy Practices

> Transfer in meaning-making practice … puts the transformed meaning to work in other contexts or cultural sites.
>
> *(NLG, 1996, p. 88)*

Transformed practice is a cornerstone of multiliteracies, and conceptions of it have changed and evolved across time (Kalantzis & Cope, 2012). In its 1996 article, the New London Group argued that it is not enough to reflect on and learn from our work as literacy teachers; we must also redesign our practice and apply our new learning in embodied ways that manifest the goals and values of students. Moreover, this process of reflecting on and learning from experiences, then redesigning our practice in light of students' values and goals is, or at least should be, an iterative and recursive process. This recursive process involves both struggle and tension as we and our students strive to learn, grow, and improve. In essence, we, and they, are redesigned in the process of redesigning (Cope & Kalantzis, 2009). In 2009, Cope and Kalantzis revisited the multiliteracies work, including transformative pedagogy, put forth by the NLG in 1996 and reframed some of their initial ideas. In their later 2012 work, they highlighted the application aspect of transformed practice. Here we discuss transformed practice as application across twelve chapters in the book. We begin by exploring themes relative to who or what was transformed. Then we examine themes relative to how the process of transformation unfolded.

Who or What Was Transformed across the Twelve Chapters?

The most common kind of transformation discussed across the chapters was participants' beliefs, understandings, and perceptions relative to some aspect of diversity; this type of transformation was addressed in nine chapters. Moreover, participants' transformed beliefs, understandings, or perceptions were discussed retrospectively in some chapters and prospectively in others. For example, in chapters 2, 4, 5, 7, 8, and 10, authors discussed participants' retrospective transformations with respect to beliefs, understandings, or perceptions. Retrospective transformations refer to transformations that occurred in the past, such as Goodman's work (chapter 2) where she explained that once teachers' beliefs and understandings about dialect were transformed, they were open to new ways of designing literacy instruction in their respective classrooms. Salas and Pennington (chapter 4) discussed how preservice teachers' instructional practices during tutoring changed once they reconciled their beliefs and understandings about the children and their communities as a result of engagement in their community literacy course. In chapter 8, the authors discuss how Swords changed her literacy instructional practices once her beliefs and understandings about dialects were transformed after studying the work of linguists and experimenting with different instructional approaches.

Three chapters (i.e., 3, 6, and 13) focused on prospective transformations with respect to beliefs, understandings, and perceptions. Prospective transformations refer to transformations that have not yet occurred, but might occur, based on new learning. Chapters 3, 6, and 13 had something in common; they did not report on work done in a specific context. Rather, each of these chapters dealt with a central problem with respect to diversity. Chapter 3 focused on the role of ideology with respect to language varieties. A key goal was to help readers understand the role that ideology plays in people's perceptions of different language varieties and to promote positive beliefs about and understandings of language varieties. The same approach applied to chapters 6 and 13, except that chapter 6 focused on sexual identity and chapter 13 dealt with English learners at the secondary level.

Seven chapters (i.e., 3, 6, 7, 8, 9, 12, and 13) discussed transformed practices in specific classroom contexts; however, the classroom contexts varied. Chapters 3, 6, 8, 9, and 13 addressed specific instructional practices that were transformed in K–12 classrooms. Concrete examples include but are not limited to the bi-dialectical teaching that occurs in classrooms in Western Australia (chapter 3), the contrastive approach to dialect instruction in Sword's elementary classroom (chapter 8), and the revised literacy instructional practices around *Charlotte's Web* in Haag's elementary ESL classroom (chapter 9). Chapter 7 focused on transformed instructional practices in Boyd and Tochelli's university classroom, and in chapter 12, Turner focused on transformed instructional practices in a juvenile detention center. Different kinds of transformed practice overlapped in some contexts; thus, some authors described more than one kind of transformed practice.

Finally, four chapters (i.e., 4, 10, 11, and 12) focused on other kinds of tangible transformations. Salas and Pennington (chapter 4) transformed their university literacy program by adding a much-needed community literacy course to their program. Chapters 10 and 11 focused on transformations in two different communities. Walker-Dalhouse and Dalhouse (chapter 10) worked in conjunction with other community advocates to create a community reading clinic in a local church to meet the literacy needs of Sudanese refugee children and their families in North Dakota. McMillon and McMillon (chapter 11) worked with other community advocates in an impoverished community in Michigan to create a community program for local school-aged students. Turner (chapter 12) and his colleagues revamped the literacy curriculum to make it meaningful and engaging for the incarcerated youth at the juvenile detention center where they worked in New York.

How Did the Transformation Process Occur across the Twelve Chapters?

Two predominant themes cut across all twelve chapters with respect to the process by which transformation occurred. First, in every single context, participants recognized a need for change. Sometimes this recognition came about as a result of personal reflection and experience. For example, in chapters 4, 7, 9, 10, 11, and 12, key participants recognized that they needed to make a change to their practice. Salas and Pennington (chapter 4) recognized that the preservice teachers in their university literacy methods course were not "getting it" with respect to the strengths and backgrounds their mostly English learners brought to their classrooms and schools where the preservice teachers tutored. Swords (chapter 8) recognized that she was not successfully "reaching" the mostly African American children in her classroom and that she needed to change her instruction in order to do so.

In other chapters, however, key participants in the context engineered a situation to bring about the recognition that transformation needed to occur. For example, in chapter 3, Brock, Carter, and Boyd carefully crafted an argument to convince readers that unexamined assumptions and ideologies about dialect or language varieties may lead to ineffective instructional practices. In chapter 5, McVee skillfully designed a university course to help her students see the need to challenge their own perceptions/expectations/assumptions about diversity. This recognition that one needs to change, whether the recognition occurs on one's own or as a result of a gentle nudge, is eminently significant. Indeed, change cannot occur without it. This relates to Prochaska and DiClemente's (1992) groundbreaking historical work on the stages of change model. In Prochaska and DiClemente's terms, when we are at the stage of precontemplation, there is no recognition that change needs to occur. However, once we recognize the need to change, we move from precontemplation to contemplation. As humans, we begin to grow and change when we recognize that we need to do so (Prochaska & DiClemente, 1992).

A second predominant theme regarding the "how" of transformation was that key participants puzzled through the transformation process in the company of concerned others. This process of puzzling through specifics of transforming practice as it was unfolding relates to the notion of emergent practice (Cole & Pullen, 2010) that we introduced in chapter 1. Emergent practice is literacy learning that is co-constructed with key participants in immediate contexts. This process of puzzling through issues occurred in every chapter throughout the book from chapter 2, where Goodman worked with her university students as they designed projects to explore dialect use in their local contexts, to chapter 13, where Roy-Campbell drew on input from Afron and Mumina (high school English learners) as well as scholarly literature to craft an argument for best instructional practices for English learners in secondary disciplinary coursework.

Transforming Conceptions of Social Diversity

We end this chapter and book asking you to consider the following question: How does a multiliteracies perspective help us to consider what it means to be literate with respect to social diversity? We begin to address this question by referring you to Figure 14.1. You will likely recognize that Figure 14.1 is the original Figure 1.2 in chapter 1. Recall from chapter 1 that this figure presents an overview of key elements of a multiliteracies framework: multimodality, social diversity, and teaching and learning. The two key aspects of multiliteracies, multimodality and social diversity, are filtered through teaching and learning. Moreover, we list the word "multiliteracies" at the bottom of the figure to indicate that it is the primary theoretical foundation on which the chapters in this book rest. We draw your attention to the ball that represents social diversity, the aspect of multiliteracies we highlight in this book. While that ball is empty except for the words "social diversity" in Figure 14.1, we flesh out two possible renditions of conceptual ideas that could be considered content to be labeled on that ball representing social diversity; one version, represented in Figure 14.2, is an "old basics" version of social diversity. The other version, represented in Figure 14.3, is a "new basics" version of social diversity.

In their 2012 book on multiliteracies, Kalantzis and Cope articulate differences between "old basics" and "new basics." In a nutshell, old basics focus on what Guerra (1998) calls "literacy as entity," the essential components of literacy including phonics, phonemic awareness, fluency, comprehension, vocabulary, writing,

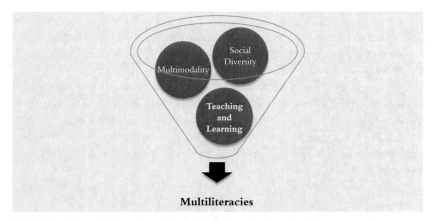

Multiliteracies

FIGURE 14.1 Social Diversity within a Multiliteracies Framework.

and so forth. While responsible educators must consider these components of literacy, an *exclusive* focus on them is problematic because it ignores the social contexts in which literacy practices are embedded. In short, a sole focus on these literacy components without attending to social context ignores issues of power, privilege, poverty, and injustice and assumes equality of opportunity (Guerra, 1998; Macedo, 1994). Indeed, our work in this book extends earlier notions of "old and new basics" because the work reported here discusses "old and new basics" as related to social diversity rather than reading and writing from a skills based perspective only. Figure 14.2 provides an overview of key aspects of social diversity that go unexamined when we, as a field, focus solely on decontextualized conceptions of literacy.

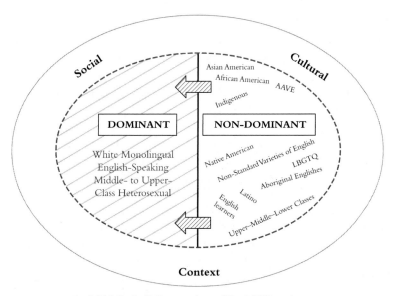

FIGURE 14.2 An "Old Basics" Conception of Social Diversity.

In particular, as indicated in Figure 14.2, an "old basics" conception of social diversity establishes a dualist approach toward social diversity privileging white, monolingual, standard English-speaking middle- to upper-class heterosexual people. Moreover, an educational goal from an old basics perspective would be to "help" everyone in the "non-dominant" category learn the norms, values, and dispositions of the dominant group; recognizing, of course, that many people in the dominant group see their group membership as the taken-for-granted norm (Delpit, 2012). Hence, the arrows in Figure 14.2 face toward the dominant group since that is the focus of education for advocates of an old basics perspective toward social diversity.

Kalantzis and Cope (2012) argue that a "new basics" conception of literacy values multiple "literacies" in a world of multimodal communication. This conception of literacy resonates with Guerra's (1998) "literacy as practice" perspective. From this perspective, "literacy is no longer considered a singular, monolithic, or universal entity; instead, scholars who take a practice-oriented perspective contend that there are many literacies in any society serving multiple and culturally specific purposes" (Guerra, 1998, p. 57). Guerra (1998) argues the following:

> The goal, from this perspective, is not to master a particular form of literacy, but to develop one's ability to engage in a variety of social practices that require us to operate in a plethora of settings and genres to fulfill different needs and goals … [I]t becomes our responsibility to identify and understand the varied ways in which different groups of people make use of literacy in their lives and to assist everyone in becoming more adept at making use of whatever literacies they deem important in their present and future lives (p. 58).

Figure 14.3 presents an alternative "new basics" approach with respect to literacy and social diversity as emphasized by each of the authors of the chapters in this book.

Although all of the chapters represent this "new basics" approach, we highlight three examples here. In chapter 3, Brock, Carter, and Boyd discussed the bi-dialectical work being done in Western Australia whereby teachers and students learn varieties of Aboriginal English and varieties of Standard English; the ultimate goal of this work is the acquisition of both dialects by both Aboriginal and white Australians rather than merely the use of Aboriginal English as a means to teach Aboriginal students standard varieties of Australian English. As another example, in chapter 6, Wiest presented school scenarios where teachers understand and embrace the lives and experiences of sexual minority youth in their classroom teaching. Finally, in chapter 10, Walker-Dalhouse and Dalhouse helped us, as readers, see what happens when the backgrounds and literacy experiences of Sudanese refugees are seen as valuable resources upon which to build rather than problems to be fixed.

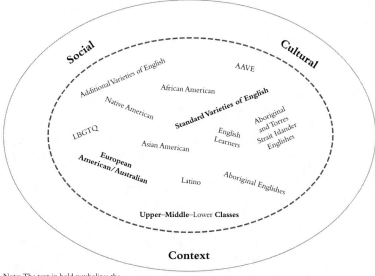

Note: The text in bold symbolizes the discourse of power.

FIGURE 14.3 A "New Basics" Conception of Social Diversity.

Notice that in Figure 14.3, there is no longer a binary between dominant and non-dominant. *All* aspects of people's identities are considered valuable and integral to effective literacy-related teaching and learning. However, you will note that we have highlighted the following words: "Standard Varieties of English," "European American/Australian," and "Upper-Middle Classes." This is because we are aware that the aforementioned groups of individuals represent the culture of power, and it would be unwise to neglect recognizing and naming this situation (Delpit, 2012). A worthwhile goal, however, is to continue transforming society so that students' and families' group-linked and individual identities are equally valued. Taken together, the chapters in this book provide both an impetus and a roadmap for us, as a field, to (re)consider and (re)conceptualize social diversity within a multiliteracies framework.

References

Barton, P. E., & Coley, R. J. (2010). *The Black-White achievement gap: When progress stopped.* Policy Information Center. Princeton, NJ: Educational Testing Service.

Cole, D., & Pullen, D. (2010). *Multiliteracies in motion: Current theory and practice.* New York, NY: Routledge.

Comber, B., & Kamler, B. (2004). Getting out of deficit: Pedagogies of reconnection. *Teaching Education.* 15(3), 293–310.

Cope, B., & Kalantzis, M. (2009). "Multiliteracies": New literacies, new learning. *Pedagogies: An International Journal*, 4, 164–195. doi: 10.1080/15544800903076044

Delpit, L. (2012). *Multiplication is for white people: Raising expectations for other people's children.* New York, NY: The New Press.

Exley, B., & Luke, A. (2010). Uncritical framing: Lesson and knowledge structure in school science. In D. Cole & D. Pullen, *Multiliteracies in motion: Current theory and practice* (pp. 17–41). New York, NY: Routledge.

Guerra, J. (1998). Close to Home: Oral and Literate Practices in a Transnational Mexicano Community. New York, NY: Teachers College Press.

Kalantzis, M., & Cope, B. (2012). *Literacies.* Cambridge, MA: Cambridge University Press.

Leander, K., & Boldt, G. (2012). Rereading "A pedagogy of multiliteracies": Bodies, texts, and emergence. *Journal of Literacy Research*, 45(1). 22–46.

Macedo, D. (1994). *Literacies of power: What Americans are not allowed to know.* Boulder, CO: Westview Press.

McVee, M. B., Dunsmore, K. L., & Gavelek, J. R. (2005). Schema theory revisited. *Review of Educational Research*, 75(4), 531–566.

New London Group (NLG). (1996). A pedagogy of multiliteracies: Designing social futures. *Harvard Educational Review*, 66, 60–92.

Prochaska, J., & DiClemente, C. (1992). Stages of change in the modification of problem behaviors. *Journal of Behavior Modification*, 28, 183–218.

U.S. Department of Education (2001). No Child Left Behind (program description and law). Retrieved July 14, 2014 from http://www2.ed.gov/policy/elsec/leg/esea02/index.html

INDEX

Note: Page numbers with *f* indicate figures.

AAE (Appalachian English) 20; study of
    23–5
Abbate-Vaughn, J. 187
Aboriginal English 6, 30–1, 34, 37
Academic English 20
Adger, C. T. 21, 34, 39, 114, 115
Adler, D. 136
Adolescent Literacy 46–7
Advanced Certificate in Teaching and
    Leading in Diversity (ACTLD) 67
affiliations, as participatory culture 156
African American English (AAE) language
    study 21, 23–5, 37, 110
African American students, failure rates of
    111–4, 111*f*
African American Vernacular English
    (AAVE) 6, 7, 8, 31, 34–5, 113, 204
Aimée & Jaguar (film) 81
Ajayi, L. 190, 192
Akiba, D. 152
Albers, P. 6
Alim, H. S. 110
All Around the Neighborhood initiative 155,
    156, 158–62, 159*f*
Alvermann, D. E. 151
Amanti, C. 36, 141
American Tongues (video) 18
Anagnostopoulous 80
Anderson, G. 152
Angelou, M. 93–4, 96
Anstèy, M. 190, 192
anti-bullying/harassment policies 83

Appalachian English (AAE) 20, 24
Apple, M. W. 59
applied linguistics, dialectally diverse
    classroom and 115–6
Aragon, S. R. 94
Arias, M. B. 47, 56
Armstrong, T. 192
attitudes, toward language 115
Austen-Smith, D. 111
Australian English 37

background knowledge, activating and
    building 190–1
bad English 115
Bailey, N. M. 61, 170
Baker, B. 113
Baldwin, J. M. 35
Barth, R. 123
Bartkiewicz, M. J. 74, 94
Barton, D. 150
Barton, P. E. 111, 204
Basic Interpersonal Communication Skills
    (BICS) 188–9
Baugh, J. 113, 118
Bay Area Writing Project 195
BBC World News 149
Beals, M. P. 66
Bearne, E. 157
Bellini, C. 80
Berg, M. 84, 85
Bernstein, B. 174
Bidell, M. P. 80
bi-dialecticalism 38
bigrams 3

Birch, B. 114
Birzin, E. 169
Bismilla, V. 133
Blackburn, M. V. 85, 98
Black English (BE) 23
Black English Vernacular (BEV) 23
body biography 93
Boesen, M. J. 74, 94
Boldt, G. 3, 201
Booth, D. 137
"border crossing" project 67, 70–1
Bouley, T. M. 74
Boyd, C. J. 94
Boyd, F. B. 1–9, 30–40, 61, 65, 71, 89–105,
    201–11
Boyle-Baise, M. 47, 49
Bradbury, A. 149
Breaking the Silence (video) 97
Briar Rose (Yolen) 93
Brock, C. H. 1–9, 30–40, 59, 61, 65, 141,
    201–11
Brokeback Mountain (Proulx) 80
Brouillette, L. 137
Bull, G. 190, 192
Bullied (documentary) 81
Burn, A. 174

Cahill, R. 30, 38
canonical texts 2
Carger, C. 63
Carle, E. 192
Carolan-Silva, A. 80
Carrillo, R. 152
Carter, J. 30–40
Cartwright, K. 114
Cazden, C. B. 7, 71, 103
Chang, S. p. 80
Chapman, M. 144
Charlotte's Web (White) 138–41, 140*f*
Chavez, C. 53
Children of War: Voices of Iraqi Refugees
    (Ellis) 149
Children's Hour, The (Hellman) 80
Chow, P. 133
Christenbury, L. 110, 114
Christian, D. 21, 34, 39, 114, 115
Chrysanthemum (Henkes) 43
Chun, C. W. 192, 193
Ciechanowski, E. M. 152
circulations, as participatory culture 156,
    157
Clay, M. 135–6
Clementi, T. 96

code-switch 110, 115, 118, 122
Cognitive Academic Language Proficiency
    (CALP) 189
Cohen, S. 133
Cole, D. 6, 208
Coleman-King, C. 152
Coley, R. J. 111, 204
collaborative problem solving, as
    participatory culture 156, 157
Collard, G. 30, 38
Collazo, T. 152
Collier, V. P. 189
Colorín Colorado (website) 195
Comber, B. 203
comics 193–4
community literacy 47–8
Compton, M. 127–42
contrastive analysis technique 115, 116,
    117–9, 122
Cooper, J. 47
Cope, B. 1–2, 3, 5–6, 15, 26, 32–3, 36, 38,
    44, 46, 48, 49, 59, 68, 69, 75, 76, 77, 82,
    84, 85–6, 90–91, 135, 137, 140–1, 145–6,
    151, 157–8, 188, 190, 202, 205–6, 209,
    210
correctionist methods 114–5
Cowart, M. 152
Craig, H. K. 113
Crawford, J. 172
critical framing 204–5; defined 204
Critical Framing (NLG framework)
    95–6
critical literacies pedagogy 90–91, 145
critical reflection 39
C.S. Mott Group for Sustainable
    Agriculture Systems 162–3
Cumming, D. 117, 118
Cummins, J. 75, 76, 78, 128, 133, 142,
    188–9
cyberbullying 83

Dalhouse, A. D. 144–52
Danzak, R. L. 192, 193
Darwich, L. 77
Daud, F. 193
Deadly Ways to Learn (Cahill & Collard)
    30–2
"Deadly Ways to Learn" project 37–8
decoding 2
de la Luz Reyes, M. 37
Delpit, L. 14, 20, 31, 34, 35, 36, 37, 38, 40,
    113, 114, 210, 211
Derrick, J. 192

dialect: conceptions of 34, 34*f*; defined 115; regional variation of 15–6; as rule-governed versions of language 36; stigmatized 20

dialectally diverse classroom 109–23; African American students and 112–4; applied linguistics and 115–6; classroom language varieties and 116–7; code-switch and 118; contrastive analysis technique and 117–9; correctionist methods and 114–5; frequently asked questions, responding to 121–2; overview of 109–12, 111*f*; plural patterns and 119, 119*f*; possessive patterns and 120, 120*f*; reading/writing language varieties and 120–1

DiClemente, C. 208

digital storytelling 192–3

digrams 4

Dilg, M. 81, 85

"Disco Rice and Other Trash Talk" (*New York Times* article) 18

discourse markers 22

diversity(ies), white male perceptions of 58–72; background and context of 60–1; border crossing and 70–1; discourses and, teacher and student 69–70; Fronczak's story of 66–8; multiliteracies relationship with 68–71; overview of 58–9; power/empowerment and 70; self-awareness/-reflection and 69; Stainsby's story of 64–6; theory and research perspectives of 59–60; troubling insights 71; White's story of 62–4

Dolan, R. 81

double negative 116

Douglass, F. 201

Dowdy, J. 114

Do You Speak American? (PBS series) 18

dual narrative 44–5*f*

Dunsmore, K. L. 61, 205

Durso, L. E. 78

Early Literacy 46

Ebonics 23, 33, 34–6, 37

Echevarría, J. 190, 191

Edelsky, C. 189

Edison, T. 136

Educational Technology and Mobile Learning (website) 195

Educational Uses of Digital Storytelling (website) 195

Edwards, P. A. 155

Egbert, J. 193

Ellis, D. 149

Ellis, L. 152

emergent practice: described 6; literacy teaching and learning as 6

encoding 2

English as a Second Language (ESL) 9, 127–9, 136–8

English double negative 116

English Education, Adolescence 91

English learners (ELs) 127, 128–9; components of 190; identity charts and 132–3; self-portraits and 129–32, 130*f*, 131*f*, 132*f*; stupid book and 133–5, 134*f*

English learners, lessons learned from 127–42; identity charts and 132–3; listening and 141–2; multimodal pathway use and 135–7; overview of 127–9; self-portraits and 129–32, 130*f*, 131*f*, 132*f*; student voice in problem solving and 137–41; stupid book and 133–5, 134*f*

English learners (ELs) multiliteracies 186–95; background knowledge, activating and building 190–1; enacting 190–4; envisioning 187–90; input, providing comprehensible 191–2; knowledge, demonstrating new 192–4; overview of 186–7; resources for enacting 195; teacher implications 194–5

Espelage, D. L. 94

"Everything Possible" (song) 81

Exley, B. 202

expressions, as participatory culture 156–7

Fargo (TV show) 22

Farm Stand Project 158–62, 159*f*, 160*f*, 161*f*; student reflections on 164–5

Feistritzer, C. E. 59

Finn, P. J. 63

Flint, A. S. 145

Flirtations 81

Florio-Ruane, S. 58, 59, 67

Flossie and the Fox (McKissack) 27, 121

Formal Standard English 116

Franklin, A. 164–5

Freedom Friendship Program 64

Freedson-González, M. 187

Freeman, D. E. 187

Freeman, Y. S. 187

Freire, P. 50

Fries, P. 14

Fronczak, D. 58–72

Fryer, R. G., Jr. 111

Gal, S. 110
Galda, L. 137
Garcia, E. 47, 56, 128
Garza, C. L. 42–3, 49, 51
Gates, G. J. 78, 79
Gavelek, J. R. 61, 205
Gay, Lesbian and Straight Education
    Network (GLSEN) 86, 105
gay life *vs.* lifestyle 84
Gay-Straight Alliance (GSA) 79, 82
Gay-Straight Alliance Network 86
GED (General Education Diploma)
    60–1
Gee, J. P. 7, 8, 18, 31, 32, 60, 70
General Education Diploma (GED) 60–1
Giampapa, F. 133
Gibbons, P. 192
Gilyard, K. 14, 27, 114, 115
Glazier, J. A. 59, 61, 65
GLBT *see* LGBT (lesbian, gay, bisexual,
    transgender)
Godley, A. J. 110
Gone with the Wind (Mitchell) 80
Gonzalez, N. 36, 141
good English 115
Goodman, D. 13–27, 34, 39, 113
Goodman, K. 16
Goodman, Y. 14, 16, 26, 113
Graff, C. M. 91
grammar 110
graphic novels 193
Graybill, E. C. 94
Green, J. 93, 96, 104
Green, L. 114
Greenfader, C. M. 137
Greytak, E. A. 74, 94
GSA (Gay-Straight Alliance) 79, 82
Guerra, J. 208, 209, 210
Guichon, N. 192
Guo, L. 3
Guthrie, L. 113
Gutierrez, K. D. 37

Haag, C. C. 127–42
Hagood, M. C. 151, 192
Haley, M. H. 194
Halliday, M. A. K. 15, 26
Hamilton, M. 150
Hamlet (Shakespeare) 169
Hard Love (Wittlinger) 98; author's style
    in 102–4; relationships in 101–2; sexual
    identity, expressions of 99–101; written
    responses to 99–104

Hard Love (Wittlinger) discussions
    98–104; author's style responses 102–4;
    relationships responses 101–2; sexual
    identity responses 99–101
Harré, R. 59
Harris Murri, N. J. 47, 56
Harste, J. C. 6
Heath, S. B. 40, 110, 137, 155, 177
Hellman, L. 80
Henkes, K. 43
heterosexist comments 77
History of the g (video) 169–70
Holbrook, T. 6
Holler If You Hear Me (Michie) 63
homophobic comments 77
Horn, S. S. 94
Houghton-Jones Resource Center 155,
    158, 161
Hughes, T. 147
Hull, G. 144
"Hyena, Lion, and the Baby" (Sudanese
    folktale) 148–9
Hymel, S. 77
Hymes, D. 7
hypervisual set 179–81, 180–1*f*

identities, multiliteracies and 7–9
identity charts 132–3
identity development 7–9
ideology, language variation and 34–6, 34*f*,
    38–40
I Know Why the Caged Bird Sings (Angelou)
    93–4, 96
Inada, L. 18
in-and out-of-school literacies,
    connecting 151
in between spaces 67
incarcerated youths' multimodal
    composing events 172–83; classroom
    182–3; event one 172–4; event two
    174–7, 175*f*, 176*f*; event three 177–9;
    hypervisual 179–80, 180–1*f*, 181;
    student identity 181–2
Informal Standard English 116
In My Family (Garza) 42–3, 49, 51
input, providing comprehensible 191–2
Inside Out and Back Again (Lai) 149–50
interrogation process 204, 205
Intersex Society of North America (ISNA)
    74, 84
intersex *vs.* hermaphrodite 84
intonational rhythms 24
It Gets Better Project 86

Jacobs, G. 2
Janks, H. 32, 39–40
Jenkins, H. 156–7
Jennings, T. 80
Jensen, B. T. 128
Jewitt, C. 174
John, V. 7
Joos, M. 114
Junior Master Gardener Program 160–1, 160*f*

Kalantzis, M. 1–2, 3, 5–6, 15, 26, 32–3, 36, 38, 44, 46, 48, 49, 59, 68, 75, 76, 77, 82, 84, 85–6, 90–91, 135, 137, 140–1, 145–6, 151, 157–8, 188, 190, 202, 205–6, 209, 210
Kamler, B. 203
Kavanagh, J. H. 32, 39
King, M. L., Jr. 53
Kitchen, J. 80
Klein, N. A. 74, 77
knowledge, demonstrating new 192–4
Koenig, B. W. 94
Kosciw, J. G. 74, 77, 78, 80, 82–3, 85, 94
Kozol, J. 68
Kramer, R. 152
Kress, G. 4, 174, 177, 178, 179
Krieger, S. L. 105
Kull, R. M. 94

Labov, W. 24, 113, 123
Ladson-Billings, G. 14, 61
Lai, T. 149–50
Language, Identity, and Power (Janks) 39–40
Language, Literacy, and Culture (LLC) course 58, 60; Chad and 62–4; David and 66–8; Jay and 64–6
Language of Wider Communication 110
language stories 15
language study 13–27; African American English (AAE) 23–5; in classroom 26–7; data-based study and, systematic 20–2; independent field projects and 22–5; learning and teaching and, reconsidering language 25–7; observation and documentation, cultivating through 15–8; overview of 13–5; readings and resources, informing with 18–20
language teachers 14
language variation; *see also* language study: ideology and 34–6, 34*f,* 38–40; literate behavior and 6–7; quiz 33, 33*f*;

Standard English and 36–8; teachers' understandings of 13–27
language varieties 115; *see also* dialect
Lapp, D. 141
Lauricella, A. M. 104
Lazar, A. M. 155
Leander, K. 3, 201
Leoni, L. 133
lesbian, gay, bisexual, transgender (LGBT) 80, 82–3, 86, 91, 94–5
Lewis, R. 81
Lewison, M. 145
LGBT (lesbian, gay, bisexual, transgender) 80, 82–3, 86, 91, 94–5
LGBT YAL class session 96–8; Captain's vignette 97–8
Life Academy Instructors 195
linguistic diversity 13
Linguistics Society of America 35
Lippi-Green, R. 113
literacy: as entity 208–9; forms of 49; as social practice framework 145; traditional, defined 49; transformation levels of 56–7
literacy digs 26
literacy event, defined 177
Literacy Specialists 91
Literacy Studies and Teaching of English to Speakers of Other Languages (TESOL) 13
Literacy with an Attitude (Finn) 63
literal level comprehension 2
literate behavior: language variation and 6–7; social diversity and 6
Little Rock Central High School, integration of 2
Lockhart, J. 80
Looking for Alaska (Green) 93, 94, 96, 104
"The Lost Boys" 144; *see also* Sudanese culture
Lowenstein, K. L. 59
Lucas, T. 187
Luke, A. 8, 9, 202

Macedo, D. 37, 209
Macklemore 81
Mainstream American English 115, 121–2
Malcolm, I. G. 31, 38
Mannheim, K. 31–2, 39
Martinez, M. 137
Martin Luther King Junior Elementary School Children v. Ann Arbor School District Board 122–3

Marx, K. 32
Mayer, R. 187–8
McClendon, B. 156, 159, 160
McClure, E. 113
McGinnis, T. 27
McIntyre, D. J. 47, 49
McKenna, T. 169
McKissack, P. 27, 121
McLaren, P. 145
McLornan, S. 192
McMahon, S. I. 65
McMillon, D. B. 154–67
McMillon, G. T. 154–67
McVee, M. B. 4, 58–72, 59, 61, 65, 71,
    104, 205
McWhorter, J. 18, 19–20, 115
meaning-making 14, 32, 44, 77, 104, 157;
    investigations of, systems 59–60
meaning representation 59–60
Mecuria, S. P. 190, 191, 192
Meier, T. 113
Mercuri, S. P. 187
Meyers, J. 94
Michaels, S. 60
Michie, G. 63
Milk (film) 79
Milk, H. 79, 96
Miller, S. M. 4, 104
Milroy, J. 110
Mitchell, M. 80
Moesha (TV show) 22
Moghaddam, F. M. 59
Moje, E. 8, 9, 152
Moll, L. 26, 36, 141
Moreno, R. 187–8
multiliteracies; *see also* multiliteracies, English
    learners (ELs); multiliteracies, for youth
    living on margins; preservice literacy
    programs: advancing, framework 5–7;
    border crossing and 70–1; conceptual
    framework 32–3; discourses and 69–70;
    explained 32, 75; exploring framework
    reach of 3–5; facets of 59; identities and
    7–9; impact of 3–5; introduction to
    1–2; new basics of 157, 158, 163, 210,
    211f; old basics of 157–8, 163, 209f,
    210; outside in view of 42–57; power/
    empowerment and 70; resources for
    enacting, with English Learners 195; safe
    places, designing 91–6; self-awareness/-
    reflection and 69; as sexual diversity
    in classroom framework 75–6; social
    diversity within 5–6, 5f, 209f; teacher

implications for 194–5; topics studied
    using 3; transformative literacy practices
    and 202–5; troubling insights 71
multiliteracies, English learners (ELs)
    186–95; background knowledge,
    activating and building 190–1; enacting
    190–4; envisioning 187–90; input,
    providing comprehensible 191–2;
    knowledge, demonstrating new 192–4;
    overview of 186–7; resources for enacting
    195; teacher implications 194–5
multiliteracies, for youth living on margins
    168–85; *see also* incarcerated youths'
    multimodal composing events; case
    examples 171; challenge of 169–70;
    lessons learned 183–5; narrative 170–1;
    overview of 168–9; *Through Our Eyes*
    production 171–2
multimodality, defined 4
multimodal literacies 157
Multiplication Is for White People (Delpit) 40
murals: of Aztec Warrior 50–1, 51f;
    of Cesar Chavez 53, 53f; of Earth
    and Chains 54, 54f; of *La Virgen de
    Guadalupe* 51–3, 52f
My Cousin Vinny (TV show) 22
"My Princess Boy" (news article) 81

National Assessment of Educational
    Progress (NAEP) 111
National Center for Education Statistics
    (NCES) 111
National Center for Lesbian Rights 97
National Center for Transgender Equality
    (NCTE) 86
National Clearing House for English
    Language Acquisition (NCELA) 187
National Council of Teachers of English
    117
Neff, D. 141
Nelson, E. S. 105
Nettles, M. 187
new basics, of multiliteracies 157, 158, 163,
    210, 211f
New London Group (NLG) 1–2, 8, 32,
    59–60, 61, 69, 75–6, 91, 92, 94, 201–2,
    203, 204, 206
New York Times 18
Ngram models 4
Ngram Viewer 3–4, 4f
Nieto, S. 14, 114, 122
non-dominant English 6, 37
nonstandard English 110, 115

Norton, B. 190
Nykiel-Herbert, B. 152

Oakland Ebonics case study 33, 34–6, 37
Of Borders and Dreams (Carger) 63
old basics, of multiliteracies 157–8, 163,
   209f, 210
Osborne, S. 31
O'Shaughnessy, T. 81
Other People's Children (Delpit) 40
overt instruction 203–4
Overt Instruction (NLG framework) 94–5

Pahl, K. 6
Paley, V. G. 137
Palmer, N. A. 74, 94
Pandya, J. Z. 142
Parents, Families and Friends of Lesbians
   and Gays (PFLAG's) 80
Park, S. L. 169
participatory culture: benefits of 157;
   defined 156; forms of 156–7
patterns of meaning 14–5
Payán, R. 187
Pearson, J. 82
*Pedagogy of Multiliteracies: Designing Social
   Futures, A* (NLG) 1, 3
Pellegrini, A. D. 137
Pennington, J. L. 42–57
Pennycook, A. 31
Pernicek, T. 152
Perry, T. 31, 35, 114
PFLAG's (Parents, Families and Friends of
   Lesbians and Gays) 80, 85, 86
phonics, described 16
Phonics Phacts 16
plural patterns 119, 119f
possessive patterns 120, 120f
Postman, N. 31
Poteat, V. P. 94
power, teachers and 142
preservice literacy programs 42–57;
   author's narrative histories 44,
   44–5f, 46; classroom instruction
   and 55–6; community literacy and
   47–8; development of 46–7; forms
   of literacy and 49; multimodal
   experiences and 50–5, 51f, 52f,
   53f, 54f; overview of 42–3; situated
   learning experiences and 49–50;
   transformation levels of 56–7
Prochaska, J. 208
Proulx, A. 80

Puchner, L. 74, 77
Pullen, D. 6, 208
Pullum, G. 115

Quart, A. 80–1

Rainbow Books 80, 87
Ranker, J. 192–3
Raphael, T. E. 65
Ravi, D. 96
Rayford's Song (Inada) 18
Rea, D. M. 190, 191, 192
Reading Diagnosis 47
ReadWriteThink (website) 195
recontextualization 174
Redd, T. 37
Reed, C. 160
Reeves, J. 189
reflection, defined 58
Regional Standard English 116
register, defined 115
Reyes, M. 14
Reynolds, R. 113
rhetorical patterns 24
Richardson, E. 113
Rickford, J. R. 111, 112, 114, 116, 118, 122
Ride, S. 81
Robertson, K. 195
Rodemeyer, J. 96
Romeo and Juliet (Shakespeare) 80
Roosevelt, E. 136–7
Roosevelt, F. 137
Rosenblatt, L. 136
Roser, N. 137
Rowsell, J. 6
Roy-Campbell, Z. M. 186–95
Ruiz, R. 26
Rustin, B. 96

Sadowski, M. 77, 82
safe places, designing 90–105; Critical
   Framing 95–6; *Hard Love* discussions
   98–104; LGBT YAL class session
   96–8; multiliteracies pedagogy 91–6;
   Overt Instruction 94–5; overview of
   90–92; points to consider 105; Situated
   Practice 92–4; teacher snapshot 91, 92f;
   Transformed Practice 104
Safe Schools Coalition 87
Saint Lucious Preparatory Academy 164
Salas, R. G. 42–57, 141
Sally Ride Science 81–2
"Same Love" (song) 81

Sandhu, P. 133
Sarroub, L. K. 151, 152
Sastri, P. 133
Savage Inequalities (Kozol) 68
Schieffelin, B. B. 110
Schierloh, J. M. 118
Schilling-Estes, N. 34, 113, 115, 116, 122
Schmidt, S. J. 80, 85
school language 20
Schrock, K. 195
Schultz, K. 144, 152
Schuster, K. 37
Schwartz, G. E. 192, 193
Scott, J. 169
Scribner, K. P. 128
self-awareness 69
self-censoring 95, 96
self-portraits 129–32, 130*f*, 131*f*, 132*f*
self-reflection 69
semantic variations 22
Serna, C. 47, 56
sexual diversity, in classroom teaching 74–
    87; adult learning and communication,
    create culture of 84; discussing, openly
    and honestly 81–2; human experiences
    and 80; inclusive/nondiscriminatory
    policies, develop 83–4; literature,
    news media, writing, film, and music
    curricular 80–1; multiliteracies
    as framework for 75–6; offensive
    comments/behaviors, addressing 83;
    overview of 74–5; resource listing 86–7;
    resources, availability of 85; safe spaces
    and 82–3; school curriculum and 80–1;
    sexual minorities needs and 76–9, 77*f*,
    78*f*; supportive relationship development
    82–3; teachers and schools role in 79–85
sexual diversity resources 86–7
sexual minorities: consequences of issues
    faced by 78*f*; described 74; issues faced
    by 77*f*; needs of 76–9
sexual-minority youth, defined 74
sexual orientation *vs.* sexual preference 84
Shanahan, L. E. 61
Sheltered Instructional Observation
    Protocol (SIOP) 191
Shepherd, M. 96
Shi, L. 144
Short, D. 190, 191
Situated Practice (NLG framework) 92–4
Skilton-Sylvester, E. 144
Skinner, E. 151, 192
Small, F. 81

Smith, J. M. 85, 98
Smitherman, G. 35, 114, 122
social diversity: literate behavior and 6;
    within multiliteracies 5–6, 5*f*, 209*f*;
    new basics conception of 211*f*; old
    basics conception of 209*f*; transforming
    conceptions of 208–11
social equity teaching 154–67; community
    as classroom and 162–4; Farm Stand
    Project 158–62, 159*f*, 160*f*, 161*f*, 164–5;
    implementing 165–7; multiliteracies
    framework 157–8; overview of 154–6;
    participatory cultures framework 156–7
Sohmer, R. 60
The Sopranos (TV show) 22
South Sudan News Agency 149
Sparks, S. D. 59
*Spreading the Word: Language and Dialect in
    America,* (McWhorter) 19
Stainsby, J. 58–72
stand and deliver approach 188
Standard American English (SAE) 110
standard English 37, 115; children from
    non-dominant backgrounds and
    37; language variation and 36–8;
    responsibility to teach 37; in Western
    Australia 33, 34
"Start Again" (song) 81
Steffensen, M. 113
stigmatized dialects 20
Stonewall Book Awards 80, 87
Strauss, S. 16
Strecker, S. 137
student identity 181–2
Stufft, D. L. 91
stupid book 133–5, 134*f*
style-shifting 115
Sudanese culture 144–52; Ethan's
    interviews 148–9; in Fargo, ND 144–6;
    literacies and practices, Samuel's 146–7,
    150–1; overview of 144; Samuel and
    Ethan, introduction to 146; school
    implications for 151–2; social literacy,
    Ethan's 149–50
Sudan Net 149
Sudan Tribune 149
Sweeney, T. 152
Sweet Home Alabama (TV show) 22
Swords, R. 6, 33, 39, 109–23
Sze, C. 144

Taylor, D. 26
Taylor, H. U. 116, 118

Taylor, O. 114
teacher talk 187
Teaching Tolerance School Leader
  Guide 87
technology nights 166–7
This is Water (Wallace) 38–9
Thomas, W. P. 189
Thompson, M. 68, 104, 195
Through Our Eyes production: *Birds of
  a Feather* play 172; critical principles
  involved 170; *Mega/August* play 171–2;
  Mexico/Brooklyn play 172; *Mommy
  Dearest* play 172; *Oranges* play 172;
  overview of 169, 171; teachers stance
  on 170
Tochelli, A. L. 2, 90–105
Tom Brown's School Days (Hughes) 147
Toohey, K. 190
Top Dog Underdog (Park) 169
Townsend, D. 141
Tracks to Two-Way Learning 39
Tracy, B. 90–91
Transamerica (film) 81
transformative literacy practices:
  classroom transformation 206–7;
  critical framing and 204–5; described
  205–8; inquiry and learners' lifeworlds
  202–3; multiliteracies and 202–5;
  new knowledge overt instruction and
  203–4; prospective transformation 206;
  retrospective transformation, participant
  206; tangible transformation 207;
  transformation process 207–8
Transformed Practice (NLG framework)
  104
TransYouth Family Allies (TYFA) 87
Truscott, A. 38
Turner, S. 168–85, 169
"'Two-Spirit' People of Indigenous North
  Americans, The" (Williams) 84
"two-spirit" terminology 84
two-way bi-dialectical teaching 30, 37

unigrams 3–4, 4*f*
Urbina, I. 18

Valdés, G. 189
Valenzuela, A. 26, 27
Valuing Language Study (Goodman) 26, 27
van Leeuwen, T. 4, 174, 182
Van Sluys, K. 145
Varjas, K. 94
vernacular: defined 115; dialects 110, 116

Very Hungry Caterpillar, The (Carle) 192
Villegas, A. M. 187
Virtue, D. C. 144
Vogt, M. E. 190, 191

Wadjella (Aboriginal English white fella)
  30
Walker-Dalhouse, D. 144–52
Wallace, D. F. 38–9
Walters, E. 149
Wardhaugh, R. 34
Warriors Don't Cry (Beals) 66
Washington, J. A. 113
Waterhouse, T. 77
Watson, L. B. 94
Ways with Words (Heath) 40
Wedding Banquet, The (film) 81
Wei, M. 96
Wells, G. 14, 188
What Works Program 38
Wheeler, R. 6, 33, 39, 109–23
When Elephants Fight (Walters & Bradbury)
  149
"When Girls Will Be Boys" (Quart)
  80–1
White, C. 58–72
White, E. B. 138, 141
Whitman, J. S. 94
Wiest, L. R. 74–87
Wilde, S. 16
Wilkinson, C. 111
Wilkinson, L. 82
Williams, J. 142
Williams, L. J. 37, 38
Williams, W. L. 84
Williams Institute, The 87
Wittlinger, E. 98–104
Wolfe, S. A. 137
Wolfram, W. 21, 24, 34, 39, 113, 115,
  116, 122
Word on the Street, The (McWhorter) 18
*Words at Work and Play: Three Decades in
  Family and Community Life* (Heath) 40
writing 114
Written Standard English 116

Yolen, J. 93
Yoon, B. 189, 190
young adult literature (YAL) course 90–92;
  NLG framework of 92–6
youth slang 22

Zimmerman, W. 195